AF540293

The Indian Diaspora :
A Study on Expatriates' Narratives

The Indian Diaspora : A Study on Expatriates' Narratives

Dr. Nagraj G. Holeyannavar

The Indian Diaspora : A Study on Expatriates' Narratives

Edition 2024

ISBN 978-93-87537-06-4

Published by:
CRESCENT PUBLISHING CORPORATION
4806/24, Mathur Lane,
Ansari Road, Darya Ganj,
New Delhi - 110 002
Ph.: 011 - 23244131
Mob.: + 91 - 9711991838, 9999021668
E-mail: crescentbook@gmail.com
Website: www.crescentpublishingcorp.weebly.com

Typesetting by
Priyanka Graphics
New Delhi

Printed at:
Roshan Offset Printers
Delhi

Printed in India

Preface

There is a tendency among the human beings to look back to ones' own root and ancestry. And further to find out the whereabouts. This finding out of one's ancestry makes the person to trace one's origin and identity or the socio-cultural patterns or the society to which he belongs. Thus, he quintessential tries to indentify one's ethnicity just to have better social relationship with that group. Moreover, this identification gives him a kind of oneness. Therefore, the impact of outsider in the alien soil tries to create a different outlook and to identify one another with the same social group. And in words of Salman Rushdie "— one physical alienation from India at almost inevitably means that we will not be capable of redeeming precisely the thing that was lost, that will, in short, create fictions not actual cities or villages, but invisible ones, imaginary homelands, Indians of mind."(Rushdie, 1991:10).

Moreover, the Diasporic study is not only based on the displacement or replacement from its roots but it is expressed with various factors in narratives which are taken into consideration by creating new space of explanation. Thus, these narrative forms to explain the diversified factors, which have affected many people or the group. These writers depict their narratives depict to create a world of their experiences which is based on memory or experience of someone of previous generation. They depict to highlight with comparison of life of previous and present generation with the change in culture norms and mores. Further, they try to give a new thought or new way of explaining the idea which may capture the attention of many readers through the writers' real or imaginary expression of life with their masalas and girmit in their narratives. These are often ingredients which are written in diasporic writing just to instigate the minds of readers and to understand the situation of an individual in an alien soil. Another factor is about psychological aspects which has become panoramic view point of an individual or group at present as it is the aspects which has affected them to find their inner psyche : the loss of homeland and yarning to get it, alienation in new culture: its adversities, compromises and redefining one's identity. Thus, all these channelize a new aura of study in diaspora.

Therefore, Uma Parameswaran rightly defines as it is first is one of nostalgia for the homeland left behind mingled with fear in a strange land. The second is a phase in which one is busy adjusting to the new environment that there is little creative output. The third phase is the shaping of diaspora existence by involving themselves ethno cultural issues. The fourth is when they have 'arrived' and start participating in the larger world of politics and national issues. (Parmeswaran, 165)

II

The diasporic writers are try to speak about the life and problem faced by an individual or the group on alien soil. These are writers who imagine/sensed themselves about the condition have written about their pain and sufferings in their writings. On the other, there are few writers have faced and sensed the real pain of cultural alienation and assimilating with the culture. Their saga of adjusting to different culture are presented in a hyped manner and also various sources and methods are incorporated through quoting so as to sense of the reality can be imagined through lyric, letters and memoirs etc which will help in establishing the true source. Thus it will exhibit the local culture and standard of life in which they live what they were facing in it. Indian writers therefore, have been categorised into two groups on basis of their Indianness and how much they are really faced the problem.

The first group is the migrants who belong to India and have Indianness in them. They carry their cultural notion in them and they feel difficult to assimilate with the host culture. They face problems of racial discrimination, hostile conditions and cultural onslaughts in foreign soil which make them difficult to adjust and survive on the other the opportunity which they have academic and materialistic prospects make it more difficult to return back to home land. This situation makes them to feel that they are being torn between two polarities they develop a sense of in-betweenness, a sort of 'hybrid', 'diasporic identity', always in a state of flux. This identity crisis is seen in novels of Salman Rushdie, Bharati Mukherjee, Vikram Seth, Rohinton Mistry, Anurag Mathur and others belong to this group.

The second generations of Diaspora writers are educated elites to Indian born parents and they are brought up outside India, migrated to developed countries like the USA, UK, Canada & Australia. They present Indian life in an imaginary manner as they have not experienced or sensed culture clash as their parents might have been. Their Indian or Indianness in their writings is totally removed from sense of social reality. They have presented different Indian life through their secondary sources or bits of information. Thus many critics have stated about this condition. Kiran Desai, Jhumpa Lahiri, Ramchandra Guha, Arvind Adiga and others belong to this group.

This anthology is collection of scholarly papers written by scholars.

—Author

Contents

1

Diaspora : Writing from The Margins

Dr. Annie John

Asso. Prof. & Head Dept. of English,
A. R. Burla Womens' College,
Solapur

The term 'Diaspora' literally means *'to be scattered'*. Other words which carry similar shades of meaning are expatriate, exile, refugee, immigrant etc.

The Oxford Advanced Learner's Dictionary defines the term 'Diaspora' as:

The movement of the Jewish people away from their own country to live and work in other countries.

It also refers to the movement of people from any nation or group away from their own country.

The Britannica Encyclopedia explains the term 'Diaspora' as:

The dispersion of Jews among the Gentiles after the Babylonian exile (586 BC); or the aggregate of Jews outside Palestine or present day Israel. (Vol 3)

This term also carries religious, philosophical, political, and eschatological connotations, as the Jews perceive a special relationship between the land of Israel and themselves.

Jewish Diaspora

The year 70 A.D. marks the end of the Jewish state, since the Romans drove them away from their homes. This was home for the Jews for over a millennium. In reality, however, the Jewish Diaspora had begun long before that. During the year 722 A.D., the Assyrians conquered Israel; and the Hebrew inhabitants were scattered all over the Middle East. The years between 597-586 B.C. witnessed the Judeans being deported to different parts of Babylon, by king Nebuchadnezzar. They remained as a unified community. Few fled to and settled down in the 'Nile delta of Egypt.' Therefore, the Jewish community settled in the different parts of the Middle East. As such, the year 597 can be safely considered to be the beginning of the Jewish Diaspora. During the year 538 BC, Cyrus, the Persian, came to power; and the Judeans were permitted to return to their homeland. A majority of them preferred to remain in Babylon. While a few converted to other religion, the majority retained their religion, culture, and social customs. After 73 AD, the Hebrew history became the history of the Diaspora, since the Jews and their world view spread over Africa, Asia and Europe.

The word 'Diaspora' comes from the Greek term 'dia' which means 'through' and 'Speirein' that is 'scatter'. Thus Diaspora refers to the process of dispersion. The notion of the centre and a home are essentially associated with the term; and the images of journey / voyage, displacement, seeking roots, and finally seeking anchor in alternative homes are all evoked.

A closer analysis of the term 'Diaspora' reveals that there are more dimensions to this term.

The offspring of an area who have spread to many lands.

(mcgraw-hill.com/sites)

The movement, migration, or scattering of people from their original homelands. (www.indianahistory.org/programming/immigration/glossary)

This definition can safely be applied to the Parsi community and their migratory movement. The invasion of Persia, by the Arab conquerors and the persecution of the Parsis at their hands, resulted in them fleeing away from Persia. They landed in Diu, off the coast of Gujarat in India, some 1200 years ago; and made this their new home. Although, there were few conditions imposed upon them by the local leader, the Parsis were free to follow their own religion. This was the beginning of their new life in a new country.

Similar migratory movements were found in India during the year 1947. The gruesome act of the Partition caused many Indians to cross to the other side of the border. The pain, and agony undergone; and their quest for identity were akin to what other immigrants encountered.

Migration sometimes takes place out of choice and freewill.

The dispersion or spreading of something that was originally localized. (www.cogsci.princeton.edu/cgi-bin/webwn)

The situation of the people of one country dispersed into other countries. (www.yeshuahuadonai.com/glossary.htm)

No doubt, the earlier Diasporas were often products of forced migration. They were people running away from economic hardships, social/ political persecution, and religious discrimination. However, there was a second group of migrants who voluntarily moved to other countries, in search of a fortune and better prospects. The lure of the West, with promises of greater economic benefits, prompted this group to undertake this voyage. In addition to this, there were others who left to the West for high studies. Marriage and moving away with the spouse was yet another factor that encouraged migration.

Therefore it can be said that the reasons for migration are as follows

- Indentured labour / economic hardships.
- Political persecution / religious discrimination.
- Better prospects / marriage / higher education.

Biblical Evidence of Diaspora

The Bible begins with the book of Genesis, which narrates the first nomadic story. God placed Adam and Eve in the Garden of Eden as its gardener, to tend and care for it. He also warned them regarding the fruit from the 'forbidden tree' and the dangerous consequences, if they disobeyed him. However, man sinned and fell short of the glory of God.

So the Lord God banished him forever from the Garden of Eden, and sent him out to farm the ground from which he had been taken. Thus God expelled him, and placed mighty angels at the east of the Garden of Eden, with a flaming sword to guard the entrance to the tree of life.

(Genesis.3:23, 24)

Man's disobedience and his fall from Eden suggest a diasporic state. As a result of his sin and disobedience, the Almighty drove him away from his 'original home'. He was forced to move out in search of a new home and some way to fend for himself. The Lord further said:

And you shall disappear from the land. For the lord will scatter you among all the nations from one end of the earth to the other. There you will worship heathen gods that neither you nor your ancestors have known. There among those nations you shall find no rest; your lives will hang in doubt. You will live night and day in fear, and will have no reason to believe that you will see the morning light. In the morning you will say, 'oh, that night were here!' And in the evening you will say, 'oh! that morning were here!' You will say this because of the awesome horrors surrounding you.

(Deuteronomy.29:63-67)

The Bible also refers to the greatest event that occurred in Israel's history; the details of which are stated in the book of Exodus. The term 'exodus' means 'departure', the departure of the people of Israel from Egypt, where they had been slaves. The Egyptians exploited the Israelites ruthlessly in fields, with bricks and mortar. The Israelites suffered during their slavery and their cry went up to God, who liberated them and formed them into a nation, promising them a blessed future. This is the Biblical evidence regarding the advent of the Diaspora. However, the exile produced some positive things too. It is likely that many of the books of the Jewish scriptures (Old Testament) were written during the period of exile. The book of Daniel in the Bible provides a glimpse into the problems faced by faithful Jews living in exile. The men in Diaspora were in touch with the natives of the host country, who in turn got attracted to the Christian faith. As such, 'dispersal' helped the spread of Christianity throughout the Roman Empire. A detailed account of this is found in the New Testament, in the book of Matthew, Luke and Acts.

All these definitions have a strong undercurrent of diasporic tendencies. The dimension of the definition includes all the people who have moved away from their homeland (for some purpose) and sought refuge in an alien country. The term 'Diaspora', which once implied to the Jewish community, has now become an umbrella term and accepts every immigrant from across the globe.

The Indian Diaspora

Both Naipaul and Mukherjee are writers of the Indian Diaspora. Therefore, it is necessary to trace the nature of the India Diaspora.

The subjugation of India and its incorporation into the British Empire gave rise to the Indian Diaspora. A large part of India came under the British rule, by the year 1830. The British Government of India permitted the transportation of Indians to far off alien lands to nurture their political and economic gains. The decline in the Indian economy, the rise in natural calamities, the destruction of industries, and the increase in the number of the unemployed, encouraged indentured labour. The Indo-Trinidadian scholar, Kenneth Permasad states:

Indentureship recruitment took place in an India reeling under the yoke of colonial oppression.

(http://www.sscnet.ucla.edu/southasia/diaspora/reflect.htm)

Although, a very small fraction of the emigrants left 'voluntarily'; the majority undertook this voyage to escape the economic hardships and their wretched lives. Over the period 1834 to 1917, nearly 1.5 million Indians had sold themselves into debt bondage. They were sent to different places like the British Guiana (present Guyana), Jamaica, Trinidad, and other Caribbean nations The Barbadian novelist, George Lamming, recognizing this, says:

These Indian hands, whether in British Guiana or Trinidad, have fed all of us.... there can be no creative discovery of this civilization without the central and informing influence of the Indian presence. There can be no history of Trinidad and Guyana that is not also a history of the humanization of those landscapes by the Indian labour. (http://www.sscnet.ucla.edu/southasia/diaspora/reflect.htm)

However, the Indians rose from the painful experience of their indentured migration; and during the last few decades succeeded in building their lives anew. They have also earned an 'inestimable and indispensable' position in the countries to which they migrated. Today, the Indian Diaspora constitutes an important force in world culture.

The Indian Diaspora began in the 19th century with the Indians being sent as indentured labourers to far off places like Mauritius, Fiji, Guyana, Malaysia, South Africa, Trinidad, SriLanka and various other places. In addition to this, over two million Indians participated in the World wars, Boer wars; and refused to come back, claiming the land on which they fought as their own. It is undoubtedly true that the post war Europe was reconstructed with the assistance of the Indians and South Asians.

Similarly, their unskilled labour also helped the physical transformation of the Middle East. It is seen that the Indian community, today, occupy a place of considerable privilege in the United States.

Writers of the Indian Diaspora

The writers of the Indian Diaspora, through their literary contributions have greatly enriched the English literature. They have been aiming at re-inventing India through the rhythms of ancient legends, the cadences of mythology, the complexities of another civilization, cultural assimilation and nostalgia. They dive deep into the realms of imagination and the ocean of memory to paint something quite different and distinct from that portrayed by fellow novelists, so far, in English language. To name a few, V. S. Naipaul, Bharati Mukherjee, Salman Rushdie, Vikram Seth, Amitav Ghosh, Vikram Chandra, Firdaus Kanga, Rohinton Mistry, and Amit Chaudhuri are writers of the Indian diaspora.

The writers of the Indian Diaspora write about India, even as they seek to locate themselves in the new culture. They paint the vastness and the complexities of the home country which contains everything in multitudes- multiple truths, multiple crisis, multiple realities, and this diversity is portrayed for the world wide reading public, and chiefly for the Indians. This aspect is best expressed by Shashi Tharoor who is often troubled by the question regarding the authenticity of his writings and the audience for whom he writers. He replies:

Ask not who I write for: I write for you.

(The Hindu. Aug 5th, 2001)

Characteristic features of diasporic writings

- A sense of dislocation – physical and psychical.
- Disillusionment.
- Multiculturalism.
- Alienation / Isolation.
- Identity crisis / Tracing the roots.
- Expatriate Sensibility.
- Insider – Outside view.
- A feeling of intense loss.

- Nostalgia / Memory / Reminiscence.
- Autobiographical elements.
- Nagging sense of guilt.
- Pretended sense of satisfaction.
- Racial discrimination.
- Impartial portrayal of India.
- Journey/ Voyage.

Some of the common themes re-occurring in the writings of the diasporic writers are the new home, impossibilities of going back home, inability to adapt to the new world, tracing back the roots and alienation. The crisis of being a diasporic writer is brought out very effectively through the words of Anita Rau Badami, a Canadian writer, in Makarand Paranjape's article "One foot in Canada and a Couple of Toes in India":

We are both doomed and blessed, to be suspended between two worlds, always looking back, but with two gorgeous places to inhabit, in our imaginations or our hearts. (Paranjape161)

The diasporic writer experiences dislocation and finds himself caught between a flux of two opposing cultures and two contrasting worlds. The diasporic writer tries to negotiate a new space for himself. Some writers even go a little further and create a 'third space' and move away from both the lands — the original and the adopted. This creation of the third space is only an attempt to escape from the conflictual situations that he encounters or to negotiate alternative realities. The writer begins a process of reconstruction both at the personal and universal levels. While working at the 'third space', the writer moves away from his own culture and the past. He begins to interpret something new. Drifting away from the past and rejecting even the present, he begins to interpret a culture and world which he is not born into, but acquired.

Some writers write about their adopted land and flow with the tide, just as the mainstream writers do; others write about their ethnic world and tend to be different. Normally, the immigrant writer speaks and writes from the margins. He stands on the periphery and at times tends to be a mere spectator. He writes and voices his opinion of being marginalized, alienated, obscured, peripheralised, and marginalized.

Awareness of one's past and tracing one's roots becomes a pre-requisite. Along with this, there is also the need to adapt to the changes. Immigration is nothing but a renewal of sorts. Being physical away from the motherland makes some of them undertake a literary journey back home. This journey helps them to redefine, reconstruct, and reshape their past. Both the situations of leaving home and the arrival in a new land, the way in which they intersect with each other, the social relations that crop up with this, determined by class, gender, race, and other factors configure the diaspora and its subsequent literature.

In diasporic writings, the cultural encounter plays a very significant role. This is followed by the bicultural pulls that cause the emergence of a new culture. The diasporic space acts upon the space of the home country. The centre remains the same with the margins having being expanded. It causes cultural encounters and the formation of new cultures. Immigration and its experiences vary from one writer to another, in relation to various factors such as the family background, social / cultural / economic setup, academic skills, and so on. Migration does not dislocate a person totally from one place to another. Similarly, absorption into a new culture cannot be total. Reality here is an ongoing process, which one has to face without rejecting it. The only way out of this situation is either to accept or reject it.

The diasporic writers write from their own perspective and each turn to their motherland, as per their need. V. S. Naipaul, who is twice displaced, travels back to India in order to trace his roots. Rushdie seeks refuge in India, its mythologies and history. Creative writers like Rohinton Mistry and Ashish Gupta write from their own experience of migration and the memories that make them travel backwards in time and space. Bharati Mukherjee, by the sheer power of her literary ability and meticulous details, narrates how the women immigrants are capable of relating to the two homes simultaneously.

For an immigrant, the act of writing is a sort of catharsis. It is a canvas on which they create and explore themselves. Writing helps to redefine themselves, especially, their identity which they have lost, during the process of migration. It is an intense and sentimental account of how a person dislocated in the new place feels and how he goes on to retrieves his past for the present. During the process of writing, memory is invoked in a magnanimous manner, and this helps to rebuild and renovate the past. Memory is a painful journey into the past, which is dismantled and fractured.

In an immigrant's writings, there are a number of confessional statements, philosophical commentaries, and logical assertions–all aiming towards the quest for the self. The immigrant being under disparate socio-cultural forces faces an identity crisis and feels castrated. Thus, the anguished perception of his own displacement and rootlessness is brought to the fore in his writings. His condition is that of a perpetual exile lost in the eternal search for his roots. Edward Said, in his *Reflections on Exile*, comments:

The condition of an exile and his experience is something very terrible; and the agony that he faces can't be surmounted. The exile faces a rift at various levels, that is between self and home, between self and host country and the like. No doubt, there are moments of triumph and romance, heroism and achievements in his life. However the loss of leaving behind one's homeland is so great, that it undermines all gains. (Said 173)

What lies at the roots of an immigrant's problem is the fact that he does not get the feel of belonging to either his homeland or his second home. Out of this arises a true and deep yearning, an intense longing for that which is unattainable. What lies at the heart of the diasporic literature is 'the consciousness of loss'. The world that the immigrant writers see is of course not void at all. It is densely populated with the social and physical phenomena, complications and contradictions of human endeavors and the unbearable conflict between the idea and reality. The immigrants, expatriates or exiles have been wrenched up and thrown away from their roots. The tensions that they face are multi-dimensional. The dislocation that they counter is on various levels — physical, social, cultural, and even psychical.

A diasporic writer's talent lies deep not in a particular land or culture but in the predicament that he faces in terms of isolation, alienation, homelessness, and a quest for identity. This talent comes to the surface through his literary imagination. The diasporic writer, while confronting the present, races into the past through the power of his memory. M.G. Vassanji aptly suggests this aspect of reclaiming the past. He states:

This reclamation of the past is the first serious act of writing having reclaimed it, having given to write about the present. (Vassanji 63)

India, for them is in their fond imagination. It is a fantasy land where nothing bad can happen. Quest for self-realisation and seeking fulfillment is what all diasporic writers aim at. However, during this process, they realize that the identity they possess, is all fractured and fragmented. This brings about the inevitable frustration and bafflement. Further, failing to receive the required sustenance from the foreign soil and being looked down as an alien, they suffer and deteriorate into emotional and moral depravity. The diasporic writers' works do not show their inability to leave their motherland behind, nor are they able to assimilate their past with their diasporic present. They are not in a position to a bridge the gap between the two. It is this very situation that they are thrown into, which transcends all limits of time and place; and go on to achieve a universal status.

The expatriate writer, in his literary journey, travels back homewards, down memory's lane, towards the past and all that is lost. This indicates his long journey away from home; and he makes the fullest use of this opportunity to harp upon lost moments, lost love, and lost opportunities. The diasporic writer's narrative contours the impossibility of return to the homeland, either in time or place. There seems a very remote possibility of coming back and belonging once again to that left behind. The position that he holds today is based on the aspect of temporariness. Here, there is an intense urge to make a claim and write about his sense of belonging; and this is worked out only through the device of retelling the past. All the inner conflicts are laid to rest through these retellings, and the writer finds a voice to reassert him, through a process of renegotiations.

Home becomes a mythical space of desire and also a virtual space of no return. Home, then, is portrayed through many versions. The actual 'origin' of home set in the geographical locales, is refigured and reinvented, through the imagination. Sometimes this is also juxtaposed with the present day reality with all its local sights and sounds — There lies a paradox which gives rise to conflictual tensions. A lot of diversities abound and there is no monolithic notion of home. In the diasporic literature, there is an oscillation between feelings of nostalgia, anguish, love, anger, cynicism, acceptance, and rejection. Vijay Mishra, in his article "Diaspora and the Art of Impossible Mourning", writes:

Diasporic identities are indeed formed by the grand narrative of being untimely ripp'd from a mother's womb. (Paranjape 31)

The writer's identity gives shape to his narratives and the many paradoxical tensions, energies the diasporic literature. The identity constructs lies on realities and not merely on abstractions. This aspect of identity construct takes into consideration other factors such as his allegiance to the nation, his home, the socio-cultural setup and much more. In case of the diasporic writer, his routings are a reality. However, the great distance of the present in which the writer resides with its multicultural context, in a way greatly impress and influence his literary works. The diasporic discourse, both creative and critical draws its impulses from the unique, the specific, the universal, and the interconnection they share. The sense of rootlessness combined with a notion of belonging to common homeland, the experience of dislocation, and the anguish that accompany it, have gone on to establish strong ties among scattered communities.

The writer in the literary fabric mirrors the social and political themes with all its contradictions. The contradictory aspects that he paints could also be symbolic of his own contradictory physical and psychical pulls. Cultural encounters and crucial historical / political / social crux stands at the core of the diasporic movements. The diasporic concern deals not only with the political process but moves ahead and explores its impact upon human relationships and the aftermath that follows. The cultural and historical interaction with the interplay of memory stands as new for each generation. With each generation, the dimensions gain a multiplicity, which needs to be explored. Relationship with the past is not always simple and straight, it always oscillates between different aspects. Similar is one's association with the present. Hurdles and obstacles are ever lingering around. However one cannot break with the past for good, nor reject the present. The aspect of location and dislocation contribute greatly in the making of the self, and so find its ways into the diasporic discourses. The diasporic writer is always preoccupied with the past and all that is lost. He recalls and narrates the past in various ways and rearranges them in different fashion. Jasbir Jain, a well known critic, in her article, "Identity, Home and Culture through Dislocations" very aptly suggests:

It is through these retellings that the inner conflicts are worked out and resolved, a renegotiation takes place with the self and a voice is found for self – assertion. (Jain 245)

The diasporic writers frame their realties and try to trace parallels through connections and interconnections, between the remembered, the desired, and the experienced

Diasporic literature harps on aspects such as the past, the lost, many recollections, and the interplay of memory. There is no way hoping to do away with all these things.

Vijay Mishra in his article "Diasporas and the Art of Impossible Mourning" states the need of all these elements by opining:

Without memory, without a sense of loss, without a certain will to mythologies, life for many displaced people will become intolerable and diasporic theory would lose its ethical edge. (Paranjape 46)

The status of a diasporic writer is that of a rootless wanderer, without a heritage to hold on to. Often these diasporic writers have been assailed for misinterpreting / misrepresenting Indian reality and for being inauthentic. However, the truth is, the narratives of the diasporic writers are a framework of their memory motivated by an intense urge to construct their own reality. Having faced the bitter and harsh realities, these writers consistently knock down idealized view in favour of more complex and even contradictory truth. Often being attacked for hanging dirty laundry, these writers seem not motivated out of vindication, but out of an effort to scan through the unhappy memories they hold. These writers time and again use their pathological vision to portray to the people of the world, what is not visible to their eyes, or even sometimes what they refuse to see.

In this way, great many writers of the India diaspora have been contributing significantly to the Indian English literature. All these writers are different from one another and have a very distinct personality. However, there are a few themes of the diaspora that have been a binding force between them and a focal point. The crisis between 'what is' and 'what was', or between 'reality' and the 'imaginary', also has a positive effect. It energises the narrative skills of the writer.

Right from the Indian exotica to the new genres, the writers of the Indian diaspora have been experimenting with various things. The Indian writer's are growing and greatly flourishing in various markets. The kind of literary material that the Indian writers offer is something that very few countries can boast of.

What makes the immigrant writer's works so pulsating and colourful is his ability to express himself in an adopted tongue. We can call it the 'second' or even the 'third' language. But the simplicity and grandeur that flow through their literature is surely worthy of praise and worth pondering. Using the rich English language as a powerful tool, these writers have gone ahead and enriched it further by the sheer magic of their emotions, sentiments and expression. All these writers, who write in a language which is not their own, have a purpose regarding the same. Their purpose of writing in English can be aptly summed through the words of Eva Hoffman, who justifies why she chose to write in English. In her work, *Lost in Translation: A Life in a New Language,* she states:

If I'm to write about the present, I have to write in the language of the present, even if it's not the language of the self. (Hoffman 121)

Since independence, the Indian diasporic writers have been making worthwhile, contributions to the literary world. Diasporic writings seem to be flourishing in the international market and have been critically acclaimed too.

Diaspora, is therefore, a scattering of the seed in the wind, the fruits of which are — a new creation and a fight to survive. Every diasporic movement holds a historical significance, as it carries within itself the kernel of the nation's history. The diasporic Indian's life is filled with adventure and this is opening up new vistas for daily discourses.

Large scale migration, as a result of various political and economic reasons took place during the early 19th century. The masses of the indentured labourers transported to various countries became the grave, invisible ground upon which empires were built. The Capitalistic forces saw migration and dislocation becoming the order of the day. Although, various factors were responsible for the process of migration, the truth is that no human society has been able to avoid it. The crisis that follow migration are innumerable and they are again encountered in various ways, such as assimilation, withdrawal, submission, and involvement. Since the late 19th and the 20th century, voluntary migrants to the West along with the second and third generations of the early migrants formed a part of the existing diaspora.

Diaspora / Dispersal / Dislocation and the problems associated with it are the greatest challenges of our present times. 'Self', 'Memory',

'Home', 'Rootedness', and 'Belonging' are some of the concepts that clamour for re-definition. Diaspora is a journey towards self-realization, self-recognition, self-knowledge, self-definition, and maturity.

The global movement has resulted in the emergence of new narratives, with new themes, which reflect the trials and traumas of the displaced and their struggle at recovering and reconstructing themselves. There is an element of creativity present in the diasporic writings; and this creation stands as a compensation for the many losses suffered.

Thus, we can say that, Diaspora is the global context needs a re-interpretation. In today's age of globalization, there is nothing like drawing a line. The centre remains the same with the margins having being expanded. The truth is that dislocation is not final or complete, so also absorption into a new culture is not total. Reality is an ongoing process, either accept or reject it. Dislocation does not always bring about suffering or pain. The truth is one cannot hold on to the land forever.

Raja Rao, when asked why he prefers to stay in the West, said

- Easy availability of medicines
- Easy availability of books.
- Physical health
- Intellectual nourishment

From the dislocation of Adam to the present times, it has been a long going for the men in Diaspora. The time has changed, but the concept and the reason behind it remains the same. The underlying truth is that every person born is destined to experience Diaspora. There are some factors that prompt or direct the diasporic movement. The Divine call is replaced by an inner urge, which comes in the form of force, choice, survival instinct or search for greener pastures. It is a divine destiny which no man can escape. The very first step that a child takes when he learns to walk is suggestive of the great movement that he is going to undertake in life.

Man's diasporic status began with the loss of paradise. Diaspora posed a theological dilemma, to stay outside the holy land was considered as a penalty or punishment. It is the spiritual fulfillment that man yearns for. The entire movement that he covers during his life span is aimed at regaining the lost Eden.

Reference:

- Britannica Encyclopedia Vol. 3. New Delhi: Encyclopedia Britannica (India) Pvt. Ltd. and Impulse Marketing, 2005.
- Gokhale, Veena. 'How Memory Lives and Dies'. The Sunday Review, The Times of India, Oct. 27th, 1996.
- Holy Bible- Good News Bible. Bangalore: The Bible Society of India, 1988-89.
- Jain, Jasbir. "Identity, Home and Culture through Dislocations". *Dislocations and Multicultarism.* Ed. Jain Jasbir. Jaipur and New Delhi: Rawat Publication, 2004.
- John Annie, *In Search of Greener Pastures-Vol. I,* Mumbai: Pen Craft Publication, 2012
- Oxford Advanced Learner's Dictionary.
- Parekh, Bikhu. "Some Reflections on the Indian Diaspora", *Journal of Contemporary Thought.* 1993.
- Paranjpe, Makarand. '*Indiaspora'*. New Delhi: Indialog Publications, 2001.
- Said, Edward. *Culture and Imperialism.* London: Vintage, 1994.
- Said, Edward. *Reflections on Exile.* New Delhi: Penguin India Books, 2001
- Said, Edward. *Reflections on Exile and Other Literary and Cultural Essays.* New Delhi: Penguin India, 2001
- Said, Edward. *Culture and Imperialism,* Vintage, London, 1994.

2

Reflections : Comparison Between Old and New Indian Diaspora Writers

Hetal M Doshi

Research Scholar

Bhavnagar University, Gujarat.

Introduction

..... it is from those who have suffered the sentence of history, subjugation, domination, diaspora, displacement....that we learn our most enduring lessons.

Homi Bhabha "Post-Colonial Criticism" (ed. Greenblatt and Gunn)

Unpleasant experiences of life teach more and concrete than pleasant and joyous precepts. And Diaspora literature is considered to be the best medium for spreading the lessons taught in exile experiences. The present paper tries to make a distinction between the literature of old and new Diaspora group by making a study of the most unique works of these two groups. Before doing so, it is imperative to discuss a brief history of Diaspora population and literature.

Definition

The term Diaspora, originally used for the Jewish externment from its homeland, is now applied as a metaphorical designation for expatriates, refugees, exiles and migrants. The term had been derived from Greek word Dia (over) and speiro (to scatter). In modern times, this term has been used to describe any ethnic population who resides in the country other than its native land. It generally describes dislocated people who maintain or revive their connection with their country of origin.

History

Formerly people were forced to move from their homeland for a number of reasons. Robin Cohen, a Diasporic historian, had classified diasporic population as following.

1. Victim Diaspora
2. Labour Diaspora
3. Imperial Diaspora
4. Trade Diaspora
5. Cultural Diaspora

Cohen said that there is a common element in all forms of Diaspora, these are people who live outside their territories. Their craving for original homeland is reflected in the language they speak, religion they adopt and cultures they produce. Their sense of yearning for their homeland, unbreakable connections to its traditions, religious values and language gave birth to Diasporic Literature.

Keeping it limited to the Indian diaspora population in the confined space of this paper, it is classified into two kinds.

(1) Forced Migration: To Africa, Fiji, or the Carribbeans on the account of slavery

(2) Voluntary Migration: To USA, Canada, Australia for professional, academic or earning purpose.

Another more convincing classification had been provided by Sudesh Mishra, the author of Diaspora and The Difficult Art Of Dying (2001). According to him, Diaspora population is divided into following two kinds.

(1) Old Diaspora: Those who had left the country somewhere between 1830 and 1917 as slaves and had gone to Fiji and Trinidad.

(2) New Diaspora : Post 1917 dispersal from the homeland for the sole purpose of better standard of living comprises of New Diaspora.

This new Diaspora again has been classified into two groups.

[A] Those who spent a part of their life in India and then left for other countries like Salman Rushdie and Chetan Bhagat.

[B] Those who are born and brought up in foreign countries like Meera Syal and Jhumpa Lahiri.

History of Diaspora Literature

The literature produced by such dispersed group is known as Diaspora Literature. Generally, such literature is based on the idea of homeland. It mostly narrates the harsh journeys undertaken for various reasons like marriage, earning wealth, higher studies, professional accomplishments or forcible dispersion. It is perennially believed that such literature laments the loss of protagonist's laughter, language, values, friends, home etc. Such narrations usually give impression that diasporic literature is mostly tragic. It is the expression of inner suffering and plight felt by exilic people whose purgation is otherwise impossible.

Some common traits of exile literature are as following.

1. Nostalgia and lamentation
2. Bundle of memories
3. A newly found sense of freedom among characters
4. An attempt to find a connecting link between two cultures
5. A sense of displacement
6. Experiences of discriminations
7. A process of cultural transmission
8. Protest against Discrimination

Reading above characteristics of Diaspora Literature, one can easily reach to the conclusion that it is always tragic, it is always a story of lamentation and loss. This conclusion is more apt for an old generation of diaspora writers. When the migration was forcible and unwilling, it is natural that literature produced by such writers would talk about sad exile sentiments. But when the migration is willingly undertaken, what literature offers is a wide range of buoyant themes and styles. It is a pleasant surprise to find that modern diasporic literature offers optimism, ray of hopes and desires, happy adjustments in new culture and happy acceptance of new values. This point can be made more clear by studying some most representative works of old and new diaspora authors.

Comparison of themes between old and new exile writers

A House For Mr.Biswas (1961) by V.S.Naipaul is an unforgettable story of Mr. Biswas who yearns for a place he can call home. When he marries into the domineering Tulsi family on whom he becomes dependent, he embarks on an endless struggle to weaken their hold over him and purchase a house of his own. This novel is a quest of man for sovereignty against post colonial canvas. Mr. Biswas' description in the following words is an apt old diasporic sensibility.

"He read political books. They give him phrases which he could only speak to himself. They also revealed one region after another of misery and injustice and left him feeling more helpless and more isolated than ever…and he was given strength to bear the most difficult part of his day: dressing in the morning, that daily affirmation of faith in oneself, which at times for him was almost like an act of sacrifice."

The characters of Anita Desai, even if they stay in crowd, feel alienated and exiled. She is more interested in the interior, gloomy, world of her protagonists than political and social realities. Her 'Bye Bye Black Bird' is a story of Adit who comes to England and marries an English lady Sarah. He leads a happy life. After some time, Adit's friend Dev comes to England for higher education but he hates the pomp and show of England. The novel gives an interesting paradox when Adit , an Indian with comfortable job, English wife, decides to leave England and Dev who has been critical of England decides to stay back in England. The following description about Dev speaks volume about sad exile experiences.

"There are days in which the life of an alien appears enthrallingly rich and beautiful to him, and that of a homebody too dull, too stale to return to ever. Then he hears a word in the tube or notices an expression on an English face that overturns his latest decision and, drawing himself together, he feels he can never bear to be the unwanted immigrant but must return to his own land, however abject or dull,where he has, at least, a place in the sun, security, status and freedom."

The discrimination and racial segregation against Indians were major themes of old diaspora writers. The following narration from Home To India (1945) by Santha Rama Rau gives an account of melancholic diaspora community.

"For the first time I began to feel that I was ranged on the side of the Indians. I was not clear about what our side was against, but now when I saw benches on a station platform marked "For Europeans only", it was a personal insult..."

The protagonist Salim Juma in G.Vassanji's The Gunny Sack (1989) tells her daughter,

"The running must stop now, Amina. The cycle of escape and rebirth, uprooting and generation, must cease in me. Let this be the last runaway returned, with one last quixotic dream."

Hence the old diaspora writers, in quest of 'home' and 'culture' were inclined to write melancholic themes. Their writings were marked by dejection, dislocation, sense of loss and alienation. The writers of new diaspora group can be identified through its conscious interaction between gender, class and ethnicity. They seem to be more effervescent, spirited and secure in new culture. This joie de vivre can be felt in a number of following quotations derived from their works.

Meera Syal, actress and script-writer, arrives at a less melancholic definition of diasporic selfhood:

"The place in which I belonged was wherever I stood and there was nothing stopping me simply moving forward and claiming each resting place as home."

Arvind Adiga's The White Tiger provides a comical view of modern day life in India through the narration of its protagonist Balram Halwai. The novel focuses on the disparity between India's advancement as a modern global economy and the crushing poverty of its working class people. But the amusing mode of narration makes this darkly view more acceptable. These quotes would clarify this point more articulately.

(1) The moment you recognize what is beautiful in this world, you stop being a slave.

(2) It's amazing. The moment you show cash, everyone knows your language.

(3) I was looking for the keys for years But the door was always open.

(4) Let animals live like animals; let humans live like humans. That's my whole philosophy in a sentence.

Arundhati Roy's The God Of Small Things (1997) is a beautiful description of how the small things in life affect people's behavior and their lives. Some of the quote like dialogues set the positive tone.

(1) This was the trouble with families. Like invidious doctors, they knew just where it hurt.

(2) Things can change in a day.

(3) Anything can happen to anyone. It's best to be prepared.

Chetan Bhagat's Revolution 2020- a story of three friends Gopal, Raghav and Aarthi in a holy city of Varanasi- is full of positive vibrations. The book is a mild attack on the inherent corruption embedded in India's education system. The witty dialogues and plot give an impression of a Bollywood movie script.

People come to my city to feel the presence of God but I could feel her presence everywhere.

Stupid people go to colleges. Smart people own them.

Kiran Desai's The Inheritance Of Loss is a book about the rigid class systems that exist in India and abroad amongst Indians and struggle that people face within these classes after colonialism. Though the old and new migrant writers deal with the same theme of dejection and exilic experiences, the manner with which new group deal is oscillating and ebullient.

There was grace in forgetting and giving up...everyone had to accept imperfection and loss in life.(ch.39)

How could you have any self respect knowing you didn't believe in exactly anything? (ch.40)

Jhumpa Lahiri's The Namesake (2003) describes a struggle of a Bengali couple who have gone to the United States. The story narrates how they get adjusted in a new milieu, how they chose the name of their baby 'Gogol', how Gogol starts hating his name and how he accepts his name at the end of the novel. Though the novel narrates cast out experiences, there is a vibrancy felt in every sentence spoken. Ghosh, a friendly Bengali businessman's advice to Ashoke is one of the most impressive dialogues in exile literature.

Do yourself a favour. Before it is too late, without thinking too much, pack a pillow and blanket and see as much of the world as you can. You will not regret. One day it will be too late.

Conclusion

The new diasporic writers, through their literature, break the myth that migrant literature is always sadly philosophical and its single focus is on migration and multicultural issues. They write on a wide variety of themes, in a positive style and tone. There is a ray of optimism in their words. The movement from V.S.Naipaul to Jhumpa Lahiri suggests an important rethinking of the concept of diaspora themes. Whereas for the old diaspora 'melancholy' was the imposing theme, it is the excitement to take new challenges and smooth settlement which are the preferred plots of the new Diaspora writers.

Works Cited

Primary Sources

- A house For Mr Biswas by V.S.Naipaul
- Bye Bye Black Bird by Anita Desai
- Home To India by Santha Rama Rau
- The Gunny Sack by G.Vassanji
- The White Tiger by Arvind Adiga
- The God Of Small Things by Arundhati Roy
- Revolution 2020 by Chetan Bhagat
- The Inheritance of Loss by Kiran Desai
- The Namesake by Jhumpa Lahiri
- Secondary sources
- From Sugar To Masala: Writing By Indian Diaspora by Sudesh Mishra (article in An Illustrated History Of Indian Literature In English,ed. By Arvind Krishna Mehrotra)
- Realism And Reality: The Novel And Society In India by Meenakshi Mukherjee
- New Urges In Post colonial Literature edited by Sunita Sinha

3

A Diasporic Study of Amitav Ghosh's The Glass Palaces

Miss. Gita Bhojane

Research Scholar

Yeshwant College

Nanded (MS)

Born in Calcutta, grew up in Bangladesh, Srilanka, Iran and India, studied at Delhi and Oxford stayed in Egypt and Cambodia to do the field work, settled in India, Amitav Ghosh in his writings seems to believe that an effective fiction emanates from a particular historical moment which intersects the narrator and the nation at the crucial point of their evolution and growth. As Devy says, 'Alienation between speech and life seems to have disappeared now' and so storytellers like Rushdie, Amitav Ghosh almost are poets enjoying their 'poetic rhetoric'. Ghosh uses English language skillfully and artistically to present the narrator and what is peculiar of Ghosh's novels is that he varies his choice of narrator in each of his novels. Being an anthropologist himself, Ghosh takes the readers through many parts of the work. He wanders through the ancient land of Egypt as well as the war-ravaged London during the Second World War, through Dhaka before and after partition. Coming and going, arriving and departing find a frequent place in his fiction. This is not merely a geographical or physical movement but also a movement from ignorance to knowledge, awareness and understanding. The novelist has a roving eye and perceives in depth the events of the world.

There are no barriers of time and space in his fiction. Ghosh uses 'time' to maximum effect because yesterdays, today's and tomorrows fuse into one. To him past, present, and future coalesce into one. He does not arrange events in a historical or chronological order. Instead, the reader is able to move with the characters 'to envision the way in which his past colors his present, in which the past is ever present within his consciousness'. His novels are never limited by clock-time, as they do not deal merely with externals.

Diasporic condition is the situation in which the longings and yearnings of the immigrant is expressed. The longing is for the culture, people, human-relationships and for the love and security that is offered by the native land. These longings and yearnings of the immigrant psyche are expressed in all the genres of literature. Indian Diaspora is emphasized through the diasporic writers who have migrated from India to different and distant places. Salman Rushdie, V.S. Naipaul, Bharati Mukherjee, Vikram Seth, Amitav Ghosh are the diasporic writes, who in their work represent the diasporic condition. The agonies of the diasporic people, being helpless in an alien land, who had to adopt the alien culture either willingly or unwillingly is represented in the works of these writers. Amitav Ghosh, who is an eminent and foremost expatriate writer, expresses in his novels the sufferings and agonies of the displaced people. Their disappointments, their loosening grip on life and their lives spent in a sorrowful longing for their roots can be seen as an elegy for the diasporic condition.

In The Glass Palace, Amitav Ghosh clearly shows the features of diasporic condition. The diasporic condition in the novel becomes stronger due to the arrival of the colonial power, which throws down Thebaw, the king of Burma after defeating his army in the battlefield. Through the intertwining stories of Dolly and Rajkumar, the history of the twentieth century is told across three generations; spread over three interlinked parts of the British Empire: Burma, with its conflicting undercurrents of discontent, Malaya with its vast rubber plantations and Indian-amid growing opposition to British rule. But what is the most shocking part of the novel is the zest for life and struggle for existence which one finds in it through right from the beginning till the end. It is a Saga of three generations that travel through Mandalay, to India and then finally to Malaysia. Colonialism had affected the life of both kings-king Thebaw, queen Supayalat and Princess and the commoners- Rajkumar, Dolly and the collector.

The novel opens with the protagonist Rajkumar Raha is an eleven year old orphan boy from Chittagong came in an alien land by an accident. The boat on which he used to work needed to be repaired and as the boat owner came to know that the repair work may take almost a month's or even longer. He had told Rajkumar along with some others to find a new job as he was unable to feed the crew for that length of time. So Rajkumar came to Mandalay and find a job with some Ma Cho who used to run a food stall there. She was a half-Indian woman who often provided work to the stray Indians like Rajkumar who needed a job in Mandalay. Here a sense of 'belonging' develops in him and he decides to stay there. Being an Indian, he has to suffer greatly in this alien land. When Indian soldiers were marching towards the city, obeying the orders of their English masters, Rajkumar was caught by the local people and was attacked in their frenzy. The pathetic diasporic condition is revealed by this incident-

"Twisting Rajkumar's head around, he struck him across the face with the black of his fist. A spurt of blood shot out of Rajkumar's nose.... Then the crook of an elbow took Rajkumar in the stomach, pumping the breath out of him and throwing him against a wall. He slid down, clutching his stomach as though he were trying to push his insides back in."(28-29)

The pitiable condition of king Thebaw, queen Supayalat, princesses with their maids is shown when they had to leave the royalty and were exiled to live in an alien land Ratnagiri(India). The person, who ruled the country once, has to live of a prisoner, far away from the land of his origin. It is ironic that cruel queen, who had once ordered the killings of about seventy-nine royal princes, had to leave the land of her reign and live a life of confinement, in an alien land, only for the love of her husband.

Dolly, the heroine of the novel is a faithful maid of queen Supayalat, who too had to leave the land of her origin together with the royal family. Dolly, Evelyn and Augusta and a few others girls who were orphans brought up by queen in the palace and who had nowhere else to go, except with the king and queen. In the due course of novel one by one all of them except Dolly leave king and queen. Dolly grew up in India and the idea of going back to Burma upsets her. She is afraid of being called a foreigner in her own native land. Uma, the wife of the collector, asks Dolly to leave the king and queen as she is not the prisoner of the British Empire, but Dolly's pain is clearly observe at the thought of being treated as a stranger when she remarks:

"If I went to Burma now I would be a foreigner- they would call me a Kalaa like they do Indians- a trespasser, an outsider from across the sea. I'd find that very hard, I think. I'd never be able to rid myself of the idea that I would have to leave again one day, just as I had to before."(113)

The thought of being twice displaced from their belongings, threatens the diasporic people. This torturing condition found in Dolly. The self-imposed act of dispossession because of such displaced locations on the part of the colonized people who suffer from imaginary and unreal home-land is indicated in both Dolly and Rajkumar who proclaim their right in India and Burma respectively to make their 'home'. When Rajkumar comes to India to marry Dolly, with whom he had fallen in love at first sight, Dolly refuses to marry him. She is completely devoted herself with the idea of her role as the caretaker of the royal family, particularly with the first princess who is pregnant. Uma's liberal attitude and practical approach to life helps to convince Dolly, after which she marries Rajkumar.

It is more pitiful when the colonized subject has the false identification that is living with the colonizer. The effect of mental colonization creates total disorder in the relationship as in the case of District collector, Beni Prasad Dey and his wife Uma Dey. The collector is imitating the western code of conduct, keeps the Britishers above Indians and wants to be good in the opinion of the Britishers. Uma, who plays the role of a stylish hostess, leading a mechanical and lonely life is disappointed in the worldly environment created by her husband:

"I used to dream about the kind of marriage I wanted .... To live with a woman as an equal, in spirit and intellect: this seemed to me the most wonderful thing life could after. To discover together the world of literature, art: what could be richer, more fulfilling? But what I dreamt of it not yet possible, not here, in India, not for us."(172-173)

After the departure of Dolly, Uma feels lonely. It is not possible for her to live with her husband, so she decides to leave her husband and stay at her parent's home. Due to this false perception of identity the collector had to suffer and his suffering leads him towards the end of his life. It is also miserable to see people living under illusions about the exploitation of the diasporic people. Saya Jhon also lives under the false idea of the Empire. He does not think the English as usurpers. On the contrary, he thinks that they are superior and they taught him the art of using everything for his own benefit. It makes him a successful one and he does not want to know anything beyond his immediate profit. Rajkumar also thinks like Saya John and is of the opinion that without the British, the Burmese economy will collapse.

The life of the people caught in a diasporic condition gets severely affected by the announcement of the war. It is also full of pain, sadness and breaks many illusions. To Arjun 'modern' and 'western' are synonymous. He is boasting of his connection with the west. In his mind he has accepted that the western style is better and therefore desirable. Dinu is also fascinated for the British. And hence, Arjun in conversation with Dinu replies:

"To you the modern world is just something you read about. What you know of it you get from books and newspapers. We're the ones who actually alive with westerns…" (279)

Dinu understand that it was through their association with European that the Arjun and his fellow-officers saw themselves as pioneers. Mental colonization is even worse. Arjun says:

"We understand the west better than any of you civilians. We know how the minds of westerns work only when every Indian like us will the country become truly modern."(279-80)

When Arjun joins the military Academy at Dehradun, his identification with the British Empire breaks instantly. He receives an impolite shock when his colleague Hardy remarks ironically:

"Where is this country? The fact is that you and I don't have a country…." (330)

The harsh and cruel consequences of war break only the illusion but also the heart. Rajkumar and Dolly's son-Dinu falls in love with Alison-Saya John's grand-daughter. Alison dies in the World War II before she can get married to Dinu and so they are parted forever:

"The relationship that might have bloomed and lasted a life is ruptured by the tumult of war."(Tiwari: 102)

This diasporic condition is full of confusion and sufferings and ultimately it leads for the worse in some cases. Those who can't endure the suffering of the displacement, they lose their grip on life and surrender under the pressure. Manju, Rajkumar's elder daughter-in-law is an example of such a condition. She couldn't face the hardships of war and displacement and commits suicide.

The longings and yearnings of the displaced people continue to hunt their lives for a long time. Those longing and yearnings are satisfied in case of some characters like Dolly, who being a nun attains satisfaction in it. In the case of Rajkumar, his longings and yearnings are unsatisfied till his death. Throughout his life he yearns for one or the other thing. And when he is compelled to live in India he strives for the place he considers to be his 'homeland' (Burma). He accepts to his grand-daughter, Jaya that for him....the Ganges could never be the same as the Irrawaddy (544). His longings and do not end in his lifespan, it ends only with the end of his life. He mourns for life, which he and Dolly were living in Burma and remarks:

"My father was from Chittagong and he ended up in the Arakan; I ended up in Rangoon; you went from Mandalay to Ratnagiri and now you're here too. Why should we except that we're going to spend the rest of our lives here? There are people who have the luck to end their lives where they began them. But this is not something that is owed to us. On the contrary, we have to expect that a time will come when we'll have to move on again. Rather than be swept along event, we should make plans and take control of our own fate."(310)

Apart from the diasporic element, there are various ideas in this novel. There are relevant ideas on the process of civilization, wars and their futility, the concept of boundaries, colonization, and journey. In hybridity, rootlessness, childhood and process of growing etc, one can find loneliness in this novel. Rajkumar is lonely at the beginning of the novel and at the end of the novel. Uma, who is a widow, leads her life lonely and with depression. Her husband, collector Dey, doesn't have a peaceful married life. When Uma leaves him, he feels lonely and commits suicide. In The Glass Palace, 'Glass Palace' functions as a metaphor, Glass is brittle and implies transparency; palace is the symbol of power, Glass Palace is an illusion that is created around power. Throughout the novel, Ghosh also expresses the agonies and turmoil of the expatriates. In all the works of Ghosh, one finds a continuous struggle to return to roots, on the part of the diasporic people. They are trying to conquer the exploitation and misery associated with their life. Ghosh's novels are elegies of the sad plight and sufferings of the displaced and lost people.

References

- Ghosh, Amitav. The Glass Palace. New Delhi: Haper Collins, 2000.
- Jaishree, N. 'Struggle or Surival? –A Reading of Amitav Ghosh's women in The Glass Place and The Hungry Tide. Barman Bhaskar(ed). New Delhi: Authrospress, 2011.s
- Kadam, Mansing G. 'Amitav Ghosh's The Glass Palace: A Postcolonial Novel', Indian writing in English. Binod Mishra and Sanjay Kumar. New Delhi: Atlantic, 2006.
- Nara, Rakhi and G. A. Ghanshyam. 'Narating the Diaspor'. Amitav Ghosh's The Glass Palace. The Quest24.1(Jun2010): 112-117.
- Shailaja Dr. P. and Manoja. Equality and Difference: A Reading of Amitav Ghosh's women. Poetcrit, 2007.
- Tiwari, Shubha. Amitav Ghosh- A Critical Study. New Delhi: Atlantic Publishers and Distributors, 2003.

4

Celebration of The Mythical El-dorado in Chitra Divakaruni's *Arranged Marriage*

Dr. Gunjan Chaturvedi

Associate Professor

Deptt. of English Studies & Research

B.D.K. (P.G.) College, Agra (U.P.)

Chitra Banerjee Divakaruni's *Arranged Marriage* is, as the blurb at the back of the 1995 edition (Anchor Books, N.Y.) reads, "exquisitely wrought debut collection of stories (that) subtly chronicles the accommodations – and the rebellion – Indian born girls and women in America undergo as they balance old treasured beliefs and surprisingly new desires." The eleven ravishingly beautiful stories of this canonical South Asian text feature Indian born females struggling to adapt to environments, to marriage and relationships and adapting their dreams to reality. This addition to the rich multi-cultural literature of the immigrant experience in the United States of America draws on the author's own ethnic background and all the stories together weave a rich tapestry of Indian women living new lives in the United States, walking a tight rope between traditional Indian heritage and freewheeling American experience. Though the characters vary, the basic theme of almost all these stories remains essentially the same – exploration of the nature of arranged marriages as well as the experience of affirmation and rebellion against the suffocating, stultifying and inhibiting social customs and traditions. The collection has attracted considerable critical acclaim and has been the recipient of several prestigious awards e.g. 1996

American Book Award, the Bay Area Book Reviewers' Award, the PEN Oakland Award for Fiction, Josephine Miles Prize for Fiction and many more.

A number of critics, however, have accused Chitra Divakaruni of tarnishing the image of Indian society and culture and of constructing binary oppositions that privilege a modern America over a traditional India, – a negative binary of a traditional (or non-West) country against a modern US (or West). The writers like Ms. Divakaruni, opines Dr. Asha Sen, "find popularity with American audience because they do not overtly challenge idealistic notions of American exceptionalism or colonial binaries of West and East." (Sen: 2009: 57) It is an undeniable fact that Ms. Divakaruni's thoughts and notions in *Arranged Marriage* are heavily influenced by her own westernization and adoption of American culture. "One of the things I wanted to focus on in this book," observed the author herself, "is the women who came here, how their lives have changed. And you can't say for the better or for the worse; they gain certain things, and they lose certain things. It is a very poignant and often painful process but also a very exhilarating and energetic process, and for many women it is an opportunity for new empowerment and freedom." (Divakaruni: 2000: 148) And it is this idea of America as a New world, an Eden, a Golden Mountain, a Paradise, a land of opportunities, enlightenment and promises of fairytale fulfillment, that has been endorsed by nearly all the stories in the collection. Unlike most of other immigrant writers like Bharati Mukherjee, Meena Alexander etc., who grapple with the problems and traumas, pains and erasures, dislocation and isolation, identity-crisis and sense of differentiation, Chitra Divakaruni disturbingly reconstructs the colonial binaries of East versus West as primitive versus civilized, with the premise that in an encounter of Indian and American values, the latter would be sure to prevail by virtue of an inherent superiority and progressiveness. "Divakaruni's immigrant narratives," professes Husne Jahan, "focus on celebrating immigration as a liberating agent at the expense of overshadowing the influence of any other agency." Ms. Divakaruni maligns almost every facet of Indian life and culture. While her stories, Husne Jahan continues, "rarely get declaredly into issues pertaining to colonial or post colonial politics, they do reveal striking parallels to Orientalist perceptions of many aspects of Indian culture and society... The problems, pains and erasures brought about by immigration are downplayed in Divakaruni's work, while the celebrations of the promises of immigration are emphasized to the point where some aspects of her work strongly promote neo-Orientalist and neo-Imperialist projects." (Jahan: 2007: 77-79) In the United States of America Ms. Divakaruni appears to have found her El-Dorado, the mythical city of gold that has fascinated but ever eluded countless explorers since the days of the Spanish Conquistadors. El-Dorado, which as a metaphor is used to represent something much sought after, which does not even exist so will never be found, seems to have been discovered by Chitra Banerjee Divakaruni in her adoptive country. By contrast the culture and people of her home-land i.e. India are portrayed as primitive, outmoded, inferior and evil in comparison to the Euro-derived culture and values, ways and life-styles of the new centre of the world i.e. the US of A.

Being a feminist Chitra Divakaruni certainly and vehemently raises a strong voice of protest against the subjugation of the female sex. She notices the failings of Indian patriarchy but fails to notice any fault in American males. The men from "the old country" (*Arranged Marriage* 1997: Blackswan Edition: Berkshire: 187. All the subsequent references to the collection are to this edition only) have been portrayed by her as self-absorbed, insensitive, mean, wife-abusers, servant-rapists or just plain, unpleasant men usually having a roving eye. On the other hand, she, as Lavinia Shankar points out, has "glorified the white male as the liberator of the repressed Asian female." (Shankar: 2001: 295). The very first story in *Arranged Marriage* i.e. 'The Bats' (set in India) is the tale of a young kid whose abusive father beats her mother almost every day and creates yellow blotches on her body, "with their edges turning purple" (2). He has no qualms in even flinging his young daughter against the wall if the child tries to stop him. This typical Indian male "exerts on his wife a power analogous to the poisonous traps in a mango-orchard that lure bats to their death." (Jahan: 2007: 85) Jayanti Ganguli's uncle in 'Silver Pavements, Golden Roofs' is a "low-class" (39), "ugly" (38) man who, in view of the niece is capable enough of using a ploy "to keep her (the aunt) shut up in the house and under his control." (46) Towards the end of the story, he also raises his arm (whatever may be the reason behind it) and hits Aunt Pratima "across the mouth". (53) The "tall, lean and sophisticated" Richard in 'A Perfect Life' is said to be "very different from the Indian men she (the heroine) had known back home." (173) The young Indian boys whose photos are sent by her mother for the purpose of marriage are all stereotypical "earnest, mustachioed men in stiff-collared shirts with slicked-back Brylcreem hair." (176) Richard, on the contrary, despite Meera's idiosyncratic behaviour stays by her side and even gets ready to marry her even after she extracts a promise from him never to have any children. When, on a particular occasion, Richard evinces the other side of his personality, sounds "avuncular" and "jealous", he is said to be "not that different after all from the heroes of the Hindi screen whom... (she had) left behind in Calcutta." (89) In 'The Maid Servant's Story', the husband tiptoes in the privacy of the night to seek a sexual liaison with the maid and in 'Doors' an Indian girl living in America receives a warning against getting married to a boy "who is straight out of India" (183) where "men have a set of pre-historic values". (184) And ultimately the warning comes out true as the Indian husband Deepak fails to act in accordance with his Americanized wife's concept of privacy and closed doors. The father of this Indian girl is said to have "mellowed over the years" after living in America and that is the reason why the marriage of the parents is happy enough – "You should have seen him when we first got married" (184), cries out the mother. In 'Meeting Mrinal' the narrator's husband, again an Indian male, leaves her and their seventeen year old son, after twenty years of marriage, for his red-haired secretary, and 'Affair' describes Meena, who is married to Srikant, a nerd who gives his computer an adoring feminine name 'Lalita' but fails to give any satisfaction to his wife. A middle aged American colleague, on the other hand, makes her feel "special......... understands.......(her), all of.......(her), even the bad parts. With him.......(she) can be.......(herself), like....... (she) never could before this." (269) Charles, says Meena, comprehends all her needs— "With him I didn't feel greedy or guilty or ashamed." (267) In 'The Ultrasound', Ramesh, the eldest son of a large, traditional, Brahmin family in India, forces his wife to go through an abortion only because amniocenteses test shows that it is a girl and "........ it is not fitting that the eldest child of the Bhattacharjee household should be a female" (224), while the other Indian male sitting in America, merely shrugs and says, "It is a man's world in India", (218) complacently implying that his own wife is lucky to be married to him and out of India, living in the "free and easy American culture." (218) In the story 'The Disappearance' an Indian husband allows no 'space' to his wife, makes all the major decisions in the household, raises his voice and forces her for a sexual intercourse, pulls her down on to the bed against her wishes, ignoring her explicit protests, and even then completely fails to understand the reason behind his wife's sudden disappearance because he regards his own behaviour as merely a normal exercise of his husbandly authority. He feels a bitter pleasure at the thought of his wife's meeting with an accident and her consequent death. Though he feels a bit ashamed at the thought but soon tears his wife's pictures, believes the relationship to be finished for ever, decides to go to the lawyer the very next day to find out the legal procedure for remarriage and already starts making plans for that. Indian men, thus, are "culturally, ideologically, mentally and physically diminished in comparison to their American counterparts" by Ms. Divakaruni. (Jahan: 2007: 86)

Divakaruni's portrayal of Indian males is sadly one-sided but that of Indian females is also stereotypical. They have been presented as suppressed, oppressed and submissive in the extreme, going on bearing the burden of Indian patriarchy with no hope of redemption at all. Many of the stories in *Arranged Marriage*, opines Roshni Rustomji-Kerns, "such as The Maid Servant's Story, Clothes, The Ultrasound, The Word Love and Meeting Mrinal can be read as a stereotyping of the polarized concept of freedom for a woman in America versus loss of freedom for a woman in India." (Kerns: 1995: 287) Be it the tortured wife of 'The Bats' or Aunt Pratima of 'Silver Pavements, Golden Roofs', Manisha of 'The Maid Servant's Story' or Abha or Asha of 'Affairs' and 'Meeting Mrinal' respectively—for all these Indian women, marriage, marital relationship, husband and children are the be-all and end-all of their existence. They readily accept being cheated, dominated, devitalized and sexually manipulated, but are incapable of breaking the wedding-knot. The lives of these ladies have been limited only to experiences of pain. They allow their husbands to play hegemonic role and stay in abusive marriages only to maintain the sham of social respectability, even if the relationship erodes the very core of their existence. The immigrant women, who are in the process of being Americanized, are, by contrast, shown as exercising greater freedom in comparison to the non-immigrant ones. In the story 'The Disappearance', a Calcutta born woman in America manages to escape from the clutches of an insipid marriage. In 'Affairs' Abha keeps busy in cooking and housekeeping, and constantly suffers from satirical abuses hurled at her by her husband who ridicules her for her "prudish Indian upbringing" (234). It is only when more modernized and westernized Meena succeeds in getting out of her lifeless marriage that Abha also feels the realization dawning upon herself that her own marriage is also only an unsavoury arrangement. Only then she finds herself capable enough to gather courage and free herself from the shackles of a futile relationship. The traditional Indian gender roles have thus been contrasted by Ms. Divakaruni with the life in freewheeling US, where even the most obedient and self-negating women discover that they can live a more fulfilling life. "Recently arrived from Calcutta, unsettled in Chicago and San Francisco," observes Rose Kernochan, "Ms. Divakaruni's heroines are still half submerged in the dream world of Indian femininity, in an innocence as still and dark as lake water. As America revives them, they rise to its challenges; the new freedoms of their chosen country act on them like extra oxygen." (Kernochan: Quoted by Jahan: 2007: 20)

In India Divakaruni fails to see anything that is admirable, praiseworthy or appreciable. Almost all the marriages there are orchestrated by parents who are far more concerned with status, caste etc. than in their daughter's happiness, and these marriages always bring together two absolutely ill-matched individuals. In 'Silver Pavements, Golden Roofs' the heroine wonders how a marriage could ever have been arranged between Bikram Uncle – a short, stocky, ugly, dark-skinned man with a jarring voice-and her sophisticated, sensitive, beautiful and delicate aunt. In 'Affairs' two Indo-American couples decide to break off the ties after years of affluent living in Silicon Valley even though their horoscopes had been matched perfectly. Besides the tradition of arranging lives by arranging marriages, Ms. Divakaruni holds many other rituals and customs of India for disparagement. The bangle-breaking ceremony after the death of the husband leaves a big stinging cut on the arm of the widow; the widow is forced to wear a white Saree and the red marriage mark from her forehead is cruelly rubbed off. "For all the pain and oppression of women in the traditions, myths and histories that Divakaruni invokes in her poetry, short stories and novels, the writer hardly finds anything that could be redeeming, inspiring or liberating," remarks Husne Jahan. "It seems", she continues, "that the literary, cultural and political traditions of the Indian sub-continent have never produced any resistance to oppression in its entire history, which is, of course, far from reality." (Jahan: 2007: 81). In the story 'Clothes' Sumita visualizes her own life in India as a widow and feels horrified. She cries out, "I know I can not go back. I don't yet how I'll manage, here in this new, dangerous land. I only know I must. Because all over India, at this very moment, widows in white saris are bowing their veiled heads, serving tea to in-laws. Doves with cut-off wings." (33) India is a land of such hard-hearted mothers as choose to cut off all their ties with their only daughters only because they have a 'live-in' relationship with some or the other American friend, even after the daughters assure them of an early marriage to the man, even after they apologize and promise to come back to India. India is land where the faces of the mothers may remain "blank, oval, featureless" (66) when their daughters are going through dilemmas of their lives. It is a land the "black centre (of which) ripples like a bottomless well." (65) On the one hand, mothers here are so cruel and on the other it is said that "in Indian marriage becoming a wife...(is) only the prelude to that all important, all consuming event – becoming a mother." (76) Mother-love is here said to be "Real, primitive and dangerous, lurking somewhere in the female genes-especially our Indian ones – waiting to attack." (75) The heroine of the story 'A Perfect Life' muses—"Thanks to the Pill and his easy going attitude (it was a Californian thing, he told me once) for the first time in my life I felt free. It was an exhilarating sensation, once I got used to it. It made me giddy and weightless, like I could float away at any moment." (174). The American ladies are here said to be more circumspect but Indian friends who are already wives and mothers with "their limp hair pulled into unattractive bun, their crumpled saris sporting stains of a suspicious nature, the bulge of love handles that hung below the edges of their blouses...", (75) keep on harping upon the idea of marriage and motherhood. They are said to be "intellectually diminished" and the narrator of the story blurts out—"They might as well have not come to America." (76) Almost all the characters in the book *Arranged Marriage*, as Susan Chacko complains "seem to live in a mysterious sort of time warp – although the situations and details are contemporary, their behaviour is often what we would associate with a earlier generation than our own." (Chacko: Review *Arranged Marriage*: www.sawnet.org)

America is described by Ms. Divakaruni as a panacea for all the ills of Indian women. She constantly ascribes mythical names to the country—"kingdom beyond the seven seas"(18), "Great America" (25), "distant land beyond the ocean," (110) "a far off magic land where pavements are silver and the roofs all gold." (56) and so on. She eulogizes everything related to the nation. The gun-wielding, sexist womanizer James Bond is here elevated to the stature of the magical and admirable liberator (293) while the revered Hindu mythological characters like Kunti, Arjuna, Bhim etc. are blamed for perpetrating stereotypes of female sacrifice and male power. Anju in 'The Ultrasound' attributes her sense of justice and feminism to America even though rudimentary childhood drawings evinced her as a budding feminist even earlier. Anju, however, herself denies that pre-existing feminist and places her enlightened views and thoughts on geographic and cultural boundaries of America. Indian dresses, specially 'sari' are here depicted as symbols of entrapment while the western attire of skirt and blouse is described as a symbol of liberation. The complexities of American past and present are very conveniently brushed aside by Ms. Divakaruni with nothing more than a few passing references. "Clothes", comments Asha Sen, "in the US… function as a simulacrum or a distorted version of reality." (Sen: 2009: 63) The cream blouse and long brown skirt, predicts Ms. Divakaruni, will magically provide Sumita, the heroine of 'Clothes', with a professional life. This mythical happy ending is predicted on a desired image rather than an actual reality. "Even in post-modern America," to quote Dr. Sen again, where style is substance, clothes can not disguise racial difference and it is disingenuous of Divakaruni or her narrator to pretend that this is possible." (Sen: 2009: 63)

There is only one story in the whole collection where Divakaruni has made an attempt to look at the complexity of America, though even this story is plagued by some typical colonial binaries. In the story 'Silver Pavement, Golden Roofs', the heroine Jayanti Ganguli and her aunt become victims of the racist slurs of the neighbourhood boys. These slurs problematize Jayanti's American experience for a while. She, however, reacts to racism only through literary and colonial references. The slurs, she thinks, belong to another place and time. They might have been suitable from the lips of "a red-faced gin and tonic drinking British official, perhaps, in his colonial bungalow, or a sneering overseer out of *Uncle Tom's Cabin* as he plies his whip in the cotton fields." (51) Her bereaved, grief-stricken uncle blurts out – "This damn country, like a *dain*, a witch – it pretends to give and then snatches everything back" (54) but Jayanti tries to neutralize the threat of racism by focusing on the obvious youth of the perpetrators and attempts to believe that racism in US is not an issue of exploitative policies but only a street prank of young boys. The story's conciliatory tone in the end suggests that it condones violence under extenuating circumstances. At the end when Jayanti thinks of multi-coloured hands she has encountered in America and the complexities associated with multi-racial American society, white snow falls to soften "forgivingly, the rough, noisy edges of things." (55-56) Husne Jahan very succinctly remarks—"The snow becomes an anesthetizing agent, a symbol of the kind of erasure that Jayanti is about to embrace in America." (Jahan: 2007: 84) In his essay 'The Fact of Blackness', Martinique psychiatrist Frantz Fanon describes the psychological effects of colonialism and says that they become "manifest in the self hatred when he encounters the gaze of the dominant white Other who defines him as black and inferior." (Fanon: 1967: 132) Faced with this racist gaze, as Fanon says, the black man or woman has no option but to turn white or disappear. When Jayanti Ganguli who regards herself as a beautiful, fair Indian girl of a good family, encounters the same experience, she also aspires to escape into the beauty of whiteness. Earlier she was dreaming of a white professor but that would confer upon her only an honorary whiteness. In order to achieve the privilege of whiteness, she gets prepared to transform herself completely, even if it would involve a lot of pain. She stands on the balcony, watching the snow fall and notices that the snow has covered her hands completely "until they do not hurt at all." (56) This closure of the story suggests that what Jayanti is here aspiring for, is a very Fanonian desire to turn white. In fact from the very beginning of the story it comes out prominently that Jayanti is afflicted with the European colonialist notions of equating dark skin-colour with a lower breed of humans characterized by traits of brutality, vulnerability and lack of sophistication, e.g. her opinion about and description of her uncle. In contrast, the fictive white professor she dreams about, is described as handsome, refined and romantic – a polar opposite of the uncle. What to say about Jayanti, her creator Chitra Divakaruni herself gave evident proofs of her colonial biases regarding colour of the skin when she named her collection of poetry (a poem of which suggested the name *Arranged Marriage* for the collection of the stories) –*The Black Candle* – 'black' because dealing with the women of three Asian countries India, Pakistan and Bangladesh.

In her '*Arranged Marriage*' thus, Chitra Banerjee Divakaruni has glorified America, Americans, American values, American life-style as well as the immigrants' lives in US beyond reality and reason and has celebrated Indian women's immigration to this land as a lucky escape from the suppressed and oppressed conditions of India resulting in the attainment of freedom and discovery of self with the inspiration of western influences, – an escape, as it were, from evil to good, from pain to pleasure, from negative to positive, from darkness to light. In this respect she might be described as a member of that educated class in the modern Orient who, as Edward W.Said declares, borrow ideas about "modernization, progress and culture" from the Western countries, for the most part from the United States, and participate in their own "Orientalizing". (Said: 1995: 325)

Cited References

1. Chacko, Susan: Review *Arranged Marriage*: www.sawnet.org/ Sawnet-Bookshelf-Fiction-Reviews.
2. Divakaruni, Chitra Banejree: Interview by Dharini Rasiah: *Conversations with Asian American Writers: Language, Arts & Discipline:* ed. King-Kok Cheung: University of Hawai Press: 2000.
3. Fanon, Frantz: 'The Fact of Blackness': *Black Skin, White Masks*: Trans. Charles Lam Markmann: Grove Press: N.Y.: 1967.
4. Jahan, Husne: 'Colonial Woes in Post-Colonial Writing: Chitra Banerjee Divakaruni's *Arranged Marriage* in *'Indian Women's Short Fiction'*: eds. Joel, Kuortti and Mittapalli, Rajeshwar: Atlantic Publishers & Distributors Pvt. Ltd.: N.D.: 2007.
5. Kernochan, Rose: Quoted by Husne Jahan in 'Colonial Woes in Post-Colonial Writing: Chitra Banejree Divakaruni's *Arranged Marriage* in *Indian Women's Short Fiction*: eds. Joel, Kuortti and Mittapalli, Rajeshwar: Atlantic Publishers & Distributors Pvt. Ltd.: N.D.: 2007.
6. Kerns, Roshni Rustomji: 'Chitra Banerjee Divakaruni's *Arranged Marriage*': *Journal of South Asian Literature*: 30/1 & 2: N.Y.: 1995.
7. Said, Edward W.: *Orientalism*: Penguin Books: New Delhi: 1995.
8. Sen, Asha: 'From National to Transnational: Three Generations of South Asian American Writers': *Asiatic*: Vol. 3, No. 1: June, 2009. International Islamic University, Malaysia.
9. Shankar, Lavinia: *Resource Guide to Asian American Literature*: eds. Stephen Sumaida and Sau Ling Wong: NY: MLA: 2001.

5

Cultural Confrontations in Chitra Banerjee Divakaruni's The Mistress of Spices

Dr. Ibrahim Khalilulla M.

Assistant Professor
Department of English,
Sahyadri Science College (Auto)
Kuvempu University, Shimoga-577203,

Diaspora signals an engagement with a matrix of diversity: of cultures, Languages, histories, people, places, times. Diaspora is a loaded term that brings to mind various contested ideas and images. It can be a positive site for the affirmation of an identity, or, conversely, a negative site of fears of losing that identity. Diaspora is also a popular term in current research as it captures various phenomena that are prevalent in the numerous discourses devoted to current transnational globalization: borders, migration, "illegal" immigration, repatriation, exile, refugees, assimilation, multiculturalism, hybridity.

Diaspora writers have always reveled in showcasing the inalienable and ubiquitous and displacement. At the advent of globalization, multicultural societies of the present days are a result of extensive Diaspora that has been taking place especially over the last 200 years at various levels. Indian immigration in the last century was mainly a personal choice of individuals, particularly for academic pursuit or economic gain either towards the Middle East or to western countries particularly the US. The inhabitants of these countries reacted differently to the ways of immigrants. In almost all the cases the expatriate face a close of contrasting cultures and feeling of alienation, which was then followed by the attempts to adjust and to acclimatize, either from a separate identity as racial group or be assimilated. These are reflected in the writing now generally placed under the Umberalla of "expatriate writing" or "writing of the diaspora". Currently, diaspora writings has become popular and the diasporic women writers have special place in Indian Diasporic writings. Meena Alexander, Sunitra Gupta, Jhumpha lahiri, Bharathi Mukherjee, Chitra Banerjee are the some of the prominent contemporary diasporic women writers. These Diasporic women writers who have portrayed the cultural dilemmas, the generational difference, and transformation of their identities during displacement. These writers are deeply attached to their centrifugal homeland and they are caught physically between two worlds. Their experience as living in-between condition is very painful and they stand bewildered and confused. Diaspora women writers sought to find words and froms to fit their experiences and have chosen narrative strategies like auto-biography, the novels and the short stories to do so. These Diasporic women writers while depicting migrant characters in their fiction explore the theme of displacement and dilemma of cultural identity. The diasporic Indian writers have generally dealt with characters from their own displaced community.

Indian-born Chitra Banerjee Divakaruni brought new perspectives to contemporary Diasporic women's writings in the United States with a series of highly praised novels and short stories, after she was first honoured as a poet. Positioned at the interface of various cultures—originally from Kolkata and now residing in Houston, Texas—Divakaruni is herself the embodiment of the themes prevalent in her writings. Chitra Banerjee Divakaruni excels at depicting the cultural dialectics of immigrant experience, like many other contemporary writers. In her works she unveiled the complexities of discrimination, assimilation, social and demographic change, which not only affected the society itself but the lives of the various ethnic groups and the immigrants. She also depicts the cultural barriers, identity crisis, racism, and violence faced by the immigrants. In her first full-length novel *The Mistress of Spices* (1997) explores the various cultural confrontations encountered by immigrants. The novel explores the typical immigrant experience showing the mirror to Indian women wriggling out of stereotypes in American urban landscapes.

The novel *The Mistress of Spices* (1997) adopts a more complex strategy for portraying Diasporic Idenity. She makes use of fable in order to explore the various kinds of problems encountered by immigrants. Divakaruni herself says for what reason, she has written this novel : " I wrote in a spirit of play, collapsing the divisions between the realistic world of twentieth century America and the timeless one of myth and magic in my attempt to create a modern fable"(1). In The Mistress of Spices, the process of self-perception is the foundation of identity formation for the central character Tilotamma (Tilo). As Tilo strives to define herself as South Asian and American, she develops multiple consciousnesses that manifest themselves in both her experiences and her subsequent relationships with her racial and sexual identities. While Tilo is living in America, she is incapable of pure self-perception, and can only see herself through the eyes of those around her, leaving her own self-seeing as a secondary and almost marginal perspective. Tilo views herself through the lens of her surrounding society, thereby leading to various and often conflicting simultaneous visions of her identity.

In this novel the first person narrative has been adopted from the outlook of Tilo or Tilotama, who has skilled to take out the essence of the spices and make them to alleviate pain, solve problems and help people live better lives. The Mistress of spices-the deliberate gendering of the word to undercut the power associated with mastery supernatural powers is to be noted. She can foretell disasters and look into the hearts of people, only in her hands "the spices sang back", her trainer, the 'old one', had told her signifying that Tilo would never be the obedient complaint mistress that she was expected to be. But Tilotama or Tilo as she calls herself is not perfect sometimes it is too difficult to face the problems of the Diaspora. Tilo runs a spice store in Oakland, California. Where she has recreated little India which boast of all the spices that ever were even the lost ones. "I think I do not exaggerate when I say there is no other place in the world quite like this"(2). She says of her store which attracts a large group of people for whom the place is reminiscent of home, a little oasis in their diasporic lives loaded with problems. The Mistress of spices feels that the Indians come to her store in quest of happiness: "All those voices, Hindioriya Assamese, Urdu, Tamil, English, layered one on the other like notes from tanpura, all those voices asking for happiness except no one seems to know where"(3). But even within the structure of the fable Divakaruni has underscored obscure nature of national borders.

At first, Tilo allows these perceptions of herself (as created by others) to dominate her thinking, yet as she assimilates herself to American culture throughout the course of the text, Tilo comes to claim her own self-perception. Ironically, however, she finds that she is in fact comprised of the numerous identities that other people had ascribed to her, for the perceptions that others had of her are all legitimate aspects of her identity. The result of this knowledge is Tilo's recognition of her multiple consciousnesses, and although this multiplicity is replete with contradictions, Divakaruni nevertheless presents it as a possible "solution" for Tilo's dilemma of cross-cultural identity formation. The Mistress of spices is allowed by the powers that to be work magic only for the good of her own people i.e., Indians. The others must go elsewhere for their need, the first mother, the senior woman, had warned her National boundaries become violent, all important in the Diaspora, as a way of defining identity, originality that marks the form of one's experience, a platform for resisting co-optation by the dominant discourse. The spices store with its sacred, secret shelves functions as a geographical space that is the store of a monolithic national identity. The store represents a space for 'self indulgence'. "Dangerous for a brown people who come from elsewhere, to whom real Americans might say why?"(4).

The mistress of spices is the gentle spirit who hovers over Indians living in america. But for Divakaruni, assuaging the pain of diasporic life is more complex. Jaggi (Jagjit) is separated and racially marked. A timid child, he is assaulted at school for not knowing English, for not belonging: "Talk English son of a bitch" Speak up nigger wetback asshole"(5). Tilo's attempts at restoring confidence to the little boy combined with the pressures to conform transforms him into an aggressive young man who has been offered protection by a group of boys. In exchange they have asked him to carry this packet here,drop off this box there'. Jaggi is carrying out his duties carefully waiting to turn fourteen when he will get his coveted gift: "cold and black, shining and heavy with power in (his) hand, pulsing electric as life, as death(his)passport into real America "(6). Tilo is shocked and wonders whether it is her spice-remedy, Jaggi's parents or America that have driven him to become a drug trafficker, who is perhaps on his way to becoming an armed criminal. The little boy has become Jagjit by getting his back on those jeering voices, the spitting mouths, the hands; in the playground that had assaulted him.

Every immigrant in America, assimilates and grow economically and those who lost their jobs or worse, their children. The complexities of diasporic debate are underpinned by questions of identify, and Divakaruni novel tries to capture the nuances that contest the stereotypical images of south Asians as model minorities and unremarkable citizens.

But Tilo, the ministering angel, is more concerned with those who need her help. Each chapter is named after a spice and discusses the trails and problems of an individual and the special characteristics of the spices for instance: "each spices has day special to it.....color of day break and conch-shell sound. Turmeric the preserves, keeping foods safe in a land of.....heat and hunger. Turmeric the auspicious spice, placed on the.... over coconuts as pujas, rubbed into borders of wedding saris "(9).

Thus, the reader gets the glimpses of spices into a range that surrounds the life of the diasporic Indian. Mrs. Ahuja's story is a story of dispossession. She left the settled, comfortable life at her father's house, when she was married to a violent man, an alcoholic who abuses her. Unhappy in domestic life, she wants to start again in America, but she cannot drown out those voices of conditioning that outlined womanly duties for her, 'the voices, we carried them all the way inside our heads"(10). The Mistress's tools can dismantle Ahuja's houses out only when she, herself , is ready for the challenge ;the Mistress helps Mrs. Ahuja she becomes Lalita by overthrowing the tyrannical structures that have weighed her down, compelled her to be brutally raped night after night by her husband. Lalita leaves her husband's and seeks refuge at women's shelter. For Geeta, Tilo mixes several ingredients, ginger for deeper courage, fenugreek for healing breaks and 'amchur' for deciding right.

For the second generation Indian like Geeta, the questions about identity are differently poised. She challenges continuous identification with patriarchal traditions which she associates with her grandfather. Tilo empathizes with Geeta, tries to tolerate their pain and the novel tells us that she succeeds in restoring harmony within the family.

Tilo or tilotama, The Mistress of spices is really a young woman who required by the dictates of the order to disguise herself as an old woman, thus bring up her asexuality and inducing mystery and restraint. She cannot be aware of her own body: " Once the Mistress has taken on her magic Mistress-body, she is never to look on her reflection again" (12). She is required to bury her own desires and prioritize those of others: "A Mistress must carve her own waiting out of her chest, must fill the hollow left behind with the needs of those she serves"(13).

Tilo transgresses many boundaries for those who need her help, but she cannot be contained within this frame work. It is not hard to see that as in Arranged Marriage(1995), Divakaruni's script of women's rebellion against the pressure to suppress their and their bodies. The order of Mistresses clearly replicates patriarchal struggles and Tilo must be made to break free of them. She struggles with her own passions as she builds emotional relationship with Native American man, whom she calls Raven. She transforms herself in to a woman, feeling guilty about her "self indulgence", decides to brave the vengeance that she would have to face. At the level of body- politics, Tilo's re-formulations about her body, her desire to have a sexual relationship with Raven outside of institutional sanctions, go against the loss of the order of Mistress. But, Tilo knows the danger, she is in. She can always sense it. Hence, she conveys this to Raven in the novel.

The Mistress of Spices (1997) adopts a more mature structural configuration in order to discuss the Diaspora. Each chapter contains a little vignette about an individual, about a cultural encounter. The stories are then braid together through the novel, the sublets shades caught and developments depicted. A variety of cultural codes and icons are recognized as Tilo weaves her tapestry of different lives becomes implicated in the lives of Jaggi, Ahuja's wife, and Geeta.

The Mistress of Spices gives plenty of sources on Diasporic grounds. It enhances the Indian glory, into the past and present world. The intermingling of both cultures reflects more on Indian immigrants, who are curious of Indian land. The magical realism of the east, the exotic land viewed by western eyes, glance the Indian beauty of spices and their magic.

The novel closes with Tilo renaming herself Maya, which "can mean many things. Illusion, spell, enchantment, the power that keeps this imperfect world going day after day"(71). Tilo chooses a name that "can mean many things," a name that embodies the multiplicity of her identities, the many consciousnesses that lie within her. Interestingly, “Maya” is also an ancient Sanskrit name, and the juxtaposition of a name so representative of a cultural past with Tilo’s present power suggests that Tilo still lives in between spheres, with contradictory spaces and times comprising the rather ambiguous landscape of her existence. In naming herself, Tilo reveals that which she is made of: multiple consciousnesses that allow her to exist as not as South Asian or American only, but rather as everything in between, living a life that spans the endless boundaries of space and time and in which identity is filled with the promise of endless possibility and eternal evolution. The novel deals with the problem of expatriates, torn between the values of their own society and by those of the west. Divakaruni’s writings raise themes of alienation and self-transformation at various levels and try to voice such questions by exploring their roots, allegiance, family, origin, community and identity through her works.

Referencs

- Ashcroft, Bill. *Post-Colonial Transfromation.* London: Routledge,2011.
- Bhabha, Homi K. *The Location of Culture.* London: Routledge,1994.
- Brah, Avtar. *Cartographies of Diaspora: Contending Identities.* London: Routledge, 1996
- Brown, Juidith M. *Global South Asians: Introducing the Modern Diaspora.* Cambridge: Cambridge University Press, 2006.
- Braziel, Jana Evans, and Anita Mannur,eds. *Theorizing Diaspora: A Reader.* Melbourne: Blackwell, 2003.
- Divakaruni, Chitra Banerjee’s. *The Mistress of Spices.* London: Abacus, 1997.
- Nasta, Sushelia. *Home Truths: Fictions of South Asian Diaspora in Britain.* New York: Palgrave, 2002.

6

Diasporic Comparison: *The Namesake* and *Brick Lane*

Chowdhury Omar Sharif

Lecturer, Dept. of English,

East West University, Bangladesh

Monica Ali's *Brick Lane* and Jhumpa Lahiri's *The Namesake* deal with the similar theme of immigrant identity and cultural loyalty. Both the writers are immigrants. Monika Ali, who is of Bangladeshi origin, lives in England and Jhumpa Lahiri, whose parents are from India, lives in America. As a result, they are migrant-experienced. Both of the writers deal with the similar subject matters of immigration, and exploration of identity in different places. They have taken traditional approach of locating the newly migrant couple. In *Brick Lane*, the story is about the migration to London and 'back home' to Bangladesh. Similarly, in *The Namesake,* the story is unfolded as a chronological narrative both in the US and in India. While *Brick Lane* focuses on the new rural migrant Nazneen in London and in almost similar time frame Ashima of *The Namesake* gets focused in Boston. In *The Namesake* it puts more emphasis on changing relationships focusing more on 'Gogol' the second generation son of Ashoke and Ashima Ganguli.

In today's multicultural countries, diaspora, hybridity and the confusion of cultural identity (identity crisis) are key issues. Immigration has resulted into a multi-ethnic society and cultural diversity as well as the problems of discrimination, assimilation, social and demographic change, which not only affected the society itself but also the lives of the various ethnic groups and of the individuals.

Gayatri Spivak's use of concept of "Resident Alien", which describes the status of permanent residents that do not hold American citizenship, becomes a useful theoretical tool in a debate on migrant people's identity. It creates problems on the survival of the immigrants. It also shows the problematic nature of rigid identity. The term has been used by Spivak at first to analyze the experience of inhabiting a foreign country, "Spivak says 'Large-scale movements of people, renamed 'diasporas', are what defines our time'" (Uncategorized N. pag.). Spivak says that the survival of identity-defining categories that are no longer relevant to contemporary experiences:

The figure of the long-term Resident Alien belongs to a tenaciously held territoriality that is, also, of course, abstract; as all territoriality must be; yet it robs the figure of the more salient abstractions of an everyday civility, a willing suspension of civil rights. The virtuality of the new demographic frontiers is accretive rather than privative, it enlarges rather than shrinks. It creates the kind of para-state collectivities that were part of the predication of the shifting multicultural empires that had written the spatialized temporizing of the planet before monopoly capitalist colonialism – colonialism in the narrow sense. The figure of the Resident Alien seems to belong, by contrast, to postcoloniality in the narrow sense. (Alexandru N. pag.)

Although immigrants have similar difficulties in settling and adjusting in their new countries, there may be differences in their situations and conditions. They have to go through a long process of assimilation and have to try to find the right balance between taking up a new culture and their own roots. However, minority groups recognize the importance of their old traditions and national language.

"M. Kozár also notes that assimilation is an integrative process within the family and between generations, and is not socially and culturally equable, thus resulting in hybridity and the confusion of cultural identity. The assimilation of the first generation is never complete, they are in an in-between state where they have already left their culture behind but have not integrated the new culture yet. On the other hand, the second generation tends to aim at total assimilation, by breaking away from the roots and traditions (M. Kozár, „A magyarországi szlovének asszimilációja az 1980-as évektõl napjainkig" 2005)." (Pataki N. pag.)

This type of cultural assimilation can be observed in the case of American Asians and British Asians as well. The biggest populations among South Asian immigrants in America and in London are of Indian, Pakistani and Bangladeshi origin. They are forced to face a new way of adjustment. This time, they have to ignore the feeling of home. They get confused by the opposing nature of native culture and their own and as a result they suffer from the confusion of cultural identity.

Consequently, these immigrants preserve and transmit their culture to their children, who are surrounded by and taught to live according to two often contrasting cultural and social sets of traditions and expectations. In this culture-clash, they may transform into a serious confusion of cultural identity. Naturally, the process of doing away with the confusion is evident and the realization is also there that there is no one who has right identity. They think that identities are fluid and constantly changing. Jhumpa Lahiri and Monika Ali have focused on that type of confusions and difficulties of adjustment in *The Namesake* and in *Brick Lane* and at the same time, they have shown that it is neither easy nor natural for South Asian immigrants as they have had to face the overt and indirect racism, poverty, exclusion and assimilation caused by the natives. In-betweenness is a constant feeling of dislocation and identity confusion, and a feeling that characterises first generation immigrants the most. As for the second generation, a less strong bond with the home-country, and culture and the natural acceptance of the 'new' world around them tend to result in another condition of cultural existence, hybridity.

Brick Lane portrays the position and identity-confusion of Bengali women in the isolated community of Tower Hamlets in multicultural London through the story of the 18-year-old heroine, Nazneen, who faces the immigrant-experience for her arranged marriage with the immigrant Chanu, who is twenty years senior to her. Through Nazneen's eyes, the reader gets acquainted with the position and struggles of the women of the Bangladeshi community. The novel follows Nazneen's life from the first confused and obedient years through her affair with the young radical Karim until her final decision to start a new, independent life, not as a duteous Bengali wife but as a strong British Asian woman. This process of Nazneen's emancipation is accompanied by the emotional and cultural shock of migration, the everyday reality of racism, the hardships of settling in and adapting to in an utterly unfamiliar country, the feeling of dislocation, and identity confusion.

Ashima in *The Namesake*, represents a certain kind of relational identity which, is a good Indian tradition. Brought to America by her arranged marriage, she finds herself in the middle of a completely unknown culture to which she does not know how to relate and there is nobody around to tell her. She goes through the experience of motherhood alone. They are never going to return to India and that it is her duty as a wife and mother to become an American, Ashima never really manages to do so consciously. For most of her married life, she clings to an Indian model of the family as an indestructible unit outside which individual identity cannot be conceived and she finds it very hard to accept her children's wish to become independent as all their American friends are. She brings up her children in strong connection with the Bengali immigrant community on the East Coast as she takes them to Bengali school and Kathakali shows. She always conceives herself as someone who is indestructibly connected to her family back in Calcutta, from whom she should never have been separated and whom she constantly misses. The death of her husband deprives her of any real connection with America. Her decision to go back to India is the only other option.

The characters of these two novels are immigrants. They come from various cultures, have different beliefs and their own individual stories of immigration and assimilation. They are similar in their experiences and are going through the long process of trying to find or restate their identities. For South Asians, the main reasons for migration are education and economic interest, or for seeking political exile but they all have to face the hardships of settling, adjusting or assimilating in an increasingly hostile atmosphere. Besides, finding their place in their new home is further complicated. Ashoke Ganguli in *The Namesake*, and Chanu of *Brick Lane* try to resolve their identity crisis, but eventually they fail to do so, which reinforces their feelings of 'in-betweenness' and forces them to re-think of their identity. By admitting their faults, they can come to terms with identity confusion and accept their fate.

In *The Namesake*, Jhumpa Lahiri shows a newly couple, Ashoke Ganguli and Ashima Ganguli, goes to America from India. They have a son named Gogol who is considered to be the second generation immigrant in America. Gogol does not like this name which is called by his parents at home rather he feels more comfortable with another name, Nikhil. Since, he is a second generation immigrant; he needs to accommodate himself with the multicultural society in America. He needs to maintain two cultures at a time- one is Indian (with his parents) and another is American (with his friends and outsiders). As a result, he becomes a hybrid person from cultural context. Sometimes he suffers from identity crisis because it sometimes becomes a very unusual thing to him, and for this; he needs to mimic or to repeat the various contents of American multicultural society. All these become very problematic for the Gogol family in an alien culture.

Then, in *Brick Lane*, Monika Ali deals with the very similar theme as *The Namesake*. Here, in this novel, a South Asian Bangladeshi immigrant couple, Nazneen and Chanu, lives in Tower Hamlet at Brick Lane in London. Although they live in London, they constantly feel for their native land and they become nostalgic every moment. As an immigrant community, they cannot express their words and ambitions properly in multicultural London. Chanu does not let Nazneen go out or learn correct English because he feels insecure if Nazneen acts like the English women. But when Nazneen meets Karim Amir, a Bangladeshi guy, she forgets her culture and becomes a hybrid one. And, Chanu returns to his home in Bangladesh at last as he could never welcome the English society.

The third part of this chapter shows the comparative study between these two novels. Jhumpa Lahiri and Monika Ali, both of the writers are diasporic personalities which I have already mentioned. So there are so many similarities between themes of these two novels. Both the writers have focused on two immigrant families from two neighbouring Asian countries. They have used both Bengali and English language in their writing. Most highlighted issue of the novel is the problems of immigrants in an alien society.

Foucault's objective "has been to create a history of the different modes by which in our culture, human beings are made subjects" (Besley, Peters 50). This line tells the basis of novels, where characters or human bodies are also made into subjects within a framed context, propagating a historiography of culture through the different genres of horror, comedy amongst others, but more forcefully. In this respect, *The Namesake* undeniably sheds some light on how culture affects the dislocated body but also moulds an identity and thereby creating the sentiment of empathy with its spectators. This is a "culturally rooted" novel dwells amidst the complexities of the intermingling of two cultures and a search for identity which eventually culminates in the triumph of knowing, who you are and where you are.

Jhumpa Lahiri's *The Namesake* would be called a diasporic novel because like many other post-colonial novels, *The Namesake* deals with the issues of the dislocated body as a result of those same post-colonial effects of race and identity. The novel revolves around a Bengali family but Jhumpa Lahiri takes a polycentric multiculturalists' approach, rather than targeting a particular group of people or a segment of society. The novel tries to bind people together and speaks to everyone irrespective of their cultural background within a reality that exists. It can be said that *The Namesake* is an experiential piece of work since it embodies the reality of Jhumpa Lahiri's life as har life is also being a part of a diaspora.

It is seen that the story of *The Namesake* is set for the most part in America. Ashoke Ganguli, who has been studying in America for the past two years, goes back to his hometown, Calcutta, India, and marries a Bengali girl, Ashima. Together they head back to the USA and embark on their new journey there. They eventually have a son, Gogol and a daughter, Sonia. The plot revolves around this family and the intricacies, that come with being first generation Migrant, bound so much to their tradition and bringing up second generation American-Indians perpetually conflicted by identity crisis. *The Namesake's* opening credit shifts continuously from Bengali script to English presenting the ambiguous nature of the novel's theme which is that of cultural identity. This could either be seen as a crisis between east and west or a harmonizing nature depicted through the mélange of both languages.

Many of the diasporic novels "explore the identity complexities of exile- from one's own geography, from one's own history, from one's own body- within innovative narrative strategies" (Shohat, Stam 318). *The Namesake* does not deal with forced exile in the literal sense, but an existentialist choice, that Ashoke and Ashima made, which nonetheless depicts the same sentiments of being in exile which is strewn about all over the novel through the experience of isolation. In the beginning of the novel, a contrast has been made between India which has been shot in a very colourful décor with a crowd of family at the airport bidding Ashima and Ashoke farewell and the consecutive scene portraying an almost deserted like, snowy and grey America. The wintery atmosphere outside is reflected in the couple's room which also seems very gloomy.

This creates a stark difference setting the tone for the novel that Jhumpa Lahiri has tried to create in order to enhance this feeling of loneliness one feels in a foreign land through strategic use of a fitting colour palette. It grips the reader and everybody can easily identify to this scene of loneliness which is so true since one feels the loneliness through the body, where anyone feels like just curling up his/her body in a cocoon to protect his/her against the slicing loneliness while perceiving this scene. As the readers go through this scene and relating back to Ashima's traditional ways, there is a part where she prepares some cornflakes which are traditionally a very American food, but instead of pouring milk in it, she puts chili powder, this can come as a bit of surprise to the western readers. Having the cornflakes this way is a part of her cultural background and identity, for it is the only way she has learnt to eat it. This scene, on the other hand, also reveals her first experience of being in a new country to which she would have to adapt and learn certain rules of the road in order to build her niche and to fit in. Globally, very little is known about other cultures outside of the western context, where most people naturally would not know that India has a dish which is quite like cornflakes but is called 'chivda' or 'chaat' (in India) eaten with spice or 'masala' (Indian word). Ashima would simply be seen here as defying what is accepted as "normal". The west blamed Third World nation's underdevelopment due to the fact that they kept to their cultural traditions rather than following in the latter's footsteps. Ashima also, wearing her sari throughout the novel, shows her relationship in keeping with her tradition and at the same time evolving and learning what is best from her new environment.

Another equally important character in the novel is that of Gogol. The namesake, Gogol has been named after the Russian, Nikolai Gogol, who was Ashoke's favorite author. The story of Gogol Ganguli is that of an American-Indian boy and his struggle in situating himself in between these two worlds where he is bound to a hyphenated identity. He situates himself within a present culture but brings on the luggage of another, where one is always more obvious than the other. Based simply on the appearance, Gogol would be termed as an Indian, but accentually an American. It is tautological but whereby any meaning leads to that same individual. Gogol's case is complex, as he is an American-Indian but has a funny Russian name which makes him the centre of taunts. *The Namesake* tries to evade from that usual conflict of a person from any diaspora who faces having a traditional name, which becomes hard to pronounce and therefore the name is westernized. In the novel, Gogol's name is changed to Nikhil to make it easier on the boy, but as one family friend, in the novel, rightly remarks that the name would be regressed as Nick and that obviously happens later on. As Gogol grows up and taking the name of Nikhil, there is a distance that has been formed between his parents and himself. He is living his own life, which at times is difficult for Ashima. But she is constantly reminded by Ashoke that "this is America" and children do as they please. Amongst these conflicting cultures at times, it becomes difficult for children to situate themselves. Nikhil ultimately ends up dating a white American girl, Maxine, and feels closer to her family than his own. Her family represents the mass and the culture he has been trying to emulate while growing up. Even though he is very much accepted by them, he is introduced as the Indian Architect to their friends and his name instead of being Nikhil is pronounced as Nikool. Analyzing this, there comes up the issue of "denial of difference and the denial of sameness" (Shohat, Stam 24). Here, Maxine's family denies that he is different, but at the same time denies that he is similar to them. When Gogol takes Maxine home to meet his parents, he tells her not to hold hands or touch him in front of his parents, because they are not used to these public displays. It reflects his obeisance to the culture that he is trying hard to escape, which could be seen as an unconscious acceptance of it as well. And, here his denial of difference and sameness is evident. Quite often, it happens that minority groups are so under scrutiny that it makes them feel that being part of that group of minority is wrong; they are therefore in a continuous rebellion with themselves in trying to prove they can be the "other."

Jhumpa Lahiri once again exploits names as "the looking glass self". As looking for self, she believes that each person experiences the self as a social object of which he becomes aware of until he attends a particular age and there is an assertion of an individual beginning to become autonomous. "George Herbert Mead believes- We achieve a sense of selfhood by acting toward ourselves in much the same manner in which we act toward other people. When we do so we are set to be taking the role of other towards ourselves." (Kamra, Maiti N. pag.)

In order to project a new identity, Gogol wants a changed name to refashion his reciprocity and to redevelop a high self-esteem. He goes to his parents who are unhappy but give their consent at the face of his unhappiness. To play defensive, he informs the judge that his name is uncanny and he cannot associate with an identity of mental discomfort. The bench condescends and the process to crystallize a new identity is Gogol's fresh enterprise. He once again wants to feel "the real me". With the aid of his material self, he encounters a stream of sensations in his relation with Ruth, Maxine and later Moushumi. Nikhil, the newly named Gogol, now lacks a physical existence for his parents and his relatives in India to whom the association with Gogol is indelible. Thinking of oneself, he is now tossed between pride and mortification. Nikhil which implies, "he who is entire, encompassing all" now fails him for the self is not merely an experience but is a consciousness of self-worth. In the process of shaping and reshaping, directing and redirecting, forging and reforging himself as a social being Gogol fails to sustain his selfhood through the process of self-interactions. Once again, Gogol realizes the trappings within the system of concepts which we employ to define ourselves. His frame of reference provides him an illusory frame which would soon disappear for making place for the real. Erik Erikson (1959) defines identity as a signature mark and asserts "the self is the individual" as known to the individual in a socially determined frame of reference.

Exploring the utility of names, Jhumpa Lahiri's attempt is directed to socio-psychological field of strangeness. Commonly, we accept names as passively as we accept innovations in signboards. Hence, the novel is an exemplary attempt with a catchy newness embodied to a wonderful display of language.

Thus, we find Jhumpa Lahiri's handling of names in her stories is thoughtful and masterly to represent the cultural identity of a diasporic family. Names, for her, are closely interlinked to the art of characterization. Jhumpa Lahiri is well-equipped in the technique and subtleties of fiction. Thanks to the course in creative writing attended by her. Her technique is so unobtrusive, subtle and unimposing that at times the reader feels that she is not resorting to any technique at all. Jhumpa Lahiri in this regard becomes a living example of the adage, "Still waters run deep."

Monica Ali places special emphasis on South Asian/Bangladeshi geographical locations through highlighting a few of her chapters (e.g. chapter one, Mymensingh district, East Pakistan, 1967; Tower Hamlets, London, 1985; chapter 7, Dhaka, Bangladesh and chapter 8, Tower Hamlets, February and 2001). In a way, through the broken English letters of Hasina, Nazneen's life in the diaspora oscillates between Bangladesh (both urban and rural) and London (essentially in Brick Lane). While she lives physically in East London, she romanticizes (suffering from nostalgia) about her bygone days. In a way, there is no 'contestation of spaces' between 'back home' in Bangladesh or her current diaspora in London.

Brick Lane expands far beyond the walls of Nazneen's small flat in Brick Lane, the Bangladeshi enclave in London, Ali has been hailed by critics for her fine descriptive skills, adept ability to combine humor and pathos, and her creation of a truly global novel. Though set in today's multicultural London, fraught with race riots, post 9/11 hate crimes, drugs, gangs, and

Islamic fundamentalism, *Brick Lane* also paints portraits of Nazneen's rural upbringing in

Bangladesh and also paints the diasporic condition in a South Asian immigrant community. The product description of the book, Amazon describes it as "...an Asian immigrant girl deals cogently with issues of love, cultural difference and the human spirit" (N. pag.)

Monika Ali writes *Brick Lane* perceptively about the Bengali diaspora in Britain. Whether Muslim or Hindu, Bengalis share a culture that she describes to perfection. She opens a window onto the world of the deracinated and, as a counterpoint, onto the life of those left behind in an impoverished, Islamic homeland.

As a lonely, homeless, rootless immigrant Bangladeshi in such a multicultural society, Ali explores Nazneen's emerging independence and sexuality with all of the appropriate emotions, pleasure, shame, guilt, happiness. Ali's novel is one of silence, both the silencing of women and the silence of the community. What becomes unavoidably apparent in *Brick Lane* is the gaping black hole of a gap between the numbers of words immigrant dare to utter out loud (especially to the natives) and those that are forever locked up in their own minds. Sexuality, adultery, sexual assault, drugs, and exploitation are not only avoided, but actively silenced within the South Asian diasporic community.

The story of immigrants encompasses almost all of human history. Mankind has been seeking new pastures and safe havens for millennia. Success lies in assimilation: making new homes, settling into new territories, and adapting to new cultures. Failure lies in ghettoisation and segregation. But sticking to people of your own kind in an unfamiliar environment is a survival technique and makes perfect sense. Then the people try to suit them appropriating the new culture through repetition which Homi Bhabha calls 'mimicry'.

In mimicry, the representation of identity and meaning is rearticulated along the axis of metonymy. As Lacan reminds us, mimicry is like camouflage, not a harmonization of repression of difference, but a form of resemblance, that differs from or defends presence by displaying it in part, metonymically. Its threat, I would add, comes from the prodigious and strategic production of conflictual, fantastic, discriminatory 'identity effects' in the play of a power that is elusive because it hides no essence, no 'itself'. (Bhabha 90)

Brick Lane is an x-ray of an enclosed community living in a kind of London ghetto situated very close to the centre of the metropolis, yet almost invisible to it other than as an abstract exotic other, a self-contained world with little connection with what is going on around it. The Tower Hamlets Bangladeshi community concentrated around the highly tourist Brick Lane area. Ali's novel looks at this world from within, seeing it through the shy eyes of Nazneen, the girl, who was brought to London from a Bangladeshi village to marry Chanu Ahmed, a man twice her age, whom she learns to care about in years of secluded, lonely life in London. Her life is designed to be like that of many Muslim immigrant wives whose only function in a foreign country is to look after their husbands and to bear them children. Her husband does not encourage her to learn English for the fear that this might spoil her peasant innocence – a quality that weighs much in his choice of a wife – and it is not until she has to communicate with her England-born daughters Shahana and Bibi that Nazneen learns to inhabit the language of the adopted country. Placed from birth under the sign of Fate by her all-fearing mother Rupban, a total victim of Muslim female subordination, Nazneen is brought to England against her will. Yet it is in England – the country she, like her daughters, chooses not to leave when her husband does – that she finds a power she had not known she had.

After the birth of Shahana and Bibi, Chanu flaps around longing for home, vowing ultimately to return to his golden Bengal, the land of Tagore and Kazi Nazrul Islam. He sees Bangladesh as a safer, more dignified place for his growing, nubile daughters than the country he has made his home for decades; a country that hasn't recognized his true worth, nor rewarded his years of constant service, and thus doesn't deserve his allegiance. Chanu makes all the right moves to go back, lock, stock and daughters, but he hasn't taken into account the obdurate Shahana, and ignores at his peril the rumbles of discontent he senses in his wife. Ali paints a memorable portrait of the growing rebellion among second generation Bangladeshi Brits struggling with their identity, as do immigrants the world over.

Nazneen starts developing a more flexible nomadic identity when, pregnant, yet curious and bored with being alone at home, she gets out of the house on her own for the first time and explores the Brick Lane area with the fresh eye of the total stranger:

Nazneen walked. She walked to the end of Brick Lane and turned right. Four blocks down she crossed the road (she waited next to a woman and stepped out with her, like a calf with its mother) and took a side street. She turned down the first right, and then went left. From there she took every second right and every second left until she realized she was leaving herself a trail. (Ali 44)

Until Nazneen meets Karim, she negotiates well between the two separate worlds. Firstly, with Karim's attention and later with the radicalization of the 'cultural space' of East London, Nazneen seems to compromise her Bangladeshi values and becomes a 'hybrid' South Asian woman with acquired virtues of the western liberalist views. Unlike Nazneen, despite living for over thirty years in the East End's Bangladeshi diasporas, Chanu remains quite uncompromising and contests with oppressing western culture in his own way. While Nazneen continues to dress like a traditional Bangladeshi village woman in London, Chanu from the very outset has old fashioned English outfits but retains his traditional eastern values of life.

Then among young second generation immigrants, and that is embodied in the hybrid character of Karim Amir in *Brick Lane*, whose multiple and fluid identity represents a "new way of being British" (Kureishi 18). He considers himself to be the first and foremost English, but at the same time he acknowledges a sense of cultural responsibility towards his roots and learns to accept his identity confusion and hybridity.

In *Brick Lane*, the narrator appropriates the English language to incorporate words and idioms from native language to bring a regional tonality to the novel. Moreover, we discern the presence of a central consciousness, which is an experiencing soul, sharing the sense of displacement and alienation of the diaspora existence. *Brick Lane's* narrator sounds as an inmate of first generation immigrants coming from Bangladesh. The problem of emotional conflict is felt acutely and immediately. As the novel focuses on the predicaments of only Bangladeshi immigrants clustered in apartment complexes, it can present the lurking problems in a very intense and precise manner. This empathy brings a homely tonality in the novel, which is very much aware of the feeling of homelessness. Though the reality is made no less harsh, the narrator's virtual participation in the suffering of displaced existence makes it more humane.

Brick Lane attempts to fathom the underlying factors that have given birth to such radical groups. *Brick Lane,* shows us that it is often nationalist and racist uprising against which these Islamic groups take their positions; and in such groups, we have different kinds of voices-not all are for radical change. *Brick Lane* presents reality as complex and problematic; we need to go beyond the surface to see the intricate workings of various factors, which determine the social and psychological makeup of a migrated population.

This paper discusses the process of acquiring a voice through a revaluation of a limiting migrant condition as a more empowered nomadic dislocation or relocation in two novels. Both novels focus on immigrant families coming from practically the same Bengali culture, even though they are working-class Muslims in Ali's novel and Hindu Brahmins in Lahiri's. The female protagonists in the two novels learn, throughout years of inhabiting the foreign country, to perform themselves in a more empowered condition that makes it possible to inhabit the space of the target culture. The comparative analysis of the two novels will examine the discourses built around the two female protagonists as they develop in relation to the different (British and American) contexts of their relocation.

Brick Lane and *The Namesake* both set off as migration stories of young couples – Bengali in both cases – brought together by traditional arranged marriages that involve the relocation of the female protagonist in England in the former and the United States in the latter. In both novels, the main storyline develops through the protagonists' consciousness, with little variation. The main centre of consciousness in the third-person singular narrative is represented by the female protagonist, wives with a limited knowledge of the new country they are expected to inhabit and, at the beginning, even of English. Language is played upon in ways that challenge its relation to the self mirrored in it. In both novels, someone goes back to the country of origin, even though for different reasons: Chanu in *Brick Lane* and Ashima in *The Namesake*.

In *The Namesake* we find two interesting characters of Gogol's two lovers (one indigenous white American, Maxine and the other transnational second-generation Bengali woman, Moushami), who are sympathetically portrayed with tragic consequences. In a way, this mix of confused identity and loyalties of second generation Karim in *Brick Lane* could be compared with Gogol in *The Namesake*. The second-generation Gogol's lover (and for a brief period his wife, Moushami) and sister (Sonia) show more adaptation of western culture than either Gogol or Karim. We see a similar resemblance between Gogol's sister Sonia and Nazneen's older daughter Shahana who are more resilient to keeping traditional Bengali culture. Probably the main difference between the characters in *Brick Lane* and *The Namesake* is in the class representation of two immigrant families in London and Boston. Both Nazneen and Chanu come from lower class rural and lower-middle urban Bangladesh where Ashoke and Ashima are from a more established middle class in Calcutta, and, therefore we see marked differences both in their adaptability and acceptances of western cultures although both parties have strong respect and yearning for 'back home' Bengali or Bangladeshi cultures.

Monica Ali's *Brick Lane* and Jhumpa Lahiri's *The Namesake* share an attempt at a migrant experience in the multiple and dynamic society. It does not involve the fluidization of the identity. The identity performances of female characters have been projected as more adaptable than male characters. And this is from the knowledge of reality of the writers. It is a permanent trace, and about the uprooted people who have migrated to an alien society may be for political or economic reasons. Till now, the immigrants are socially and politically marginalized. The feeling of homelessness, together with the sense of being cornered, makes the diaspora experience very unique, and *The Namesake* and *Brick Lane* tell the story of such experiences.

Moreover, focusing on the immigrant population coming from particular countries, *Brick Lane* and *The Namesake* create a strong regional sound by appropriating the language. There are so many words and proverbs from the native language (Bengali). Most of the time the meaning is not given, but it is recognizable from the context. Besides, there is a whole parallel depiction of the story of Hasina, a garment's worker living in Dhaka. She writes letters in Bengali, and Asahima Ganguli reads Bengali magazine, pronounces of her native Bengali language. And, here we see the classic post of colonial problem of representation.

Moreover, Chanu in *Brick Lane* and Ashoke Ganguli in *The Namesake* are middle-aged expatriates with frustrated aspirations. They suffer from 'going home syndrome'. Concentrating in keeping alive their own racial and cultural identity, they overdo their roles as parents. Consequently, it creates misunderstanding with their offspring. These unlucky men retreated to their own personal worlds. In spite of these similarities between these two characters, we view them in quite different lights in their respective contexts. The treatment of this confusion differs according to age and gender, as every generation, every man and woman, every individual, immigrant or native alike, have their own tasks and ways of realizing their fluid, hybrid identities. And if they all succeed in adapting to such multi-racial countries, multiculturalism can finally be a functioning reality, where diversity is celebrated and hybridity is a part, and a natural and accepted phenomenon of everyday life.

Both in *The Namesake* and *Brick Lane*, the reality of the diaspora existence is viewed primarily from a feminine perspective. The doubly marginalized protagonist of the novels, Ashima, Mousumi and Nazneen as married women experienced double migration. They leave not only their native lands to settle in abroad, but also their parental household to live with their husbands. Their feelings as immigrants, therefore, are quite different from that of their husbands. But both of their feelings of deprivation come mainly from the sense of homelessness, bondage in foreign countries, and lack of moving space in both literal and metaphoric sense. Freedom is the thin they value most and aspire for. Once they come to know about their power to choose their own destiny, they just cannot leave a country which gives them the opportunity to do so. Thus for them, America and England are not the places only to earn money or a degree, but also places where they can exercise their power to choose their own destiny.

All the immigrants all over the world have to deal with the confusion of cultural identity throughout their lives as the confusions of cultural identity and hybridity seem to be the inevitable and inescapable consequences of immigration, assimilation and multi-ethnicity. These notions are highly important for immigrant writers in expressing their thoughts about the immigrant experience and being "other". And, these have been marked in Jhumpa Lahiri's *The Namesake* and in Monika Ali's *Brick Lane* as Asian diasporic literature.

References

- Alexandru, Maria-Sabina D. "From the Subaltern to the Female Nomad in Narratives of
- Transnational Migration by Jhumpa Lahiri and Monica Ali." TRANS. Internet-Zeitschrift für Kulturwissenschaften: n. pag. 11 Oct. 2008. Web. 26 Mar. 2013.

  < http://www.inst.at/trans/17Nr/5-4/5-4_alexandru.htm>.
- Ali, Monica. *Brick Lane*. London: Doubleday, 2003. Print.
- Amazon. "Product Description." Amazon.com, Inc: n. pag. Web. 27 Mar. 2013.

  < www.amazon.ca/Brick-Lane-Novel-Monica-Ali/sim/.../2>
- Besley, Tina, and Michael A. Peters. "Subjectivity & Truth: Foucault, Education, and the Culture of Self." Amazon.com, Inc: p. 50. 2007. Web. 27 Mar. 2013.

  < books.google.com.bd/books?isbn=0820481955>.
- Bhabha, Homi K. *The Location of Culture*. London: Routledge, 1994.
- Kamra, Dr. Madhoo, and Sumiparna Maiti. "Jhumpa Lahiri's The Namesake : A Study In Emotional Denotations." LitIndia.org: n. pag. 10 Jan. 2010. Web. 27 Mar. 2013.

  < www.litindia.org › Criticism › Novel Criticism>
- Kureishi, Hanif. *My Beautiful Laundrette and The Rainbow Sign*. London: Faber, 1986.

- Lahiri, Jhumpa. *The Namesake*. Australia: Harper Collins Publishers, 2003. Print.
- Pataki, Éva. "CAUGHT BETWEEN TWO WORLDS." theroundtable: p. 2-3. Web. 26 Mar.

  2013. <http:// www.theroundtable.ro>.
- Shohat, Ella, and Stam, Robert. *Unthinking Eurocentrism: Multiculturalism and the Media*.
- London and New York: Routledge, 1994.
- Uncategorized. "MISSION AND MIGRATION." MUSINGS OF THE JAZZGOAT BLOG: n. pag. 8 July 2012. Web. 26 Mar. 2013. <http://jazzgoat10.wordpress.com/2012/07/>.

7

Unearthing Diasporic Identity and Journey in Jhumpa Lahiri's *The Namesake*

Barnali Dutta
Research Scholar
Dept. Of English
Banaras Hindu University

In the present era of transnational migration, the flow of the people among the different countries, convergence of the heterogeneous cultures, creolization of languages and hybridization of identities have broken the concept of fixity or absolute territoriality. The intersection between the terriorialization and deterritorialization creates the 'third space' or liminality where the 'cutting edge of translation and negotiation' occurs. Therefore, the concepts of homeland and identity in this age of global migration form a complex framework. According to the critics like Homi K. Bhabha, Avtar Brah and Stuart Hall, the floating nature of home and fluid identity have replaced the age-old concepts of fixed 'home' and identity as well. The idea of 'home' evokes the spatial politics of home, the sense of self, its displacement, intimacy, exclusion and inclusion. The flow of the people across different countries breaks the concept of true home. The notion of home not only construes the sense of self, but also ties with the human emotion, feelings, sentiments, proximity and intimacy. Beyond the spatial territory, 'home' is associated with emotional territory.

The hybrid identity that the immigrants carry creates a tumultuous situation regarding the belongingness. In the opinion of Bhabha, hybridity is the 'third space' which makes the other positions to emerge. The identity as suggested by Bhabha, indicates the impure identity rather than fixed identity. Dual or hybrid identity construct an identity crisis in one's creating home of familiarity in the overseas countries. The second generation immigrants find it hardly possible to adhere to the identity of the parental land. The national identity of the first generation may be changed politically, but they are able to fasten with their original homeland culturally, linguistically and ethnically. In the contemporary era, immigration, exile and expatriation are related to home, identity, nostalgia, memory and isolation. These are the recurrent theme in the diasporic writings of the post-colonial writers like V. S. Naipaul, Salman Rushdie, Bharti Mukkerjee, Agha Shahid Ali, Jhumpa Lahiri, Kiran Desai and many others.

This present article focuses on the first-generation and second-generation immigrants' adherence to the old and new lands as can be found in Jhumpa Lahiri's *The Namesake* (2003). In this novel, Lahiri has explored the psychic condition of the first generation immigrants, Ashima and Ashoke and the second generation immigrants, Gogol, Sonia and Moushumi. The novel critically demonstrates how the concept of homeland creates an atmosphere to construct home and identity of proximity. In this age of transmigration, 'home' signifies its impermanence, displacement, and dispossession. For many critics, the idea of home is more conveyed as a sense of being between the two places instead of rooted one. In the novel, Ashima's sense of being at home is connected with the original homeland, i.e. India. And the selves of Gogol, Sonia and Moushumi are supposed to be attached with the USA, their birth place. The questions however arise as – is this land for which they seem to negate the Indian ideological values and principles? And how far they are able to create the true home?

In an unknown city of Massachusetts, Ashima's pang for abandoning the home country is emphasized through imagining the picture of the family in Calcutta. And the feeling of nostalgia seems to mitigate the pang and anguish of Ashima. When she is about to give birth a child, her Indian ethnicity reminds her of the conventional social code and customs of the Indian Bengali culture: "...women go home to their parents to give birth, away from husbands and in-laws and household cares..." (p.4). Again the solitary atmosphere in the hospital makes her recapture the particular moment of the domestic life of the Calcutta. The reference of the 'fractures of memory' can aptly be mentioned in this context. Ashima's anxiety over giving birth and rearing up the child in the alien land is poignantly revealed: "... it was happening so far from home, unmonitored and unobserved by those she loved, had made it more miraculous still" (p.6). Regarding the immigrants' situation abroad, scholars like Rayaprol quotes Gupta and Ferguson as follows:

"... Remembered places have often served as symbolic anchors of community for dispersed people. This has long been true of immigrants, who use memory of place to construct imaginatively their new lived world" (Gupta and Ferguson (1992: 10-11).

Similarly Ashima's recollection of the lullaby from the Bengali songs, remembrance of 'dida I'm coming' for 'good bye' are intimately associated with the Bengali social conventions which is hardly evadable for the first generation immigrants like Ashima. Her recollection of the past and imagination of the present Calcuttan family life are encapsulated within the tapestry of the isolated life in the USA. Her feeling of nostalgia captures the very moment of the far away Calcuttan life where "a servant is pouring after-dinner tea ... arranging Marie biscuits on a tray" (p.5).

In comparison to Ashima's nostalgia, Gogol's apathetic attitude to Indian culture is critically examined in the novel. The lack of tie with the Indian family makes Gogol seldom recognize the photos of the family members of Ashima. Ashima endeavors to transmit in Gogol the convention of the Bengal by introducing him with the Bengali rhyme, names of Gods and Goddesses and prevalent Bengali tradition of calling every child by two names.

Generally immigrants attempt to linguistically bind themselves with their original homeland. The present novel also orchestrates this. The tie of the language specially the Bengali of the indigenous land is presumed to make Ashima link with the Indian soil. The American English seems less important to Ashima than the Bengali language in which she is accustomed with the Calcuttan life. Ashima's grasping 'a tattered copy of desh magazine' in the foreign hospital indicates her temporary relief in the far-off country. Ashima seldom feels uncomfortable with any other language but the Bengali. The solitariness of Ashima in America seems to encapsulate the present and the future as well. Ashima's solicitude over rearing up the child without her family surrounding in this strange city, impels her to think of "... a person entering the world so alone, so deprived" (p.25).

The bipolarity of forging the cultural performances between the first generation and second generation Indian immigrants is viewed in the present novel. Cultural performance generally plays an instrumental role to construct immigrant's identity. The nurturing of the Bengali culture through Nazrul and Tagore songs, argument over the films of Ritwik Ghatak versus Satyajit Roy, as well as debate over the political parties of the West Bengal among the Bengali immigrant community in the USA illustrate their proximity with the Indian soil. Cultural performance generally plays an instrumental role to construct immigrant's identity. In the overseas countries, native cultural activities such as dances or songs construct cultural identity of the immigrants and endeavor to negotiate with other cultures too (Aparna Rayaprol,1997). Inversely, the second generation immigrants like Gogol gets involved with the American music than the Indian classical music: "... a cassette of classical Indian music he'd bought for Gogol months ago … still sealed in its wrapper" (p.78). The utmost effort of Ashima and Ashoke to make him acquainted with cultural activities like *Kathakali* dance and *Apu Trilogy* plays.

Ashima's preservation of the varied Bengali rituals in the new land epitomizes the bond with native India. The celebration of Gogol's *Annaprasan* (rice ceremony) as per the Bengali convention provides Ashima a temporary relief in this foreign atmosphere. On the other hand, to perform this ritual, absence of the family members overshadows Ashima which denotes her longing to create the Bengali atmosphere in the new unknown country. Ashima, Ashoke and Bengali immigrants obey the religious festivals of Christmas and New Year celebration probably to reconcile with the culture.

Reversely, the eagerness and excitement of the second generation Bengali immigrants is observed in celebrating the American festivals than worshiping of Indian Gods and Goddesses.

The confusion regarding the names like Gogol, Sonali and Moushumi, the American born offspring of the Indian parents creates a problem defining their identities. The names like Gogol, Nikhil, Sonali and Moushumi indicate Russian and Indian identities respectively instead of the American. The 'self' of the male protagonist of the novel is embedded in the Americanization, not in Indianness. But Gogol may be considered as 'other' in this land, his birth place. Ashima is supposed to be the 'other' in the unknown American atmosphere, as she usually observes the disparity between the home and host cultures.

Similarly, ethnic food and costume act as the symbols of one's ethnic identity. Ashoke-Ashima's preference for the Indian Bengali food like rice, *dal*, *samosa* etc symbolizes their shared root. On the other hand, Gogol-Sonia's preference for the American cuisine like Shake' n Bake chicken or Hamburger Helper than the Indian food is critically examined: "Gogol savors each mouthful, aware that for the next eight months nothing will taste quite the same" (p.81). Ashima's maintenance of wearing traditional sari than any other western dresses conveys the preservation of the old ancestral culture.

The dichotomy between Ashima's sense of alienation and solitariness in the USA, despite the prolonged staying and Gogol-Sonia's disinclination and monotonous sojourn in India, is pointed out in the novel. Hence, Gogol's returning from India to Boston symbolizes his escaping the loneliness of India which usually projects his reluctance to negotiate with the Indian environment: "... for Gogol, relief quickly replaces a lingering sadness" (p.87). In the new atmosphere, Ashima's inability to adopt with the social rules and systems and sense of embarrassment and anguish comes out regarding raising baby-son Gogol. Her yearning to move back to India is embedded in this solitary atmosphere: "I'm saying I don't want to raise Gogol alone in this country. It's not right. I want to go back" (p.33).

Similarly, Gogol-Sonia's apathetic attitude to accept the Bengali customs and rituals seems to evade his Indian identity. Their hyphenated position, Indian-American, within two different ethnic identities gives them no specific identity for the preservation of the particular ideological value of any country. The seeming manner of their adherence to the American customs makes them to impart less significance of the Indian one. Another situation can be observed through Gogol-Sonia's changed behavior of endeavoring to obey the rules and regulations of the Indian religious ceremony after their father's death: "... it was a Bengali son's duty to shave his head in the wake of a parent's death" (p.179). Hence, the inability of the second-generation immigrants to create the true home of familiarity and bond in America or in India generally can be analyzed due to the pendulumic situation.

Moushumi, the British born off-spring of the Bengali parents can be viewed from the point of transnationalism. Her continuous moving from one country to another seldom makes her to adhere to any particular cultural ideological values of the countries like Britain, America and France. Hence, her belongingness is moving among different countries instead of a fixed country. Moushumi's preference for the French literature, food and feeling of oneness with the French friends usually signify her reconciliation with the French environment instead of the Bengali. Maintaining the distance from the Bengali assembly denotes her aloofness in this unknown atmosphere: "always with a book in her hand at parties" (p.192). Her fragile married relationship with Gogol symbolizes her negation to cling to the holy bond of the marriage institution. Again her reluctant acceptance the surname 'Ganguli' of the spouse in the codes and conducts of the Bengali marriage institution, pinpoints her willingness to enjoy liberty and independence by being not confined under this particular or fixed system: " When relatives from India continue to address letters and cards to 'Mrs. Moushumi Ganguli,' "she will shake her head and sigh"(p.227). Her escape from the Bengali convention and culture to cling to the French culture does not explicit her feeling at home with the later one. Moushumi's fluid identity belongs with the varied ethnic identities like the Bengali, the British, the American and the French. Her continuous moving from one country to another is supposed to re-create the home in France: "Here Moushumi had reinvented herself, without misgivings, without guilt (p.233).

The floating nature of home and fluid identity are explicated in her lack of feeling with the previous bond with native Calcutta, which she used to nourish in Calcutta and the USA. It seems to be emerges as foreign, a new land. Moreover, she is presumed to be connected with the USA through the rumination over the past days across boundary after returning to Calcutta: "... to the city that was once home and is now in its own way foreign" (p.278). Hence, she would be sandwiched between the dual cultures and identities as well. The portrayal of Ashima by Jhumpa Lahiri reminds us of the female protagonist Taralata, the Bengali immigrant in the USA. The city of San Francisco never emerges as the sweet old home in Calcutta but is only the place of residence without any attachment: "I'm feeling just a little alien and uncomfortable, a tinge of not-belonging, in the midst of such welcoming comfort ..."(p.75).

The vacillating condition of the first-generation and second generation Bengali immigrants, their vain endeavors to tie with the particular tradition and to carry the pure identity coalesce with the vain attempt of creating the true home elsewhere. Due to the effect of global migration and cross-cultural networks the first-generation immigrants generally try to be attached with the indigenous land through the recapitulation and the feeling of nostalgia. And the second generations seem to build any connection of the unknown parental land. The second generations usually adhere to their birth land. The national identities get eroded and replaced by the hybrid identities in which both the first and the second generation immigrants are wavered. Hence, the belongingness of the immigrants hardly clings to any singular place than the multi-places. In the contemporary age, all these issues like global migration, the intersection between the different territories, impure identity and cross-cultural elements seem to disavow the popular hearsay 'Home is where the heart lies'.

References

- Blunt, Alison. Domicile and Diaspora: Anglo-Indian Women and the Spatial Politics of Home, USA: Blackwell Publishing, 2005.
- Huddart, David. Homi K Bhabha, London. Routledge, 2006.
- Lahiri, Jhumpa. The Namesake, Great Britain: Flamingo,2003.
- Mukherjee, Bharati. Desirable Daughters, the USA: Theia, 2002.
- Parker, Kenneth. Home is Where the Heart ...Lies. Transition, No. 59 (1993), pp.65-77

  http: \\www.jstor.org\ stable\2934872
- Rayaprol, Aparna. Negotiating Identities: Women in the Diaspora, Delhi. Oxford University Press, 1997.
- Rushdie, Salman. Imaginary Homelands, Great Britain. Granta Books, 1991.
- Stefano, John Di. Moving Images of Home. Art Journal, Vol. 61, No. 4 (Winter, 2002), pp. 38-51

  http: \\ www.Jstor.\org\stable\778150

8

Diasporic studies in Jhumpa Lahiri's *The Namesake*

L. T. Hemalatha

Research Scholar

Department of English, Telangana University

Nizamabad

The word Diaspora is derived from two Greek words 'dia' – 'spora' namely the dispersal or scattering of seeds. The term 'Diaspora' is biblical. It was initially used to refer to the forced dispersal of the Jewish people from Palestine. Diaspora generally refers to communities of people who have been dispersed from their own geographic homeland, and are re-located elsewhere. Indian Diaspora comprises approximately 20 million people and is the second largest in the world after the Chinese. There are more people living outside their country of origin today than ever before and 1 out of every 35 persons is an international migrant accounting for 3% of global population. Diasporic writing comes across so may new concepts relating to creativity, hybridity, linguistic experimentations focusing upon race, ethnicity, belonging, otherness gender and subalternity and so on. The diasporic production of cultural meanings occurs in many areas, such as contemporary music, film, theatre and dance. It is interesting to note that the history of diasporic Indian writing is as old as the Diaspora itself.

In fact the first Indian writing in English is credited to Dean Mahomed, who was born in Patna, India and after working for fifteen years in the Bengal Army of the British East India Company, migrated to "eighteenth century Ireland and then to England" (Kumar xx) in 1784.

His book The travels of Dean Mahomet was published in 1794. It predates by about Forty years the first English Text written by an Indian residing in India.

The first Indian Novel English Novel, Bankimchandra Chatterjee's Wife, was to be published much later in 1864. The novels of the older generation of diasporic Indian writers like Raja Rao, G.V Desani, Santha Rama rao, Balachandra Rajan, Nirad Chadhuri and Ved Mehta predominantly look back at India and rarely record their experiences away from India as expatriates. It is as if these writers have discovered their Indianness when they are out of India. When these writers in the alien land, they have the advantage of looking at their motherland from the outside. The Indian English Writers , notably, Raja Rao became an expatriate even before the Independence of the country. Salman Rushdie's "Imaginary homeland" Encompasacs the world over. Rushdie says that "Swift, Conrad, Marx are as much our literary forebears as Rabindranath Tagore or Ram Mohan Roy".

Indian English writers like Anita Desai, Bharathi Mukherjee, Shashi Tharoor, Amitav Ghosh, Vikram Seth, Sunetra Gupta, Rohinton Mistry, Jhumpa Lahiri and Hari Kunzru have all made their names while residing abroad. Their concerns are Global concerns has today's world is afflicted with problems of immigrants, refugees and all other exiles.

The Expatriate experience implies the meaning of a person who lives outside their native country. Expatriate theme has been considered to be one of the major discourses among Indian writers. Some of the prominent Indian settlers in Western countries are Expatriate writers such as Bharathi Mukherjee, Jhumpa Lahiri, Gita HariHaran, Anitha Desai etc.,

Diasporic writers are of many types. Old Diaspora Writers, New Diaspora Writers, Modern Diaspora Writers and Common Diaspora Writers. When one looks at Diasporic writing, one comes across many new concepts relating to Hybridity, Identity, Loneliness, Alienation, Ethnicity, Belonging, Otherness Gender, Multiculturalism and so on..

My paper focuses on the alienation and identity struggle of Gogol, the character in Jhumpa Lahiri's novel, *The Name* THE WRITINGS OF JHUMPHA LAHARI".

JHUMPA LAHIRI, the winner of the Pulitzer Prize for Fiction (2000), O'Henry Award for short stories (1999) as well as many prestigious awards, and a member of President's committee on the Arts and Humanities, appointed by Barack Obama, established herself as a writer of repute with her debut collection of short stories, *Interpreter of Maladies* (1999) and a remarkable novel, *The Namesake* (2003) and another exhilarating collection of short stories, *Unaccustomed Earth* (2008). Lahiri shows in her fiction how the characters attempt to Navigate between the cultural values of their birth place and their adopted home. But they are completely at home in neither, given more melancholy observation then whole-hearted participation. She examines her characters struggles anxieties and biases to chronicle the nuances of immigrant psychology and behavior. Lahiri's later short stories portray how the succeeding genarations of expatriates try to consolidate their existence by assimilating into American Culture, overcoming the constraints of their immigrant parents.

The Namesake is the vivid characterization about an American-Indian who is unhappy with his given name which threatens his very existence. The novel is a narrative about the assimilation of an Indian Bengali family from Calcutta, the Gangulis, into America, over thirty years(from 1968 to 2000); the cultural dilemmas experienced by them and their American born children in different ways; the spatial, cultural and emotional dislocations suffered by them in their efforts to settle "home" in the new land. The story unravels beginning with Ashok and Ashima Ganguli, A Bengali couple who immigrated to the U.S. with high aspirations basing on the concept of American Dream. Like many "professional Indians" who "in the waves of the early '60's" went to the United States, as part of the brain drain,"1 Ashoke Ganguli too leaves his homeland and comes to America in pursuit of higher studies to do research in the field of "fibre optics" with a prospect of settling down "with security and respect."(The Namesake,p.105). Ashima often feels upset and homesick and sulks alone in their three room apartment which is too hot in summer and too cold in the winter, far removed from the descriptions of houses in the English novels she has read. She feels spatially and emotionally dislocated from the comfortable "home"of her father full of so many loving ones and yearns to go back. Home is "a mythic place of desire"9in an immigrants imagination, says Avtar Brah. She spends her time rereading Bengali short stories, poems and articlesfrom the Bengali magazines she has brought with her. She "Sometimes two letters arrive in a single week. One week there are three. As always Ashima keeps her ear trained, between the hours of twelve and two, for the sound of the postman's footsteps on the porch,followed by the soft click of the mail slot in the door. The margins of her parents' letters, always a block of her mother's hasty penmanship followed by her father's flourishing, elegant hand, are frequently decorated with drawings of animals done by Ashima's father" (p.36) waiting for the letters which she keeps collecting in her white bag and rereads them often.

The novel begins where in we can find the pangs of Ashima and Ashok, a Bengali immigrant family, being far away in a foreign land - Ashok and Ashima Ganguli immigrate to Cambridge, where Ashima gives birth to son. Ashima and Ashok welcome their son happily into their world. Their joy knew no bounds and while they are there in the hospital, three Bengali friends visit them. Having allowed Ashima's grandmother to name their child, Ashima and Ashok have to wait for the grandmother's letter. But, they did not get any letter. As, the hospital won't discharge the baby without a name, Ashok decides to name him Gogol. Gogol, the name entered in the birth certificate Bureaucracy. Gogol- a pet name that becomes permanent, when his formal name, traditionally bestowed by the maternal grandmother, is posted in a letter from India, but last in transit. Ashima suffers the alienation and pain of becoming a mother in an alien land and delivers a child where she is related to no one. Throughout the experience, in spite of her growing discomfort, she had been astonished by her body's ability to make life, exactly as her mother and grandmother and all her great grandmothers had done. She brings up the baby in the Bengali "way." "She put him to sleep, she sings him the Bengali songs her mother had sung to her. She drinks in the sweet milky fragrance of his skin, the buttery scent of his breath."(p.35). She keeps all her emotional hazards and disappointments to herself and not intending to worry her parents and she presents in her letters a good picture of the domestic facilities and cleanliness. She is terrified to raise a child in a country where she knows so little, where life seems so tentative and spare. She comes on her own, takes pride in rearing up the child. At first depressed and overwhelmed by the burden of caring for a new one, Ashima soon begins to develop some independence and goes out into the world. She shops, she takes her son out on walks learns everything new for her newborn. She moves out alone in the market with her baby in the pram, communicates with the passers-by who smile at him and goes to meet her husband on the campus, thus growing confident. But the displacement is felt more by her after their migration from the university apartments to a university town outside Boston when Ashoke is " hired as an assistant professor of electrical engineering at the University. In exchange for teaching five classes, he earns sixteen thousand dollars a year. He is given his own office, with his name etched onto a strip of black plastic by the door."(p.48)

The novel follows the life of Gogol Ganguli from birth until middle age, chronicling his struggles, first with his unusual name and later with the traditions his parents insist on upholding that embarrass, Gogol in front of his American friends.

The name becomes a metonymy for the grateful feelings of the Ganguli couple on one hand and the frustration of their son on the other.

Ashima suffers the alienation and pain of becoming a mother in an alien land and delivers a child where she is related to no one. They name their first born child 'Gogol' and the life has changed as Ashoke goes to teach at the university, Gogol goes to nursery school, and Ashima hangs out at the library. A couple of years later Ashima become pregnant again. Like immigrants of other communities Ashima and Ashoke too make their circle of Bengali acquaintances, get known through one another. They know Maya and Dilip Nandi, " Ashoke and Ashima meet the Mitras, and through the Mitras, the Banerjees. More than once, pushing Gogolin his stroller, Ashima has been approached on the streets of Cambridge by young Bengali bachelors, shyly inquiring after her origins. Like Ashoke, the bachelors fly back to Calcutta one by one returning with wives. Every weekend, it seems there is a new home to go to, a new couple or young family to meet. They all come from Calcutta, and for this reason alone they are friends. Most of them live within walking distance of one another in Cambridge. The husbands are teachers, researchers, doctors, engineers. The wives, homesick and bewildered, turn to Ashima for recipes and advice, and she tells them about the carp that sold in Chinatown, thatit's possible to make halwa from Cream of Wheat. The families drop by one another's homes on Sunday afternoons."(p.38) As Gogol is in nursery, Ashoke tries to get the folks at school to call Gogol by a more formal name, Nikhil, but everyone calls him as Gogol.

After few months, Gogol's sister Sonali born. Her parents settle on Sonia as a nickname. As the years go by, more of Ashima and Ashok's relatives in India pass away and the Gangulis start to fit into American culture a bit more. They start celebrating Christmas but they try to keep up Bengali customs when they can. But, their kid detests the way they hold on to Indian traditions and functions that are of no importance to his American mind. Gogol is neither able to become an American at heart nor remains as an Indian. One day at the party, Gogol introduces himself as "Nikhil" to a girl named Kim and he was infatuated towards her and he feels up the courage to kiss her. In the summer before he leaves for college Gogol goes to the family court in Boston and officially changes his first name to Nikhil. At Yale, everyone knows him as Nikhil, and he makes sure that all the official paperwork at the university reflects his new name. In college, he develops a love of architecture in his drawing class. After earning his graduate degree in architecture, Gogol settles in the Big Apple, an architecture firm. He's totally with his American dream. Their American values clash with their Indian culture and sentiments. Both Gogol and Sonia, as representations of young generation American born Indians, fail to find any practical significance in the values and ideals of their parents ; and the paradoxes of their attitudes and responses with that of their parents lands them in an identity-crisis. Both of them find it extremely hard to equally belong to a cultural plurality.

He's totally with his American dream visits his parents rarely and barely ever goes home to his own apartment. One day Gogol's mother calls him and asks him to visit home before his father leaves for a research fellowship in Ohio. But, Gogol never feels their importance in his life. At some point life is pretty quiet for Ashima. Ashima in home alone addresses Christmas cards, which she has decided to make herself. Lahiri shows that the immigrants in their enthusiasm to stick to their own cultural beliefs and customs, gradually imbibe the cultural ways of the host country too. Though initially Ashoke did not like the celebration of Christmas ans Thanksgiving but as Gogol recalls that "it was for him, for Sonia[his younger sister], that his parents had gone to the trouble of learning these customs."(p.286). Ashoke comes to visit from Ohio every three weeks, where he helps her with household chores and pays the bills. When she is alone, she works at her part-time job at the library. Days pass by and one day Ashok telephoned Ashima from hospital that he had stomach pain. He promises he'll call her back after his hospital visit. By the next morning, Ashoke still hasn't called. She finds the phone number for his hospital and gives it a ring. They informed her that he is no more. Ashima completely breaks down.

Sonia calls to tell Gogol about his dad's death. Refusing Maxine's offer to come with him, Gogol heads to Ohio to arrange his father's cremation. At his parents' house, Ashima, Gogol, and Sonia go through ten days of mourning, and they receive a lot of visitors and condolences. A year passed in no time, but Gogol is still working as an architect in Manhattan, but he is no longer dating the lovely Maxine. She is also engaged to another man. Sonia has a job as a paralegal in Boston. To find him a suitable match Gogol's mother convinces him to call the daughter of a family friend, Moushumi Mazoomdar. Within a year they are married in New Jersey organized by their respective families.

Alienation in Sonia's case, however, triggers a relatively much less. Like her mother, she has a sense of duty. Like the traditional Indian Sonia marries her boy friend – a half Chinese boy, Ben and is happy in their shared world. Only once Ashima Ganguli feels attached to America because of the memories of her husband after his death. She doesn't want that the house should be altered after it is sold to someone else. Her husband has made his living in this country. The situation of Gogol is no better. He is neither able to become an American at heart nor remains as Indian. He does not fully belong to anywhere. He is a "nowhere man". Jhumpa Lahiri not only explores modern life but also paves way for the ties and bonds that overarches frustration and agony , desolation and identity –crisis, which creeps in the lives of global families .

In the United States, Ashima struggles through language and cultural barriers as well as her own fears as she delivers her first child. The baby boy is healthy and the new parents are prepared to take their son home. But Ashima and Ashok are stunned to learn that they cannot leave the hospital before they give their son a legal name. The traditional naming process in their families is to have an elder give the new baby a name. They have chosen Ashima's grandmother for this honor. They have written the grandmother to ask her to give the baby a name. But the letter never arrives and soon after, the grandmother dies. In the meantime, Ashok suggests the name of Gogol. He chooses this name for two reasons. First, it is the name of his favorite author, the famous Russian author. The second reason is that Ashok, before he was married, had been in a very serious train accident

The Namesake exemplifies the perpetual dilemma encountered by immigrants as they struggle to maintain their identities while trying to shake them off at the same time. In many of her writings, Lahari deals with the interpersonal relationship between man and woman, husband and wife, parent and child. She highlights the problem of identity in the novel in a poignant manner. Ashima Bhathuri, a student in a Degree class in Calcutta who becomes Ashima Ganguli after her marriage to Ashoke Ganguli. Ashoke shifts home to Boston for pursuing his Ph.D. in fiber optics. Later on he has been hired as an Assistant Professor of Electrical Engineering at the University of Boston. Ashima leaves her home, her family and her life to settle in a Nation where her isolation and alienation rule her environment. She is always nostalgic of her home and Spence her leisure in reading Bengali poems, Stories and Articles. After eighteen months life in Cambridge (United States). She is admitted to the local Hospital for her first delivery. She feels restless being the only Indian Hindi Hospital with three other American Women in an adjoining room. She gave a birth to Gogol. She expresses their joys and jubilations as well as the stress and strain in the characters. Her stories clearly reflect the sweeter and bitter moments and feelings of life.

Lahiri expresses the struggle of first generation immigrants and their children struggle of first generation immigrants and their children struggle to find their places in the society. She creeps into the lives of global families with the exploration of modern life. Lahiri shows that all migrants carve their own "routes" in the course of time and it is not necessary that they want to settle in the countries of their origin. Gogol (Nikhil), though having passed through many emotional setbacks because of his 'bicultural' identity, is shown to be feeling dejected, distressed, displaced and lonely in the end not knowing what to do after the thrwarting of his dreams, his father's death, his mother's impending departure to India, but his desire to settle a home and rise professionally in other countries hint at his quest for the new 'route' which will dawn on him after his reflections in the company of the stories by his namesake, Nikolai Gogol-gifted to him by his father.

Diaspora literature is cross-cultural crisis of east and west. A survey of the Indian Diasporic literature produced by the Indians living in various parts of the world reveals some common characteristics running through the gamut of the Diasporic writings.

Diasporic discourse compels us to contemplate about fundamentals of nation and nationalism, while determining the affinities of citizens and nation- state. It is the search for selfhood in the world between two cultures that of homeland and embraced land. So, the main concern of Diasporic literature is a cross-cultural crisis of East and West.

Gogol and Sonia, as representatives of young Generation American born Indians, Fail to find any practical significance in the values and ideas of their parents and the paradoxes of their attitudes and responses with that of their parents lands them in an identity-crisis. Both of find it extremely hard to equally belong to a cultural plurality. Ashima Ganguli feels attached to America because of the memories of her husband after his death. She doesn't want that the house should be altered after it is sold to some on else. Her husband has made his living in this country. The situation of Gogol is no better. Gogol suffers loneliness quietly. Gogol lives in two Worlds, two different cultures but as two different personalities- Gogol and Nikhil. Nikhil was an American where he struggles to find an identity in a nation which treated one as an alien even one was born there. Gogol was torn between two nations, India and America, between two names, Gogol and Nikhil, and between two value systems of traditions and conventions. Gogol has an identity dilemma between the duality of cultures which threatens his identity as is reflected in his personal relationships. Gogol is alienated due to the racial feelings. Jhumpa Lahiri's descriptions are filled with diasporic elements but occasionally marked by comic touches, which could be either in the form of a pictorial phrase or through short or extended images. In each of Lahiri's stories, a number of details keep striking the face of the reader, making him wonder what significance do they have, till he comes to the end of the story and at that time the details become quite relevant, meaningful and significant by becoming an indispensable part of a well-crafted texture.

Notes & References

1. Gayatri Chakravorty Spivak's observations about the Indian Community in the United States were made during a discussion with Sneja Gunew concerning the post-colonialism, anti-imperialism and multicultural politics in Australia in 1986. These are published under the heading "Questions of Multiculturalism" in the book The Post- Colonial Critic: Interviews, Strategies,

Dialogues, Gayatri Chakravorty Spivak, ed. Sarah Harasyam (Routledge : New York and London, 1990), p.61

2. Avtar Brah, Cartographies Of Diaspora: Contesting Identities (Routledge, 1997), p.192
3. Jhumpa Lahiri, The Namesake (Flamingo, 2003)
4. Rupkatha, a Journal on Interdisciplinary Studies in Humanities.
5. Ghosh, Amitav. "The Diaspora in Indian Culture" Extracted from *The Imam and the Indian Prose Pieces*, New Delhi.
6. Nityanandam,Indira.Jhumpa Lahiri: The Tale of the Diaspora. New Delhi.
7. Das, Nigamananda. Ed .Jhumpa Lahiri : Critical Perspective. New Delhi: Pencraft International 2008.
8. Boehmar_Elleke. Colonial and Postcolonial Literature: Migrant Metaphors, Oxford: Oxford University Press, 1995. Chadhuri, Amit (ed.). The Picador Book of Modern Indian Literature, London: Picador,2001.
9. Dharwadker, Vinay, "Formation of Indian-English Literature" from Literary Cultures in History: Reconstructions froms South Asia, Ed. Sheldon Pollack, New Delhi: Oxford University Press, 2004.
10. Mehrotra, Arvind Krishba(ed.). An Illustrated History of Indian Literature in English, New Delhi: Perminant Black Publishers, 2003.
11. Das, Nigamananda. Ed. Dynamics of culture and Diaspora in Jhumpa Lahri. New Delhi: Ahyayan Publishers and Distributors, 2010.

9

Diasporic Identity and Cultural Transformation as an Empowering Process in Anita Rau Badami's *The Hero's Walk*

Vikas Yadav Raskar

Assistant Professor of English

Hutatma Ragguru Mahavidyalaya, Rajgurunagar

Pune, Maharashtra,pin-410505

Diaspora brings various contested ideas and images in mind. It can be a positive site for the affirmation of an identity, or, on the contrary, a negative site of fears of losing that identity. Diaspora indicates an engagement with a medium of diversity: of cultures, languages, histories, people, place, times etc. Every country has its own special way of life. Canada is also not exception to this. It is a cultural mosaic, which allows elements of many cultures to be integrated into one. Canada's culture has many influences because the numerous people who immigrate here are encouraged to keep their cultures. Culture is the way of life of a particular society or group of people, including patterns of thought, beliefs, behavior, customs, traditions, rituals, dress, and language, as well as art, music, and literature it's rather our way of thinking and perception. Culture plays very important role in the formation of a person's identity. Cultural differences occur when two or more cultures disagree about their beliefs or ways of life. Our perception of the world is shaped by our cultural identity which is the outcome of location, gender, race, history, nationality, religious beliefs etc. The diasporic Indian women writers have achieved distinction in the field of fiction by portraying the diverse manifestations of the rich and valuable Indian heritage as well as the immigrant experiences of expatriates in a great deal. It is important that Indian diasporic women writers like Kamala Markandaya, Anita Desai, Bharti Mukherjee, Kiran Desai, Chitra Banerjee, Sunetra Gupta, Amulya Malladi and Anita Rao Badami remained successful in depicting the diasporic culture, quest for dignity, diasporic identity, problems caused by migration, displacement, cultural dislocation existential dilemmas, East-West encounter, emotional loss and psychological trauma arising out of ongoing migration and cultural transformation due to the impact of globalization and multiculturalism etc. The present paper is an attempt to explore how diasporic identity and cultural transformation prove as an empowering process in Anita Rau Badami's *The Hero's Walk.*

Anita Rau Badami has been in Canada since 1991; she received prestigious literary prizes, including the Regional Commonwealth writer's prize for *The Hero's Walk* in 2001. In all of her works, she shows a long-lasting concern with issues of gender, identity cultural psychic dislocation, the formation of transnational identities and the cultural transformation etc. Badami's fiction manages to develop an incisive critique of Indian cultural politics and custom. Through her characters, the reader is able to witness the consequences of the clash between the individual's desire for recognition and personal fulfillment with the politics of heritage and nostalgia.

Anita Rau Badami's *The Hero's Walk* represents the pattern of diasporic identities as an empowering process shaped by multiple changes on the local level rather than by transnational mobility. It is set in a fictive seaside town in Tamil Nadu, southern India. The novel has been transformed into six languages and continues to be best seller. *The Hero's Walk* reflects on the contemporary phenomena of globalization and transnationalism as the encroachment of the global in various forms is visible in the small Indian town-Toturpuram. The novel develops the disjunction that occurs between parents and their children as a result of conflicting desires and commitments. The book is not about the travails and tribulations of adjustment, assimilation and integration in an alien and somewhat inhospitable culture but assumes that the conflicts between the East and the West are prominent but those are also found in our long standing tradition.

The Hero's Walk is about the complexity of family relationships. There are three generations living together in a large and decaying house which they cannot afford to maintain. Ammayya is a mean and caste conscious woman, who controls her son Sripathi, her daughter Putti and her long suffering daughter-in-law Nirmala. While Sripathi, more than anything else, he has abandoned his aspirations of becoming a New Delhi journalist in order to remain a dutiful son to his mother Ammayya. He knows that he has disappointed his parents, his wife, his daughter, his son and even his boss, but he persistently refuses to change. Only his secret, pseudonymous letters to the local newspaper gives him little bit of pleasure. Sripathi is certainly an existential hero, and his dilemmas and choices make sense only if understood within a particular social, cultural and familial context; he is a man who acts without believing in action, he is unable to express his grief and longing for his dead daughter.

There is Sripathi's wife who worships the Hindu Gods and keeps her pain and anger silent under commitment to her family. She is a timid woman, who spends most of her life observing what she considers are the rules and regulations set down by family and society. She even doesn't ask her daughter to come home because her husband had cut off all ties with her. Putti is a sweet, loving and badly misused by her mother. At her age forty two, she weeps for the many suitors who have approached her mother and her brother over the years only to dismiss on one pretext or another by Ammayya, who wants only to keep her daughter with her until she dies. Sripathi's son Arun is seriously involved in political activism, he is a continual disappointment to his father, rather than engaging in a profession, he lives a "hermit-like" existence. Arun persists in an attempt to prevent environmental disaster, even after being badly beaten at a demonstration. Working on a doctorate while engaging in protest, which is entirely mysterious to his father. He is an unemployed young man, whose attempts to change the world annoys Sripathi.

Sripathi feels proud of being the father of her daughter Maya, one who receives scholarship for her Ph.D research in one of the universities in North America. Here Maya falls in love with her Canadian classmate. She breaks off her engagement with Indian boy Prakash, which humiliates and embraces to her father. Angry and humiliated Sripathi had already sacrificed so many passions for family obligations, now refuses Maya to return her home. It is the first time that he has been unshackled from his sense of duty. What offends him is not his daughters marriage to some one of another caste or another race, it is the fact that she has not done her duty by him by marring the man he has found for her and with whose family they have already established a relationship. So, it is humiliating for him. He himself has spent his entire life doing his duty in a sort of reaction to his father's neglect of his duty.

Initially in the novel, Sripathi appears as a scornful and egoistic character. He feels uncomfortable with his son's work as an environmental campaigner and also his anger towards his daughter Maya for having married a white Canadian rather than the guy of his choice, Sripathi has isolated himself from his wife and children. Instead of confronting why he "allowed himself to forget" the reasons for the present disintegrated state of his family, Sripathi finds it easier to "express his deepest thoughts- those blatant, embarrassing emotions that he was so reluctant to display in speech or action" in letters to the editors of various local newspapers. Ironically, he writes these letters under his chosen pseudonym "Pro Bono Publico. on behalf of the people" his imagination, makes him a secret hero, "a crusader, who tried to address the problems of the world with pen and ink" , when, in fact, his letters ironically contrast his impending unemployment as a writer and emphasize his increased alienation from his family and social community.

One of the features of Badami's writing is her liking for using "double words" in conversations between Indian characters. For instance Ammayya, in conversation with Putti, says "Chintamani told me that one should always watch the eyes. If they are yellow, then it is jaundice or some other liver trouble. If the skin inside the eyelid is pale, it is leukemia. Mine is too-too red. My blood pressure is high, that's why. I can feel it going ghash-phash in my veins, my pet." other example includes simply simply, yes-yes, what what really really etc. perhaps this is an attempt to stake a claim to authenticity by trying to catch the sound of conversation in an Indian language within a work written in English a long in which many of the characters probably do not speak.

Badami appears to present a rather depressing picture of her country of origin as compared to that of Canada "Huts made of rags and tins and stolen bricks crowed around open drains" "Ragged clothes to dry on flat stones beside thee festering drain" should serve to highlight our point. India has remained, for many in the "West," a land of snake charmers, horse-drawn carts, and elephant riders; a land run over with sick children, a country of dangerous pests and stinking drains.

The Hero's Walk explores national and local configurations of diasporic space. In The Hero's Walk, it is Sripathi's traumatic loss of his daughter and his journey to Canada that compels/makes him to remember and recreate the past, and eventually mark him as a diasporic character. When Sripathi comes to know about the death of her daughter Maya and her husband in a car accident in Canada, suddenly he experiences a dramatic disorder. This incident changes him drastically and then we see cultural and personal transformation in him at different levels. In order to bring his granddaughter, he requires traveling to Canada to arrange Nandana's reverse journey to India, a shift that marks her as doubly diasporic.

As a result of Maya's death, Sripathi starts revaluating his commitment to tradition and custom. He decides to fly to Canada to bring her granddaughter from there. When he sees that airport is a multi cultural holding ground and there is every nationality flying in and out every day that gives him cultural shock, one who has not yet left India in his fifty seven years of life. What Sripathi calls his "foreign trip" to Vancouver turns out to be an experience of profound psychic and cultural dislocation, "Vancouver dazed by the sensation of flying, of being unmoored from the earth after fifty seven years of being tied to it" After he returns, he knows that "he could never be sure of anything in the world again, not even his own body This short trip proves massive displacement for him. He goes there to acquire a space of world that he had preferred to blank out in his life. It is an emotional journey for him. He had never owned a passport. He did not need a passport where he lived. This short trip helps him to ask himself who he was all those years. Now, he comes to know that he should feel regretful, miserable and sad for what he did throughout his life.

For Sripathi, Nandana's presence acts as a constant reminder of his regret that "he had not known his daughter's inner life, the secret world of dreams and fears, the complexes and affections that follow children through their youth" as well as her life in Canada. He now recognizes that in the past he denied his daughter in order to uphold his authority over his family in light of a materially alienated and politically insecure world around him. To maintain a sense of patriarchal control, if not power, Sripathi relies on culturally purist narratives of belonging and rejects what appears to have shaped his life all along, namely his fear of social downgrading and the diasporic reconfiguration of his family and social relationships. Both of these aspects are connected in that Sripathi is initially unable to consider his situation in the larger context of Toturpuram's belated entry into changing global modern world.

Diasporic identity that is not necessarily bound to transnational border crossings, instead it shows the effects of ecological and financial universal reorganization along with the breakdown of established confined forms of national and cultural recognition change the micro spaces and communal life. Diaspora designates less a postnational phenomenon than diverse communities that might generate or regulate political dissent/ rebel. Arun's political activism is directed against both India's environmental politics and their locally depriving effects and ecological catastrophe generated through irresponsibility of global economic politics.

The present paper also observes that the formation of diasporic identities as an interdependent process of individual self-discovery and social reconnection on a local rather than a global level. Sripathi never left his hometown, until he moves to Canada to bring her granddaughter Nandana. It is only then he comes to inhabit a diasporic space. But such a space, as Avtar Brah argues, is "inhabited not only by those who have migrated and their descendants, but equally by those who are constructed and represented as indigenous. The concept of diaspora space includes the entanglement, the intertwining of the genealogies of dispersion with those of 'staying put" Brah's notion of diaspora raises certain questions which seriously need to be solved. It implies that diaspora is used as an idealized umbrella term for all kinds of cultural dislocation but in actual fact, it is required to make the distinction between old and new diasporas.

After Maya's death, Sripathi is forced to face the mistakes of his decisions in the form of his silent and brooding granddaughter Nandana, one who seems caught between the cultural forces and social demands represented by Canada and India. Nandana is a silent child whose life, now is so changed, sensitive portrayal of ordinary life in an old culture with old traditions and values, all of which are different to Nandana, who has grown up in Canada. Nandana is keeping her sentimental problems to herself and is still holding responsibility of her parent's death. Nandana moves to India with her grandfather, whom she never met in her life. Now, Nandana needs to transform her cultural identity to adapt her new existence in India. Here, she brings the gulf between the two worlds Canada and India.

In The Hero's Walk, we get a glimpse of Canada through little Nandana's eyes. Her Canada is small, pretty and simple. It is home. There are no complications and no complexities. Nandana finds life in Toturpuram uncomfortable and scary. She is a foreigner in India. She runs several times, planning to fly to her parents and their orderly safe Canadian life. When the child is returned to the house on Brahmin Street, she maintains protest through muteness, as if speaking to the Rao's or her teachers and classmates would break the spell of her parent's survival.

Nandana experiences the shakiness of her environment and the illusion of safety and harmony often attached to the notion of home. She feels no-belonging and lives in a space of in-betweenness. Nandana brings the postcolonial moment of what Homi Bhabha Homi K. Bhabha (1949-), one of the major figures in the field of postcolonial studies, describes this sense of ambivalence or 'inbetweenness' as "unhomeliness" into the privacy of the Big House, Sripathi's family home. The unhomely individual disrupts the clear-cut relationship between the dominant power and the subject. Therefore, according to Carole Boyce Davis, "the rewriting of home becomes a critical link in the articulation of [a new] identity" and a resistance to the domination of imperial power. Nandana's entry into the lives of the Rao women brings cultural transformation into their lives. Finally, Putti Sripathi's sister goes against her convention and marries a man from the dalit caste.

While crossing borders, the diasporic subject can carry his identity transnationally and could translate it into new cultural terrains therefore his identity is a process of evolving or becoming. It may either prove as an empowering process or loss of originality in the age of globalization. Globalization of the modern workforce is placing people from various cultures in constant and intimate contact with one-another. In the process of globalization geographical and cultural boundaries are blurred down.

Badami celebrates daily heroism like Nirmala's tolerance; Putti's optimism about a late marriage; Arun's political commitment; Ammayya's bad-tempered and Sripathi's ignorance and dedication etc. Even Nandana is described as a heroine after she boldly accepts the dare of her new "friends" and enters a dark tunnel. It is a portrayal of ordinary life in an old culture with old traditions and values, which are quite different to Nandana, who has grown up in different setting. the Hero's Walk captures with sensitivity the sense of uprooting and un-belonging that both Sripathi and his biracial Indo-Canadian seven year old grandchild experience as they cross physical and psychological borders for transforming their identities to acquire diasporic space. Sripathi's family has to cope with this little ghost of Maya and the years of strange western cultural values that brought her more varied experiences and opportunity in her short life.

During the course of the novel, the characters begin to realize the importance of compromises that must be made in order to sustain and improve their relationships with their near and dear people. Sripathi Rao is torn between regret and guilt about the past and later he gradually becomes a more tolerant and loving person. The process of cultural transformation begins within him. Materially alienated & politically insecure world around Sripathi in India, created fear of losing his social status is rooted in his estrangement from his community. Sripathi makes a compromise to accept Arun as more of his son, and tries to improve their father-son relationship. He also starts motivating Nirmala to raise Nandana in a proper and loving manner. It's heroic that Nirmala gets the courage to face the situation courageously; she realizes that heroism isn't simply about following rules. Sometimes it's about doing what you think is right, at the cost of displeasing people around you. She comes to this realization that she has to stand her own feet to become individual. Now, Nirmala keeps aside her fears and tries to cope with changing scenario by taking a little bit of assistance from her husband. She becomes the hero walking with dignity, courage and humility. Here, Putti finally rebels against her controlling mother and against the caste prejudices by marring a man from the dalit caste. Badami finds a wicked absurdity in tradition of India in social conflict at caste level system. Nandana's entry into both Sripathi's household and the narrative has the potential to transform both. She herself gets affected with this transformation after having stayed in the Canada for years. Nandana transfers her diasporic values and love she had learned in the west to the east. The consequences of this transference in the form of a child, cause each member of the Rao household to finally let go of their commitment to Indian tradition and get on a future that is, ultimately unknown.

Works Cited

- [1] Rau Badami, Anita. *The Hero's Walk.* Ballantine Books: New York, 2000.P.46

- [2] Ibid., p.8
- [3] Ibid., p.9
- [4] Ibid., p.9
- [5] Ibid., p.22
- [6] Ibid., p.56
- [7] Ibid., p.56
- [8] Ibid., p.140
- [9] Ibid., p.162
- [10] Ibid., p.147
- [11]Brah, Avtar. *Cartographies of Diaspora: Contesting Identities.* London: Routledge, 1996.P.209
- [12] Bhabha, H. K. *The Location of Culture*. London: Routledge, 1994,p.9
- [13] Davies, C. B. *Black Women, Writing and Identity: Migration of the Subject*. London and New York: Routledge,1994.p.85

10

A Study of Amitav Ghosh's *Shadow line* with a perspective of Diaspora

Imtiaz Qurrat
Research Scholar
CUK
Gulbarga

The origin of the nation –states can be traced back to the French revolution of 1789.since the 'nation's' modern and recent conception;Nationalism, the feeling arising out of nationhood or belonging or devotion to the interests or culture of one's nation, has been defined by various scholars, researchers and artists in the past two centuries in insightful yet conflicting fashion. Benedict Anderson, in his ground breaking work *Imagined Communities,*defines a nation as an "imagined political community that is imagined as both inherentlylimited and sovereign" Rabindranath Tagore is rather critical and denounces nationalism as "a cruel epidemic of evil".Eqbal Ahmed classifies nationalism as "an ideology of difference" and Collective identity [built] on the basis of the other. Through his work *Shadow Lines*, Amitav Ghosh too, is joining the fray, questioning the fixity if culture and whether cultures can be contained within boundaries demarcated by maps .He brings forth all sides of this intellectual dilemma through his various characters and the different opinions they hold about nations and nationalism.

Diaspora and Dislocation in the Shadow Lines

The Shadow Lines is the most appreciated novel of Amitav Ghosh. The partition of Bengal and the trauma resulted from the partition are depicted very vividly in this novel. The world largest migration in the history of the humankind as a result of Partition of India which created a vast dislocation of people in Pakistan (east and west) and India. Thus the novel questions physical borders between nations, arguing that these obfuscated the emotional and cultural ties between officially separate countries, India and Pakistan. The division of India, mainly the partition of Bengal, dictates all the courses of the novel The Shadow Lines. So the dislocation of people as refugee is one of the main concerns of the novel. The partition was the direct result of the mutual misunderstanding of nationalism of the two major religious groups. Both the Hindus and the Muslims took the idea of racism as the idea of nationalism. The partition of Bengal had such a strong trauma on the life and culture of the related inhabitants that the event dictates their mindset for generations.

In the novel there are two kinds of dislocations, forced migration and the mercantile migration or professional migration. Forced migration was due to the partition of India, mainly because of the partition of Bengal. The professional migration was due to the high skilled work force of India. Both dislocations are so strongly knitted in the novel that any of these dislocations must not be ignored in considering the novel as a text of diaspora and dislocation. The first diaspora resulted from the forced exile. And the second diaspora resulted from professional migration which produced alienation among the people.

The shadow lines primarily brings out the post partition trauma in the context of a violent incident in a race riot and raises relevant questions relating to such violence. Minoti Chatterjee in her essay '*The Bengali in the shadow lines*' - there is 'a generation of Bengalis whose collective memory still makes them believe that borders have a tenuous existence and that not even a history of bloodshed can make them real and impermeable'. They are probashis include the Bengalis. Who live outside the Bengal such probashis include Bengali-Hindus and Bengali-Muslims on both sides of border. Thus the novelist's enduring objective is to remind his readers of the historical closeness of Asian societies, transcending barriers of ethnicity. Ghosh embarks on an endeavour to systematically deconstruct the category of the nation and the process through which a sense of national identity is formed.

The Shadow lines as 'an interrogation of a political Consciousness baptised in the crucible of national division. What emerges in the foreground in the text is a subjectivity which is expressive of 'A new civilisational ethos' conditioned primarily, by the 'the overwhelming dynamics if Globalisation'.

Ghosh is deconstructing the Nation, primarily as 'an endless source of wanton brutality and violence'. To the Question of Nationalism and nation is connected the question of political freedom. It was expected that freedom won in 1947 would create a perfect order, but unfortunately, it has generated animosity and hatred in our polity. In the name of freedom what has got created are the Shadow lines or the Barriers between the communities and the nation-states. It has led to displacement and dispossession and large scale communal violence, even the individual and national identities have get messed up. In such a bleak scenario, freedom appears as a 'mirage'.

A Congent way between 'Freedom and Violence'

Freedom means different things to different characters in the novel. For tha'mma, of course, it was freedom from the colonial rule, but in the post partition scenario violence masquerades as freedom- thus there is a communal violence. At the root of it all is the question of Identity.

Meenakshi Malhotra in her essay *'Nationalism and the question of freedom'* In The 'Shadow lines' looks at the crucial question of freedom and nationalism from the view point of gender. She brings in Globalism in her discussion as Ghosh interrogates the nation from the perspective of globality. Malhotra points out that in the recent times which have witnessed the collapse of different political blocks and nation states, nationalism has been discredited and reduced to an outmoded 'grand narrative of history'. It is the legacy of the colonial political heritage that has continued to trouble us. A legacy that post-colonial writing continuously seeks to dismantle and erase. Ghosh through his interrogation of borders and boundaries, questions the relevance and the continued validity of the concept of 'nationhood'. Malhotra brings out the different versions of freedom in the text. Thus, while the narrators grandmother's idea of freedom is tied up with freedom from the colonial power and attaining nationhood, Illa's concept of freedom is basically, a struggle for personal identity or a quest for personal freedom in a post-colonial, post-modern context. As against these versions of freedom, the narrator's idea of freedom under the influence of his mentor Tridib, assumes on intellectual cast, so that he is able to perceive the Shadow lines that intersect our lives -as individuals, as a community and as a nation.

Human values and Indian pluralism as a vital 'worldliness'.

The Shadow lines presents the universal truth that human society is divided into several sections and sub sections though human beings are the same in nature and emotions all over the world. Hindus, Muslims and Sikhs have shown exemplary unity time and again, but the fanatics have turned them into enemies. So is the case of nationalism. The Home planet has been divided by national boundaries drawn on a map, but the cultural unity cannot be divided by these shadowy lines. Bangladesh was carved out of Bengal but this man made division has not affected the cultural unity of the people. Bengalis are Bengalis in both the countries. Even religions cannot restrain people from being united, since love does not admit of any obstacles. The Chaudhurys and the Prices get united in the bonds of marriage in spite of their different religions. Hindus, Sikhs and Muslims envinced spirit of unity on several occasions. When Mu-i-Mubarak, a hair of Prophet Mohammed was brought to Kashmir and installed at the picturesque Hazrathbal mosque, Kashmiris of all faiths and religions, Muslims, Hindus, Sikhs, Buddhists, marched in thousands from every part of Kashmir to get a glimpse of the relic.

The Shadow lines is organised at various level. Take for instance, the story within the story of the novel, the story of the Tristan the Hero who was 'a man without a country, who fell in love with a woman across-the-seas'. It is significant that Tridib received this story from Snipe as a birthday gift. Tridib was particularly fond of it, and had told it to the narrator before he (Tridib) left for Dhaka. Where he met his death. In a sense it is a 'legacy', which the narrator inherits from his mentor, Tridib. This universal story figures in cultures of different nations.

The narrator of the Shadow lines, towards the end of the novel, too, secures a kind of bonding with his uncle's 'love', May, by developing love and understanding with her. This is Tridib's story and the narrator's too. It makes it possible for us to imagine a world which was not divided by boundaries, where one did not have to give up one's ' Home' because of political upheavals - a place where one experienced the 'Stillness' and the quiet of the earth.

The Shadow lines, allows cultural differences to be magnified and opens up space for a multicultural definition of the "self" to emerge and hybridity to be embraced; it illustrates how diasporic displacement is not merely a loss, but a source of creativity as well, through the regeneration of a new polyglot and cosmopolitan culture that takes place as a result of it.

The idea of hybridity is further cultivated if one takes into consideration that the narration focuses on the intersected stories that takes place between the two families, one of which is Bengali (that of the narrator's) and the other English. The whole narration also moves back and forth between India and England, to emphasize the narrator's hybrid identity, as he is of Indian nationality, but has received an English education. Furthermore, in his narration, Ghosh makes use of the English language, while deviating from the British national canon of literature and thus challenging the 'privileging norms', as a means to reclaim an Indian lost to the English, a homeland from which he has been alienated. Eventually a heterogeneous version of India is portrayed in the text, through a hybrid use of English literature.

The narrator's grandmother, however, having strong feelings of Indian nationalism and patriotism, strongly disapproves this hybridity and identity of Diaspora, as she considers ideal a homogeneous society with clear borders. Thus, she does not accept Ila's decision to live in London, as in her opinion "she does not belong there" and "she has no right to live there". She is of the belief that each country solely belongs to the people that fought wars throughout the years to set its borders firmly with their family's blood. she claims that " they are a nation because they've drawn their borders with blood... war is their religion" and that this is "what it takes to make a country", supporting that the same has to be done for India, in order to build a homogeneous national identity.

Thus the author attempts to re-imagine Calcutta, to re-define its culture and identity through the creation of what is referred to as an "imaginary homeland" that is channelled within its pages, presenting the reader with a possible version of India that stems partly from the memories of the author and partly from his imagination, as not all that was lost can be ever reclaimed; The Shadow lines can be essentially characterised as "a novel of memory about memory". As a result, the heterogeneous notion of national identity is impossible, taking into consideration that no post-colonial narrative can be completely objective and accurate, or claim to possess the absolute historical truth.

References

1. Ghosh,Amitav.Shadow lines.New Delhi:Ravi Dayal publishers,1998.
2. Ahmed,Eqbal.Confronting Empire.Cambridge:South End Press,2000.
3. Anderson, Benedict. Imagined communities. London: Verso, 1991.
4. Tagore, Rabindranath.Nationalism. Newyork:The Macmillian company,1917.

11

"Home-less" Homeland

Mousim Mondal

Research Scholar

Department of English

The University of Burdwan

The emergence of various Literary Theory in the academic domain with both its thesis and antithesis heralded a new era, where the cocoon of 'a' homogenous monochromatic 'identity' was spilled open with a 'big bang' to decentralize the notion of 'identity' with a very complex intertwining matrix of 'identities'. Metanarratives became incredulous as petit –recit became celebratory, homogeneity was questioned and deconstructed to welcome heterogeneity in its place. Notion of identity thus became multilayered and multifarious rather than being single and unilinear. The canvas of identity was thus redefined to accommodate a wide "spectrum of identities" because:

> In our normal lives we see ourselves as members of a variety of groups – we belong to all of them. A person's citizenship, residence, geographic origin, gender, class, politics, profession, employment, food habits, sports interests, taste in music, social commitments etc., make us members of a variety of groups. (SEN 5)

And it is due to these enigmatic spectrums of 'identities' that one grapples with complex questions such as: Who defines our identity? Do we ourselves define it or is it the society at large which defines our identity? At any given moment, while defining one's identity without any set paradigm, what are those perspective that one likes to choose and include while defining identity? Now, coming to the question of choice of selecting some fragments of identity in preference to the others, the question that arises is, whether the selection is natural or is it motivated and controlled by hegemonic ideological discourse of the period? For example, in a world, which has witnessed much trauma of "ethnic cleansing" and where people have been made homeless in one's own homeland – like the Kashmiri Pandits of India – in that case how is ethnic identity related to national identity? Is this relationship hierarchically structured, such that the 'national' is supposed to subsume and transcend 'ethnic' identity, or will this relationship between ethnic and national identity produce a hyphenated identity, such as Kashmiri-Pandits, South-Indian Brahmin, Bengali-Muslim, North Indian – Jat, and so forth, where the hyphen marks a dialogic and non-hierarchic conjuncture, a non-viable difference that is experimentally authentic but not deserving hegemony? What if identity is exclusively ethnic and not national at all? Could such an identity survive and be legitimate?

Now since the question of both legitimacy and survival of exclusive ethnic identity needs a wider spaceo-temporal canvas for its discussion, this paper would like to narrow down its focus on 'the struggle' and need for survival— both biological and cultural — of such an ethnic race— the Kashmiri Pandits— as depicted by Rahul Pandita in his memoir *"Our Moon Has Blood Clots : The Exodus of the Kashmiri Pandits"*.

Born in the Kashmir Valley, Rahul Pandita, the critically claimed journalist and novelist, became a refugee in his own country, at the age of fourteen, when on 19th January, 1990,his family along with thousands of other Kashmiri Pandits were forced into exile because of their ethnic identity of being Kashmiri Pandits. Two decades have passed, but :

> No campaigns were ever run for us; no fellowship or grants given for research on our exodus [...] It has become unfashionable to speak about us, or raise the issue of our exodus. But I have made it my mission to talk about the 'other story' of Kashmir
>
> (Pandita 220)

Initially, Pandita didn't care when a series of untruths were spoken so many times, over the years, regarding the narrative of what led to the exodus of the Kashmiri – Pandits from the valley, but then he became "determined [...] that my memory must come in the way of this untrue history."(Pandita 220) So it is an honest endeavour on part of the author to document a 'true' 'history/ his-story' through the sufferings that he has lived and is still living along with so many other members of 'his – community.' The author also categorically emphasizes about his narrative being the 'other story' of Kashmir because he wants to convey the message that it was violence against their ethnic identity, which made them so conscious of their minority status in a predominantly Muslim state and thus they are the significant 'other' :

> A few years earlier, in our locality, a few Pandit families had tried to construct a small temple out of wooden planks [...] But as soon as the planks were assembled and the idols placed on a small, wooden platform, some Muslim men gathered and began to hurl abuses. One of them brought the whole structure down with a kick. There was no protest. We had learnt to live that way. Whenever things went sour, we would just lower our heads and walk away. Or stay at home, till at things got better [...] and I soon forgot about the incident [...] But I think it changed me a little, *and I became conscious of my identity as a Kashmiri Pandit*. (Pandita 35-37)

So it was violence against his ethnic identity that made him "conscious" of his ethnic identity and from there in perhaps grew the urge to protect this identity and thus the endeavour to write down the "insider's" version of the story of "his – people" :

> Like the tramp in Naipaul's *In a Free State,* I have reduced my life to names and numbers. I have memorized the name of every Pandit killed during those dark days, and the circumstances in which he or she was killed. I have memorized the number of people killed in each district. I have memorized how many of us were registered as refugees in Jammu and elsewhere.(Pandita 220)

Though ethnic identity is community bound and pivoted around the socio – cultural milieu, but it is perhaps the 'home', the people of the home, their acquaintance and the various other affairs and customs of the home which initiates and propagates this ethnic identity silently even when one is not conscious of it .It is in home that one is born and thus unconsciously inherit that ethnic identity, and it is society who makes one conscious of that ethnic identity by differentiating one from other by following some set of hegemonic paradigm. And maybe it is due to this fact that 'home' remains the central axis along which the various orientation of identity revolves. Home is not just the physical geographical space, it is the 'psychic womb' of every individual – that physical entity on earth where one feels most secured and connected, a place to give the feeling of rootedness, a place to relish one's being, a place where the most beautiful relations of one's life bloom. Thus, 'home' is always mottled with 'memory and desire'.

But, when suddenly one – night, one is forced out of his/ her home in the name of ethnic cleansing, how does the individual of those family negotiate with this reality? Rahul Pandita's memoir, narrates the struggle of such dislocated people, who became homeless in their own homeland :

> For me, [...] exile is permanent. Homelessness is permanent. I am uprooted in my mind. There is nothing I can do about it. My idea of home is too perfect. My idea of love is too perfect. And home and love are too interwined. I am like my grandfather, who never left his village his whole life. It was deeply embedded in his matrix, too perfect to be replicated elsewhere.(Pandita 224)

Truly enough, perhaps a man can reside in multiple houses, but 'live' in one and only one home in one's lifetime. Thus, even after several years of exile, when Rahul Pandita would regularly visit Kashmir as a journalist from Delhi – where he now owns a flat and lives with his family – would never have the courage to visit his home, maybe because he did not want to face the harrowing reality that would shatter the "too perfect" (Pandita 224) image of what Rushdie calls "Imaginary homelands". But, perhaps, the call of 'home' for an exile is too strong to resist :

> Over the past decade I have visited Kashmir regularly as a journalist. [...] But in all these years I have never gathered the courage to visit my home in Srinagar. In fact, I would avoid travelling in that general direction. But over the last few years,

> the urge became powerful, as if it were my compulsory pilgrimage to Mecca. As if some umbilical cord with memory would be severed if I did not visit. [...] So on the morning of a day in September 2007, [...] my journey towards home began. (Pandita 212-213)

In his journey back to home, he was accompanied by two journalist friends, Suhail and Zubair along with the elderly Kashmiri driver, Ali Mohammed, whom he had met during his reporting assignments and over several assignments grew fond of each other. Ali Mohammed reminded him of 'Totha' – his maternal grandfather's brother, who always pampered them during their childhood days – a person who was very close to his heart. And like Totha, Ali Mohammed – whom he calls 'Chacha' – became a very good friend:

> Whenever I went to Kashmir, I always made it a point to visit the Kshir Bhawani temple. There, I felt connected to my ancestors. A day before, I would tell chacha about my plans. He would arrive early in the morning, and together we would drive to the temple. 'It is important to be in touch with one's roots,' he would tell me. [...] On many afternoons, he would park the car outside Ahdoo's restaurant and we would sit like old friends, sharing a quintessential Kashmiri meal of rice, roganjosh and collard greens. (Pandita 213)

Significantly or coincidentally, on January 1990, it was the Muslim extremist, who drove him along with his family away from home and several years later, it is a Muslim driver, who is driving him back home...

On reaching the street of his locality, he walks ahead with Suhail and Zubair following him in search of his home :

> *I am now standing at one end of my street, my locality.* [...] *I walk ahead. Suhail and Zubair follow me.* My house should be somewhere here. Yes, yes, it is. On my left. I turn. It is in front of me. The huge blue gate is still there. The name Aabshar – waterfall – is still painted on a small board. [...]

[...] Then I am standing right in front of my house

[...] I want to go inside my house, my home, my only home

(Pandita 214)

But, 'his home' is now someone else's house and now he will have to knock at "his own door, finding someone else opening it, and then seeking permission to enter his own house." (Pandita 216). The very thought is so pathetically disturbing, but the Kashmiri Pandits lived through these!

With every step towards 'his home', the minute details of 'his home' bubbled up from his memory and all those little details of this house – which made it a home for him and his family – were now used by him as a yardstick to judge the difference between memories of past and realities of present: at the very first sight of the house, he could 'still' find the huge blue gate and the name Aabshar painted on a small board, but he could not find the apple tree on his orchard. While entering his home, he 'still' found the fish – shaped doorbell (though non – functional now), but in the living room he could not find the "show piece almari". In the attic upstairs, there were no books in the self where it used to be, but rather the self is filled with onions and garlic now! "There is no kitchen garden – there is no mountain mint, there are no rose shrubs." (Pandita 217) He still wanted to go to the attic and check if something is left of his huge collection of comics and Enid Blyton series, many of which he won by collecting lucky coupons from packs of Double Yum chewing gum. He also wanted to check if :

There is also the 'best deodar wood' that Father had procured just before we had to leave. (Pandita 218)

So the picture perfect memory of 'his home' lured him into its magical trail of inspection. But the questioning stare of the lady and the restlessness of the man – the new occupants of 'his home' – made him realize that he is the 'unwanted guest' in 'his home' or 'their house'. So to relieve them of this discomfiture he declared very emphatically (sometimes when we utter something against our heart, we try to sound loud and emphatic, in order to hide our inner turmoil, and perhaps that's why, the author too adopts this means, and thus records this entire speech in capital letters) :

> I JUST CAME TO TAKE A LOOK. IT'S BEEN A LONG TIME SINCE WE LIVED HERE. WE LIVE IN DELHI NOW. WE HAVE OUR OWN HOUSE. WE ARE SETTLED THERE(Yes, settled!) I JUST WANT TO CLICK A FEW PICTURES AND SHOW THEM TO MY PARENTS. THEY HAVEN'T BEEN ABLE TO RETURN SINCE 1990. [...] YES, DON'T WORRY, I KNOW HOW IT FEELS - THE THOUGHT OF SOMEONE COMING AND CLAIMING YOUR HOUSE. IT IS YOUR HOUSE NOW. I HAVE JUST COME TO PLACE IT IN MY MEMORY. (Pandita 216)

Thus, it is through memory and photographs that the exiles tries to rationally negotiate the loss of a 'home' : "I have no home, only images. And in those closets in my bedroom, I could only conjure up images of home."(Pandita 224) But emotionally perhaps that is not feasible. So, when the man said "The house was in bad condition [...] when we shifted [...] " he almost wanted to burst out, but said nothing. But in his mind he said **:**

> Sir, quote a price and I will buy it from you right away. Bad condition! Do you, sir, even realize what it means for me to be sitting in this house? This house built with my father's Provident Fund savings and my mother's bridal jewellery; this house where my mother sat on her haunches and mopped the long, red – cemented corridor each morning; the house we left forever to *become refugees and court suffering and homelessness.*(Pandita 216-217)

At such a juncture of life, he would perhaps be reminded of Bob Dylan's "Like a Rolling Stone" **:**

> How does it feel
> To be without a home
> Like a complete unknown
> Like a rolling stone.

Yes, the Kashmiri Pandits life became a 'rolling stone' after that fateful night of 19th January, 1990. Being uprooted from home, they were all permanently rooted in the quagmire of dislocation and thus with every passing day, a life of dignity slipped away from them :

Each day we leave behind something of our identity. (Pandita 250)

The process of exodus took away the physical belongings of life and the life after exodus in refugee camps and resettlement colonies took the psychic life away from them :

> Every memory comes back to me. The boys who had assembled on the street below on that cold evening in 1990, distributing our houses among themselves; that taxi ride to Jammu and that man showing us his fist and wishing us death; truck after truck refugees under that tarpaulin, that women's blank eyes; the heat and other horrors of those one- room dwellings; mother's tears and that young man holding the remains of a wedding feast on a plate outside our room; the humiliation of a door-less toilet; the ignominy of suffering landlords. (Pandita 217)

Thus , many a times , Rahul Pandita compared the life of Kashmiri Pandits with that of the Jewish Holocaust victims :

> In truck after truck, there were Pandit families escaping to Jammu [...] Women had been herded like cattle into the backs of the trucks. [...] In one of the trucks, a women lifted a tarpaulin sheet covering the back and peered outside. There was nothing peculiar about her except the blankness in her eyes. They were like a void that sucked you in. Years later, I saw a picture of a Jewish prisoner in Auschwitz. When I saw his eyes, my mind was immediately transported to that day, and I was reminded of that look in that woman's eyes. (Pandita 98)

The ironic tragedy of the Kashmiri Pandit's life is that in Kashmir they were persecuted and terrorized to leave their home by the pro – Pakistan Islamist militants, for their belief in Hindusim and for considering

India as their nation; while in Jammu when they settled as refugees, they were not welcomed either by the people of their own faith :

> Initially, like us, the Jammuities thought our exodus was temporary. Though they benefitted economically because of us, they developed an antipathy towards us. For them, we were outsiders. Within months, invectives had been invented for us. The most popular among them was:
>
> *Haath mein Kangri munh mein chholey*
> Kahan se aayey Kashmiri loley
> Kangri in hands, chickpeas in their mouth
> From where did these Kashmiri flaccid penises come?
>
> [...] This was the mainstream India for us. Our own Hindu brothers and sisters who took out a procession every Basant Panchami to safeguard Hindu rights were turning into our oppressors as well. (Pandita 123)

Thus, the Kashmiri Pandits "were already becoming nobody's people." (Pandita 89)

And what makes this saga of loss much more shocking is the apathy and refusal of the majority of India's intellectual and political leaders "to even acknowledge the suffering of the Pandits" (Pandita 220), let alone act for them. On the contrary :

> [...] the land owned by Pandits is being acquired ostensibly "for public purposes" under a deliberate plan to thwart their chances of return by "finishing [off] their immovable property" [...] Sadly, Government of India that depends on state authority for feedback did not try to intervene." (Pandita 133)

So, this is perhaps one of such strategic tools that is used by hegemonic discourse to subsume ethnic identity by national identity.

However much we vaunt aloud about plurality of identities in academic seminars and political meetings, but in reality even the celebration of plural identities is not completely free from the clutches of hegemonic discourse. That's why may be majority of the Kashmiri Pandits who have paid much in their life for their identity do not want to talk about it at all. For example, when Rahul Pandita was struggling to get in touch with people whose family members were killed by militants, to record their stories, "no one really says 'no'. But everyone is evasive." (Pandita 221) One of them, named Vinod Dhar – "the lone survivor of a massacre that claimed twenty – three members from his family and extended family and neighbours" (Pandita 223) – asked Rahul Pandita : "What will it achieve now, speaking of those days ? I am trying to forget it all." (Pandita 222) Then to answer him and to convince him to tell his (Vinodji's story), Rahul Pandita "quoted Milan Kundera : The struggle of man against power is the struggle of memory against forgetting." (Pandita 223) Vinodji was convinced.

Now let's hope, this clarion call of Rahul Pandita will encourage many more wretched silenced soul to give a voice to their petit recit. Only then, as Pandita says :

> May be our story will not come to an end in the next few
>
> decades. Maybe some of us will still be nicknamed Sartre.
>
> (Pandita 252)

And with all such hope when Pandita ends his memoir with a promise : " I will come again . I promise there will come a time when I will return permanently." (Pandita 253) Let's say 'Amen' for Pandita's secret prayer and also pray that no homeland ever becomes 'home-less' again!

Work Cited

- Pandita, Rahul. *Our Moon Has Blood Clots : The Exodus of the Kashmiri Pandits.* Noida. Random House Publishers India Private Limited, 2013.Print.
- Sen, Amartya. *Identity And Violence: The Illusion Of Destiny.* London.
- Penguin Books, 2006. Print.

www.notable-quotes.com/h/home-quotes-ii-html Web.

12

Indian Diaspora in Perspective With The Parsi Writers

Sanober Kahkeshan

Asst. Professor

Takshashila Mahavidyalaya

Shyamnagar, Amravati-

The word "Diaspora" is derived from the Greek word "dia" means 'through" and "spiro' means "to sow the seeds". The Oxford Dictionary defines 'Diaspora" as the movement of the Jewish people away from their own country to live and work in other countries. It also says that it is the movement of people from any nation or group away from their own country.

Robert Cohen, extends the meaning of the term 'Diaspora' to the communities of people living together in a migrated country who 'acknowledge that the old, country a nation buried deep in language, religion and customs or folktale always has some claim on their loyalty or emotion.'[1]

Over the centuries the concept and meaning of diaspora has undergone many changes. Today, diaspora addresses and assists the understanding of migration, post-migration problem, people's multiple sense of belonging and loyalties beyond the national boundaries. Diaspora is a concept which is far from being definitional. Despite problems and terminology, this may be defined with issues attached to it for a complete understanding. Diasporans are those people who have settled forever in a country other than the one in which they were born and thus this term loses its dimension of irreversibility and exile.

The present research paper is exploring the Indian Diaspora in special context with the Parsis. The Indian Diaspora is the second largest in the world. The overseas Indian community is estimated as over 25 million and is spread across the major countries of the world. Yet, it is difficult to speak of one great Indian diaspora. The overseas Indian community is the result of different waves of migration over hundreds of years driven by a variety of reasons-mercantilism, colonialism and globalization. Its early experiences make up a saga of trials, tribulations and the eventual triumph of determination and hard work. In the last three decades of the 20th century the character of migration began to change and a 'new Diaspora' led by high skilled professionals moving to the western world and semi-skilled contract workers moving to the Gulf, West and South East Asia emerged.

The Diasporans carry a longing for a memory of the homeland. They need to be sustained through a set of cultural symbols. These symbols assert the unity of that community, and visibly maintain it as different from that in the homeland, for it has been structured within a particular immutable form. Diasporic writers tend to portray the cultural dilemmas, the generational differences, and transformations of their identities during displacement. Their living in-between condition is very painful and they stand bewildered and confused. These writers are deeply attached to their centrifugal homeland and they are caught physically between two worlds and this double marginalization negates their belonging to either location. Indian diasporic writers have made their haven the adopted country and are using English language almost like a mother tongue. They are thoroughly exposed to significant modern western literary movements like post modernism and magic- realism. This has enabled them to give a fresh orientation to fiction. At the same time, the best of them continue to have strong roots in India so they remain true to the kindred points of India and the west. Indian Diasporic writing in English covers every continent and part of the world. It is interesting paradox that a great deal of Indian writing in English is produced not in India but in other parts of the continent. Many writers of Indian origin, who have settled abroad, are engaged in creative writing e.g. V.S.Naipaul,Bharthi Mukherjee, Salman Rushdie, RohintonMistry, Uma Parmeswaran etc.

As the research undertaken is on the Parsi writer; I would like to throw light on the Parsi Diaspora. Parsis migrated to India after the fall of the Sassanian Empire around 650A.D. They landed in Diu, and were later given refuge in Sajan [Gujarat] by the local Hindu King, JadhavRana. The king was not too keen to let them settle in his small kingdom so he sent them a glass full with milk signifying that the land is full and cannot support anymore; but the Parsieswere clever they mixed sugar in it and returned them. Till then this community has given enough success in the field of education, commerce, science, technology, medicine, literature etc. They entered Bombay at the most opportune time in urbanization of India, and became the most urbanized community in India. For them Gandhiji said that-"In numbers Parsis are beneath contempt but in contribution beyond compare."There are number of virtues in this community i.e. hard work, sincerity, high- thinking, peace- loving nature, sense of humour, social service, patriotic etc. They have also preserved their Zoroastrian culture alive even after their migration to India. Hence, one can easily distinguish a Parsiamongst the Indians.

The contribution of Parsis in the field of literature has left a significant mark. Writers like RohintonMistry, Firdaus Kanga, BapsiSidhwa, FarrukhDhondy, Dina Mehta, MeherPestonji, Gieve Patel and many others. These writers are fully conscious of the fact that their community is fast disappearing. The number of Parsis is dropping day by day. In India they are down from 115,000 in 1941 to perhaps 65,000 [out of 1 billion] today, by 2021 they are expected to fall to a more 21,000. Hence, creative writing is one of the media for them for the purpose. Their literature deals with their community, its religion, its customs and traditions. The trend of Parsi authors in English started a century ago with BehramMalbari, the first poet to write in English. His collection of poems called *TheIndianMuseinEnglishGarb* in 1877. In twentieth century, another well-known Parsi writer was Cornelia Sorabji who published three volumes of short-stories *Loveand Life Behind the Purdah* [1901], *Sun Babies* [1904] and *Between the Twilights* [1908]. D.F.Karka, an eminent journalist published some novels in the 40's and 50's. NergisDalal published four novels in the 60's and 70's. PerinBharucha's novel – *TheFireWorshippers* was published in 1968.Boman Desai another Parsi creative writer was awarded the Lewis Prize for Creative Writing. His first novel – *TheMemoryofElephants* was published in 1998. The novel focuses on the Parsi family of three generation facing the problem of generation gap. FirdausKanga's autobiographical novel – *Trying* to *Grow* depicts the experiences of a physically handicapped boy turning into manhood. This novel also focuses on the ethnic identity of the Parsi community in general. The problem of alienation and quest for identity is the theme of the novel. Dina Mehta is a well Parsi novelist writing in English. Her novel- *AndSomeTakeLover* [1992] and her play- *BridesarenotforBurning* has become very popular.Geive Patel is a Parsi poet writing in English. His poetry includes *Poems* [1966] and*HowDoYouWithstandBody* [1976].He is regarded as poet of the body because human body is a recurrent theme in most of his poems.BapsiSidhwa, the best known Pakistani novelist has published four novels- *TheCrowEaters*, *ThePakistaniBride*, *Ice-Candy* Man and *AnAmericanBrat*. Her theme of writings include partition crisis, expatriates experiences, women's problems, patterns of migration, the Parsi milieu and social idiosyncrasies of this minority community.

Bapsi Sidhwa, was born in Lahore in 1939. She suffered from polio but was a voracious reader. She read the novels of Charles Dickens, Tolstoy, V.S.Naipaul and many other which influenced her writings. She received the 'Lila Wallace –Readers' Digest Award for 1993 and the 'Sitara- i-Imitiaz' Award of Pakistan. She is also an eminent social activist working for woman's emanicipation. In the novel *TheCrowEaters*she describes the social nobility of a Parsi family, during the British Raj in the early twentieth century. The Pakistani Bride is based on a real incident involving a Pakistani girl who becomes Zaitoon, the sixteen year old girl the protagonist of this novel. The real story was narrated to Sidhwa when she was travelling to a remote place in the KarakoramMountains with her husband. She heard the story that a Punjabi girl, who had run away from her tribal husband, could not bear the insult of losing his wife, chased her in the valley and after two weeks killed her on the spot. This story haunted Bapsi for a long time and then she decided to write a novel. The novel focuses on the theme of marriage between two totally different cultures. The girl of a cultured city finds difficult to adjust with a fanatic tribal husband. The novel also focuses on the harsh realities of the lives of people living in the granite folds of Karakoram, who for their honor is ready to kill their wife. It also depicts on the victimization of the women characters at the hands of the age old patriarchal tribal culture, social and environmental forces to a different culture, and their victory over these forces. Sidhwa, being a Parsi expresses the age old customs and traditions from a liberal perspective of a novelist writing in English, which is an international language.

In the novel *Ice-Candy Man* the traumatic scene of partition is portrayed.The narrator in this novel is an eight year old Parsi polio-stricken girl. The paradigm of 'woman-as-victim' is depicted in the novel. The maid in the Parsi family suffers the most due to Partition of India and Pakistan. The communal riots give the Ice-Candy man the opportunity to engineer her abduction. The most tragic scene in this novel is the abduction of Ayah. She is betrayed by her own people who love her the most. The novelist gives a realistic picture of the traumatic event of the Partition. Another major issue pertaining to the Parsi paradox during the period of the Indian struggle for independence, whether they should be loyal to the Britishers is depicted in the novel. The Parsies fear the partition of India and were in dilemma as to which community they should support. The incident of the Joshan prayer to celebrate British victory at the fire temple in Lahore is neutral manifestation of the Parsi community. It expresses the insecurity of the Parsies not because of communal antagonism, but the apprehension of their status at the departure of the British. Parsi life again comes under close scrutiny in Sidhwa's novel – *AnAmericanBrat* which chronicles the adventure of a young Pakistani Parsi young girl Feroza. She is depicted as a lively and temperamental girl, who is being sent to America for a three month holiday. This act of apparent audacity arises concern by the family of Feroza because of her conservative attitudes. Her parents- Zareen and Cyrus were disturbed by the thought that her daughter has adopted a Parsi like orthodoxy in her attitude and outlook, thereby making her a misfit in her community. The fear of loss of Parsiidentity is the main concern by his father. He is constantly in fear that her daughter might marry a non-Parsi. And to avoid this would- be circumstances he plans to send her abroad. But all his plans becomefutile when her daughter falls in love with an American-David Press, who is a Jew. The novel ends with her love ending by her interference of her mother and calling her an 'American Brat'. BapsiSidhwathus in this novel stresses the fact that expatriate experiences go a long way in changing the protagonist's attitude. She highlights the sensitive issue of inter community marriage between a Parsi and a non-Parsi. The major concern of all the Parsi writers is the fast diminishing of their race due to the unwillingness to accept conversions to faith, the low birth-rate and high rate of death.

RohintonMistry is another Parsi writer, who is the recipient of 2012 NeustadtInternational Prize for Literature, thus making him one of the most important contemporary writer in English Language. His work has been published in more than 300 languages. NiluferBarucha writes in about Mistry-"As an Indian who now lives and writes from Canada, RohintonMistry is also a Parsi Zoroastrian and as a person whose ancestors were forced into exile by the Islamic conquest of Iran he was in diaspora even in India. This informs his writing with the experience of multiple displacements."[2]His maiden anthology of short stories- *TalesfromFirozShahBaag* published in 1987 was short listed for the Canadian Governor General Awards. It is a collection of twelve short stories each dealing with the aspects of the lives of the residents of FirozshahBaag, an apartment complex where Parsies lived in majority. All the ten stories are set in India depicting Parsi's busy life in the apartment. His short stories deals with ethnicity, religious rituals and customs of Parsi community. Two of the stories are set in Canada which is again autobiographical. The story 'Squatter' reveals Parsies desire for emigration and the problems of immigrant in Canada's multicultural mosaic. The protagonist- Saroshtries hard to adapt to the western culture. He promises his mother that-"If I do not become completely Canadian in exactly ten years from the time I land there, then I will come back."[3]Sarosh calls himself 'Sid' and became totally westernized after staying for ten long years. But still he is unable to adapt the western culture of using toilets. His inability to use western toilet symbolizes his cultural dislocation and its social and psychological dangers. The last story of this collection is 'Swimming Lessons' is also autobiographical deals with his personal identity, recollection of his homeland and his adjustment in a new ambience. The story is India's past and Canada's present portraying the clashes between Oriental and Occidental. Everything in Canada transfers his mind to India which makes him nostalgic. The old man in his apartment reminds him of his Grandpa. The Swimming Lessons in Canada reminds the failed attempts at swimming in Bombay. Swimming abilities is shown as a mark of high class. The clean water of Canada is compared with the polluted water of Bombay. The son Kersi in this story is again autobiographical in character. Mistry is portraying himself through his mode of writing letters. He becomes nostalgic and remembers FirozshahBaag where he spent his childhood. He memorises his rich culture and religious life of India like the Ganesh Chaturthi festival, the beating of drums, grand processions and their immersions in Chaupatty.Mistry skillfully portrays the debate surrounding multiculturalism that has held the nations intellectuals and academics for more than three decades now. The truth about the ethnic minority and the problems they face are facts which the diasporans have to adjust in a foreign land.

Apart from giving the touch of diaspora in his writings he is also concerned about the Parsies. The first story of the collection, "Auspicious Occasion" deals with the ethnicity, religious rituals and customs of Parsi community. The protagonist Rustomji, executes a balancing act between the desire to embrace modernism as well as be in touch with old religious traditions. In the story 'Condolence Visit' the character DaulatMirza is managing hard to live the life of a widow. Her distribution of her husband's clothes to the poor, especially her attachment with the beautifully embroidered pugree which she gave to a young man, who was about to marry has been beautifully portrayed by Mistry. The picturesque view of Dusmoo, i.e. the tenth day after death and the trauma of loss and how people cope with loss is beyond comparable. All the traditional customs of Parsies regarding funeral and aftermath are very well portrayed. Readers can also find in his novel- *FamilyMatters*published in 2002 where the fictional transmission of cultural attitudes actively proceeds from generation to generation. The mythology of Parsibelief is explained to the reader through the query of his grandson to his grandfather-

"It (Jehanjir) means 'conquer of the world.'

Jehanjir was impressed.

Murad came into the front room.

'What does my name mean?' He asked.

You are a boon, a blessing', said his father.

And mummy's name?

"Roxana means the dawn."[4]

There names carry unique cultural connotations. Moreover, their names are rooted in Parsi tradition and hence highlight their difference from the others.The novel deals with the Parsi anxieties concerning emigration, cross-cultural marriages and declining birth rates. Mistry believes that it is the failure to imagine a new kind of Parsi community, one better integrated in Indian life and not so absorbed in issues of cultural purity, which has been the bane of the community.

His first novel- *SuchALongJourney* published in 1989, which brought him international recognition won the Governor-Generals Award and Common Wealth Writer's Prize. The novel revolves round Bombay. The condition of Bombay during the Emergency period or the Babri Masjid aftermath is vividly drawn. It is based upon a series of real events that took place during the Indira Gandhi administration in 1971. The author saves special anger for the policies of Indira Gandhi and the growing power of Shiv Sena. The Parsis also feel insecure because of growing political power of the Maratha parties as they would upset the power structure. Same effort has been made in his second novel- *AFineBalance*published in 1995. The novel focuses onthe unlikely friendship of four disparate people – Dina, Om, Ishwar and Maneck who come to live together during the tumultuous period of Indira Gandhi 1975 bid to retain power. Bombay stands tall in all his works. Readers never feel that the writer who is writing about Bombay's reality is residing in Canada. He draws a pathetic picture of near naked people in Bombay slums, with meagre possessions, lean, emaciated babies, hungry and crying when the parents feed them half rotten bananas etc. In both the novels Mistry's characters exhibit a quiet deliberateness despite the senselessness tragedies that threaten to overwhelm their lives.

Mistry latest short story-*TheScream* is narrated by an elderly man who is living in a house with many generations. Relegating to sleep he keeps a constant vigil of men who are passing by as his bed was near the window. One night he was woken up by a scream from outside and a stranger was being assaulted.Mistry's language is typically the language of a Parsi gentleman. Though he has been living in Toronto in Canada since 1975, his English is very much Indian. His fiction focuses on the Parsi identity and also reveals how they are learning to cope with the reality of postcolonial India and how they are coming with new life in the west.

Another Parsi writer FarrukhDondhy, who was earlier a teacher in London has now became a full time writer. His stay in England inspired his award-winning children's books, *EastEndatyourfeet*[1996] and *CometoMeccaandotherStories*[1978]. He has written several collections of short stories viz. *TheSiegeofBabylon*[1978], *PoonaCompany*[1980] and *TripTrap*[1982]. He has written many plays viz. *MamaDragon*[1980], *Trojans*[1983], *KiplingSahib*[1982], *MaidsandtheMadShow* was telecast in 1981. His first novel- *BombayDuck*[1990] focuses on different kinds and consequences of cultural transferences. It is a diasporic novel which focuses the great cultural divide between the East and the West. The Parsi community also forms the thematic concern of the novel. His novel- Poona Company is specifically designed for the adults, appeals to readers of all ages and cultures. His use of language is natural as he has the ability in giving language to the characters concerned.

All the Parsi writers have mentioned their Zoroastrian religion, their culture, rites and rituals, alienation from their majority and their quest for identity. RohintonMistry has himself mentioned in an interview with Stacy Gibson that when the Parsies have disappeared from the face of the earth, his writing will preserve a record of how they lived. This shows his concern for his community, and his sense of helplessness to preserve the rich heritage of his community. The paper concludes, highlighting the Parsi writers, who are trying their best to portray their culture in their writings.

References

1. Robert Cohen: Global Diaspora: Contesting Identities, pg.84,1997, London: Routledge
2. NiluferBharucha: On the Wings of Fire: Theorising the Parsi Diaspora, 2003, Rawat Pub.
3. RohintonMistry: Tales from Firozshah Baag,pg.154, 1991, Faber and Faber
4. RohintonMistry: Family Matters, pg.281, 1995, M&C Canadian Pub.
5. JaydipsinhDodiya: Parsi English Novel, 2006, Sarup& Sons.
6. JaydipsinhDodiya: Perspectives on the novels of RohintonMistry, 2006, Sarup& Sons.
7. Jasbir Jain: Writers of Indian Diaspora: Theory and Practice, 1998, Rawat Pub.
8. RandhirPratap Singh: BapsiSidhwa, 2005, Sarup& Sons.
9. http://www.thecore.nus.edu./canada/literature/mistry.html.
10. http://theparsichronicle.com
11. http://www.sidhwa/Paper abstracts.htm
12. http://www.wikepedia.org/wiki/Rohinton _Mistry

13

Gandhi's Literature and Diaspora: A Descriptive Study of Gandhiji's Ideology

1. Mayur R. Agravat

Shri Chimanbhai Patel Institute of Business Administration Ahmedabad-380051

2. Tanvi M. Dubal

Mohandas Karamchand Gandhiji, a formative figure in Indian history, was a freedom fighter, a researcher and a poignant writer whose works do not only reflects his ideology about truth and non-violence or freedom struggle but also about a way of life. His *Satyagraha* was not only a movement of agitation but his own framework for positive thinking and purposeful action. His holistic approach was considered by mass approach and was influenced by many religious references. It would be a chance to know Gandhiji from diasporic point of view. The major change one can ever mark in Gandhiji was all his overseas experience which brought immense change in his thinking and ideology.

In this research paper it has been taken mainly his three books for study i.e. *'The Story of My Experiments of Truth'*, *'Hind Swaraj'* or *'Indian Home Rule'* and *"Satyagraha in South Africa"*. This chapter encapsulates Gandhiji's diasporic approach and experience in England and South Africa and how host-countries behaviour affects or forms Gandhiji's psychology. Gandhiji's works presents lots of issues related with the diasporic Indians. His visit to England has brought him with the contacts of Indian mythologies which he has never touched or imagined to touch it while his South African experience taught him to be a man of substance and made him sharp and powerful. In his autobiography, Gandhiji tells the story of his discovery and use of the moral power of truth and love. In naming it *Experimenting with Truth* he claims to be a sort of scientist, a seeker and discoverer of absolute Truth and the relative of this world and of action in it. As he explains formerly, his goal was *moksha* or self-realization, seeing God face to face, and his experiments in the political field were a means to that thing. He only said that such a seeker,

'must be able to love the meanest of creation as oneself'. The freedom of moksha is thus available only to one who chooses to live an egoless life.

(A Gandhi Reader, Pg. No. 10)

The current chapter *'Gandhi's Literature and Diaspora'* talks initially about Gandhiji's formation of attitude and how with this he had fight in the foreign land and won. This discusses in detail about Gandhiji's attitude and approach towards host countries. Gandhiji is a diasporic character as he had experienced all complexities that a diasporic character faces. All diasporic literature is repleted with the issues related to location, movement, crossing border, original home and adopted home and identity. His *"My Experiments with Truth"* deals with his background, childhood experience, culture, family, British rule etc but his *"Hind-Swaraj"* and *"Satyagraha in South Africa"* typically deals with his journey in foreign land, initial shock, pragmatic development and holistic approach developed at the end of his journey. Gandhi was deeply religious, but he was no blind follower of convention. He said, 'nothing in the shastras can bind us if it is repugnant to reason and the moral sense. To me God is Truth and Love. God is ethics and morality. God is fearlessness. God is conscience.'

It is this inner light which Gandhi followed with an ever-growing humility of spirit. *Satya,* truthfulness in thought and word, and *sattva,* goodness in action, gave him glimpses of the perfect *sat,* the ultimate reality. From such pursuit of truth in thought and word, and loving kindness in action, there flowed a moral power which was felt and freely obeyed by large numbers both in India and abroad.

Gandhi began the experiments in his revolutionary region in South Africa. His South African career is the clear and inspiring story of a young man discovering his true identity as a patriot and a seeker of Truth and discovering also the '*soul-force*' or the moral and spiritual power inherent in all human beings. The barrister became a Mahatma by identifying himself with Tamil coolies, Muslims and Parsi merchants and earnest Christians who supported him in a common struggle for establishing human value. He perfected here the philosophy and technique of Satyagraha and conceived the idea of 'sarvodaya' (welfare for all). The evil which he battled against in India was far greater than what he had known in South Africa. It was almost terrifying in its all pervasiveness and Gandhi's effort was prominently more heroic and more complex. Fighting that battle he touched and transformed the life of our people at so many points that he is rightly regarded as the master-builder of Modern India.

Now it is better to know about the term 'diaspora' in order to discuss Gandhiji in a diasporic framework. To study 'Gandhi's literature and diaspora', we need to know what this *'Diaspora'* connotation mean? Where from it did originate? What is the root of it? For what it had implied for the first time? What are the patterns of it? How many waves are there? Is this the new connotation or it is quite old like our ancient mythology? What role has it played in human life? Is it essential for human being's living or is it simply a way of life?

Turning to *Webster's Collegiate* dictionary, it finds that *Diaspora* is used, as a capitalized name, for the Jewish Diaspora, understood to mean colonies of Jews living outside Palestine, or the places where they live — and in recent times, those living outside of Israel. A second dictionary meaning, written without capitalization (*diaspora*) refers to the process of scattering people from their homelands, or the communities formed as a result, or the places where they live. Today it has been used for any sizeable community of a particular nation or region living outside its own country and sharing some common characteristics and bonds that give them ethnic identity. Very recent writing on the said subject conveys at least three meanings of the concept '*diaspora*'.

(1) 'Diaspora' as a Social form.

(2) 'Diaspora' as a type of consciousness.

(3) 'Diaspora' as a mode of cultural production.

The Oxford English Dictionary 1989 Edition (second) traces the etymology of the word *'Diaspora'* back to its Greek root and to its appearance in the Old Testament (*Deut*: 28:25) as such it references. God's intentions for the people of Israel to be dispersed across the world. The Oxford English Dictionary here commences with the Judic History, mentioning only two types of dispersal: The *"Jews living dispersed among the gentiles after the captivity"* and The Jewish Christians residing outside the Palestine. The dispersal (initially) signifies the location of a fluid human autonomous space involving a complex set of negotiation and exchange between the nostalgia and desire for the Homeland and the making of a new home. Diaspora Literature involves an idea of a homeland, a place from where the displacement occurs and narratives of harsh journeys undertaken on account of economic compulsions. Basically Diaspora is a minority community living in exile. People migrating to another country in exile home living peacefully immaterially but by losing home.

In current parlance the term is applied to describe any group of people who are dispersed (N. Jayaram 1998). The term Diaspora may be defined as the migration of a population or a section of it along with their ways of life to the place of destination. In the tradition of indo-Christian the fall of Satan from the heaven and humankind's separation from the Garden of Eden, metaphorically the separation from God constitute diasporic situations. Etymologically, *'Diaspora'* with its connotative political weight is drawn from Greek meaning to disperse and signifies a voluntary or forcible movement of the people from the homeland into new regions.

William Sarfan points out that the term Diaspora can be applied to expatriate minority communities whose members share some of the common characteristics given here under:

1. They or their ancestor have been dispersed from a special original *'centre'* or two or more *'peripheral'* of foreign regions;
2. They retain a collective memory, vision or myth about their original homeland- its physical location, history and achievements;
3. They believe they are not- and perhaps cannot be- fully accepted by their lost society and therefore feel partly alienated and insulted from it;
4. They regard their ancestral homeland as their, true, ideal home and as the place to which they or their descendents would (or should) eventually return- when conditions are appropriate;

5. They believe they should collectively, be committed to the maintenance or restoration of their homeland and its safety and prosperity; and
6. They continue to relate, personally and vicariously, to that homeland in one way or another, and their ethno- communal consciousness and solidarity are importantly defined by the existence of such a relationship.

History of Diaspora: Waves of Migration

1. 1st Wave – To Pacific islands as sailors
2. 2nd Wave – (1864) – Indentured labour – to Fiji under *girmit* system (5 years contract)
3. The Colonial era – inter – colony migration 'brain-drain'
4. Post-Colonial – (1940s onwards) – socio-cultural & technological

Typologies of Diaspora

1. Marginal Man (stranger) – no orientation
2. Sojourner:
   - Ethno-centric – ethnic orientation only
   - Xeno-centric – orientation to host society
   - Xenoplilia – hospitality of host country
   - Xenophobia – hostility of host country
3. 'Middle men' minorities

Characteristics

1. Sojourning
2. Ethnic organization
3. Host hostility
4. Economic concentration

"The banyan tree has thrust down roots in soil which is stony, sandy, marshy and has somehow drawn sustenance from diverse unpromising conditions. Yet the banyan tree itself has changed; its similarity to the original growth is still there, but it has changed in response to its different environment."

—Tinkar (1977:19)

The nineteenth century brought a radical change to the character of emigration. The Indian Diaspora had its strong foundation during its period. The small-scale emigration became a mass movement to provide cheap labour to British and other European colonies. Conditions of absolute poverty in many parts of India or the prospect of gaining wealth overseas motivated people to sell themselves and become bonded labour. Modern Indian emigration started with the abolition of slavery in 1833 in British Empire. After a transition period, these slaves became free men in 1838. Indian emigration, which involved with all religions, has been present in India since l9th century. Between 1834 and 1837, ten thousand people emigrated from Calcutta to Mauritius (Chali 1995). Many went to British Guiana, Jamaica, and Natal in South Africa. In 1834, slavery was abolished in French colonies and the reunion of families brought in many labours from Pondicherry. Conditions of this journey were extremely difficult and the mortality was high on both British and French boats. Within a few decades, there was significant Indian presence in Natal, South Africa, Surinam, Trinidad, Mauritius, and Fiji.

The Story of My Experiments with Truth

Social and Psychological Impact of his Childhood Experiences :

"When I despair, I remember that all through history the ways of truth and love have always won. There have been tyrants, and murderers, and for a time they can seem invincible, but in end they always fall. Think of it always."

—M. K. Gandhi.

Gandhi's philosophy and his ideologies of *satya* (truth) and *ahimsa* (non-violence) were influenced by the Bhagavad Gita and Hindu beliefs, the Jain religion and the pacifist Christian teachings of Leo Tolstoy. The concept of *'ahimsa'* (non-violence) has a long history in Indian religious thought and has had many revivals in Hindu, Buddhist and Jain contexts. Gandhi explains his philosophy and way of life in his autobiography 'The Story of my Experiments with Truth'. There are many factors responsible behind the formation of Gandhiji's attitude and psychology. Some of them are publicly known while others are not. Gandhiji's quest for '*Truth*' and '*Non-Violence*' basically depends upon his childhood experiences. And thus in South Africa he was able to stand as a man of truth and non-violence.

Gandhi and the Kokila Vratha : - Gandhiji's mother Putlibai observed a vow known as '*kokila vratha*' everyday. Every morning, after she completes her ritual she would wait for a sweet call of cuckoo and then takes her break fast. She would not touch anything to eat without doing the same ritual everyday. She was following it regularly without break. Gandhiji had been very much concerned about his mother's health. Once Putlibai was waiting for cuckoo's voice for long time in order to take break fast. She kept on waiting near the window to hear the sound of cuckoo but didn't get. Gandhiji had observed this act and crafted a plan. He went out of the house, hiding himself behind the bush, started imitating cuckoo's voice. Then he suddenly went into the house and said to his mother,

"*Mother you can eat your food now as it has made its call.*"

(http://www.4to40.com/story/print.asp?p=Mahatma_Gandhi_and_Kokila_Vratha&c=Special_Occasion)

Initially she minded it but then she realized about Gandhiji's silly prank as she was observing this oath since long and hence understood the voice clearly. She became very angry and slapped Gandhiji for his misdeed and said,

"*What sin have I committed that such a wicked liar should be born to me! Lord!*"

The Incident of '*Kettle*': Once there was an incident which occurred at the examination hall during his first year at the high school. The Educational Inspector, Mr. Giles, had come to his school for an inspection. He had set five words to write as a spelling test. One of the words was *'cattle'*. Gandhiji had mis-spelt the word. The teacher tried to prompt him with the point of his boot. He wanted him to copy the word from his colleague's, sitting next to him, slat. But that perhaps out of Gandhiji's ethics. When the result came out, all the boys had spelt the word correctly, except him. Though he was very much pleased but never learnt the art of copying.

Shravana Pitribhakti Nataka & Raja Harishchandra: Gandhiji was not a bibliophile during his childhood. But once he happened to have a glance on a book called '*Shravana Pitribhakti Nataka*'. Initially he read it with a great interest. Once, when he was of seven year of age, at his school in Rajkot, an itinerant showman came to his school. He happened to see '*Shravana's Pitribhakti*' where Shravana was carrying his blind parents on a pilgrimage. The book and the picture left an indelible impression on his mind. Gandhi's early self-identification with Truth and Love as supreme value is traceable to his identification with these epic characters.

Hind-Swaraj: A critique of the modern west

In '*Hind Swaraj*' Gandhiji has well expatiated about his attitude and approach (diasporic views) towards host culture. He said,

"*Western civilization assures progress by the progress of matter-railways, conquest of disease, conquest of the air. No one says, 'now the people are more truth-ful or more humble.'* "(Hind Swaraj - 32)

'*What I object to is the craze for machinery, not machinery as such.*'

(Hind Swaraj - 08)

Hind Swaraj is an embodiment of Gandhiji's frustration towards host countries. The book which published in 1908, during Gandhiji's return voyage from London to South Africa, in answer to the Indian school of violence and published serially in the columns of the '*Indian opinion*', edited by Gandhiji, has various illustrations of host – countries hostility and materialistic progress in rail-ways, medicine and other human convenience. In Gandhiji's own words Hind Swaraj '*is a severe condemnation of modern civilization*'. Civilization, says Gandhi, is civilization in name only. In reality it correspondences to what ancient Hinduism called the dark ages. It has set material well-being up as the only goal of life. It scorns spiritual values. It maddens Europeans, leads them to worship money only, and prevents them from finding peace or cultivating the best within them. Civilization in the Western sense means hell for the weak and for the working classes. It saps the vitality of the race. But this Satanic civilization will destroy itself. Western civilization is India's real enemy, much more than the English, who, individually, are not bad, but simply suffer from their civilization. Gandhi criticizes those of his compatriots who would want to drive out the English, to develop India themselves, and civilize her according to European standards. This, he says, would be like having the nature of a tiger without the tiger. India's aim should be to repudiate Western civilization. Gandhiji's negative opinion about modern civilization extended to all its aspects. Modern technology, machine being the fundamental constituting unit of it; and Western social institutions, particularly those pertaining to law and medicine, came in for the most severe criticism.

At one point of time, one can think that on the one hand Gandhiji's commitment to non-violence was of a high order and on the other he saw embodiment of violence in every way of modernity. It is believed that if in the value system of a person non-violence figures very high and his characterization of a particular social order or civilization is such that violence figures in it in a prominent way then the evaluative judgment of that social order or civilization being unacceptable follows immediately. Gandhiji believes that true civilizations can never be achieved through fair-or-foul means of machinery. He believes it rather creates discontent and unrest. He said,

"Formerly men were made slaves under physical compulsion. Now they are enslaved by temptations of money and of the luxuries that money can buy. There now diseases of which people never dreamt before, and an army of doctors is engaged in finding out their cures, and so hospitals have increased." (Hind Swaraj - 32)

It is said that once there is a multiplicity of values, conflicts of values are almost inevitable.

"Immorality is often taught in the name of morality."

(Hind Swaraj - 32)

Gandhiji was not only committed to non-violence; he was also committed to truth and other important human values. When two values are in conflict, willingly or unwillingly, the individual must choose the fairer one, what holds true for an individual holds for societies and civilizations as well. In Gandhiji's perception Western or Modern civilizations might have been more violent than pre-British Indian civilizations. Gandhiji believes that India is being ground down, not under the English heel, but under that of modern civilizations. Even Napoleon is said to have described the English culture *'as a nations of shop-keepers.'* Though Gandhiji called Indians as responsible for such an outcome as we are responsible for inviting them and giving them chance to trade in India and become a part of it. He himself said that,

"If the English become indianized, we can accommodate them."

(Hind Swaraj - 56)

From Gandhiji's writings it is explicitly clear that in his opinion the modern civilization placed the idea of bodily comforts on too high pedestal. The canvas that self-interest will occupy in a system where comforts and personal luxuries are not only desirable but considered of the highest achievements of civilization is bound to be large. Furthermore, Gandhiji's intuitive understanding of social institutions planted by the Britishers in India was that they sowed selfish motive among human beings. Gandhiji has very painfully talked about lawyers and doctors in *Hind Swaraj:*

'Whenever instances of lawyers having done good can be brought forward, it will be found that the good is due to them as men rather than as lawyers. All I am concerned with is to show you that the profession teaches immorality; it is exposed to temptation from which few are saved.'

(Hind Swaraj - 41)

'The latter's duty is to side with their clients and to find out ways and arguments in favour of the clients to which they (the clients) are oftenstrangers. If they do not do so they will be considered to have degraded their profession. The lawyers, therefore, will, as a rule, advance quarrels instead of repressing them. Moreover, men take up that profession, not in order to help others out of their miseries, but to enrich themselves. It is one of the avenues of becoming wealthy and their interest exists in multiplying disputes. It is within my knowledge that they are glad when men have disputes. Petty pleaders actually manufacture them. Their touts, like so many leeches, suck the blood of the poor people.'

(Hind Swaraj - 41)

In the light of above, we can say that Gandhiji's criticism on modernity was fundamentally unsustainable. It would not be inappropriate to interpret the following remark of Gandhiji in this light:S

'Indian civilization is the best and that the European is a nine days wonder.' (Hind Swaraj - 67)

Satyagraha in South Africa: As we know that Gandhiji's freedom movement is originally started from the South Africa and then it has got carried forward in India. In 19th century, there was the indenture system, which was the name given to the type of contract used in the emigration was based on hiring for work for a given period, usually three to five years, in exchange for the price of the passage and a wage. On the expiration of the contract, either they seek work in the host country or return home at own expenses. This system instituted by the British authorities to prevent abuse was nullified by employer's determination to make people sign contracts for the longest period at the lowest wages. The emigrants were almost all males. The indenture system lasted until after the First World War. General Editor, Professor Brij Lal of the Australian National University, says in his one of the books on diaspora:

"Like other movements and displacements of people, the Indian diaspora grew out of many causes and several crossings. Due to its varied origins, divergent patterns of migration and settlement and different degrees of absorption or integration into the culture of their new homeland, the Indian diaspora defies easy categorisation. It is a complex confluence of many discreet cultures, languages and histories."

(http://www.vedicheritageinc.com/bookreview/108-dispora)

In the study of Indian diaspora, it is customary to distinguish between two main phases of emigration: *'Overseas emigration in the 19th century' and '20th century migration to industrially developed countries'*. For analytical convenience, these could be termed the 'colonial and the post-colonial phases' of Indian diaspora. It is no doubt, possible to identify overlaps between these two phases: The emigration of Indians that began in the second quarter of the 19th century continued into the early decades of the 20th century. The trickle of emigration of Indians to the industrially developed countries, which assumed phenomenal proportions in the post-colonial phase, could be noticed in the 19th century itself. Nevertheless, it is important to recognize the distinctive nature of these two phases of migration, for their causes, courses and consequences.

Studies of Indian diaspora have largely focused on one or the other of the afore-mentioned phases. This is easy to understand considering the magnitude of the population involved, and the variegated nature of their economic status and political predicament in different diasporic spheres. Furthermore, some of these diasporic communities have been topical or their members themselves have begun manifesting an acute sense of *'communal self awareness'*. The history of Indian diaspora in South Africa is a fascinating tale of suffering and triumph. In 1904, while the indenture system of importing Indian labour on a contractual basis was nearing the end of its crucial period, the Governor of British Colony of Natal, Lord Milner, at that time, thought it right to describe Indians as a *'strangers, forcing themselves upon a community reluctant to receive them'*. The irony of this statement would be apparent if juxtaposed against the persistent demand, in earlier years, of the British settlers in Natal for a large scale import of cheap labours from India to shore up their sinking economy. D. F. Malan, a member of the self-governing British dominion called the Union of South Africa, declared in one election manifesto that *'Indians are a foreign and outlandish element which is inassimilable.'*

Contrary to the view that Indians had gone first to South Africa in 1860, they had in fact arrived much earlier in 1654. Dutch merchants, returning from their voyages to India and East Indies, had taken Indian labourers to their Dutch Cape Colony and sold them as slaves to the early Dutch settlers. There they were allotted duty of servants or slaves or work with African slaves who were already toiling to the newly established farms. Most of the Indians slaves had been shipped from Bengal or the Coromandal coast. In the foreign land they were unable to preserve their *'Indian'* identity because of their social and working condition. Many of them married to the slaves workers of East Asia, or parts of Africa. Their children were known as *'Malays'*. The apartheid system had been already started that point of time and Indians were come under the appellations of *'coloureds'*. Then after the *Act of Abolition of Slavery* in 1833, a group of Indian coolies, comprising of approximately 342 men, women and children, reached to Durban port on S.S. Truro on 16th November, 1860. They were the first of 384 such arrivals of 'human cargo' containing as many as 1,52,184 unfortunate persons who were about to stay for 51 years in South Africa. Most of the migrants were from Tamilnadu, Uttar Pradesh, Bihar and West Bengal. Mostly were Hindus, Muslims and Christians.

The purpose of their importing was to make them work at Britishers sugarcanes and sisal plantations. The indentured contract was about for five years. After the completion of first five years contract, labourers can renew their contract and they were promised to give return free tickets from India or small part of land. But still Britishers had not fulfilled their commitment according to their expectations. They were brutally treated, wages was so meager and even the accommodation provided was so clumsy and full of inconveniency. This was one of the main reasons for the high number of suicides among them. Though majority of indentured Indians stayed in South Africa as they have themselves banished them from their own country by crossing the seas (kalapani) which was taboo at that time and were condemned to do *prayaschit.* Later on Indians were distributed to the railways, dockyards, coal mines, municipal services and domestic employment. They were very much suppressed with the racist laws and taxes. Even Gopal Krishna Gokhale himself once said Indians, in South Africa for work, as a

'a monstrous system, iniquitous in itself, based on fraud and maintained by force'.

(http://hif.wikipedia.org/wiki/South_Africa_me_girmit)

Many of Indian indentured had later on started their free-hold businesses and they had succeeded in partial ways. Their success had inspired many Indians to come and commence business. They were known as *'free passengers Indians'* as they have themselves paid for the fares of traveling and staying there. These new migrants were a community of traders, both Hindu and Muslim, who hailed mainly from Gujarat. They had set up their small retail shops and started doing competitions with the white settlers who were running businesses with quite a high rate. These communities consisted of 10% of Indian immigrants. Much later, teachers, doctors, priests, lawyers, accountants and other professionals arrived, also mainly from Gujarat. Due to jealousy the white settlers labeled them as *'coolie merchants', 'coolie doctor', 'coolie barrister'* etc..

The major turning point between India and South Africa relations came under when one of the Gujarati businessman Abdul Karim Jhaveri of Dada Abdullah & Co. had secured his services in a 40,000 pound legal suit against a rival Indian firm in Pretoria. Mohandas Karamchand Gandhi's, a young Indian barrister from Porbandar, arrival coincided with the determination of the Whites to put an end to **'***the Indian merchant menace***'**. Gandhi had become subject of existing practices of racial discrimination by the White settlers. He witnessed that Indians were not allowed to sit on **'***European benches in public parks or bathe in beaches reserved for Europeans. Nor could they enter a restaurant, tearoom, barber's shop or a hotel as they did not have the 'uniform of a white skin'* **'**. (http://indiandiaspora.nic.in/diasporapdf/chapter7.pdf)

Gandhiji opposed this racist practices and discriminatory system. With his legal training, Gandhiji insisted that the colonial government should strictly implement Queen Victoria's Proclamation of 1858 in which she had promised her Indian subjects equality with all other subjects throughout the Empire. While opposing the powerful White settler administration he developed tools and tactics for Truth and Non-violent struggles and had even started *Satyagraha* movement. He started *Indian Opinion,* a weekly newspaper, to give expression to the feelings and aspirants of his fellow Indians, and as an instrument to guide them in their struggle for identity. He also set up the Phoenix Settlement near Durban and later on, the Tolstoy Farm outside Johannesberg, to provide shelter for the families of those who followed his advice and peacefully courted arrest and detention.

It was during his sojourn in South Africa that the Natal Indian Congress was established on 22nd May 1894 and later also the forerunner of the Transvaal Indian Congress. A mass movement of labourers, traders and industrial workers followed him in his courageous fight against the discriminatory laws that restricted even their movements. Gandhi's struggle had given edge to many of the movements. By the time Gandhi finally planned to leave South Africa in 1914 he had already redressed Indian diasporas problems and grieves, which included frustrating and delaying the Government's efforts to register Indians in the Transvaal; abolition of the 3 pound poll tax; and formal recognition of Hindu, Muslim and Parsi marriages. By the time he left on 18th July 1914, he had already sown seeds for future generations to fight courageously against injustice and racial discrimination in South Africa.

One day, walking on the streets of London, he came across a vegetarian restaurant in Farringdon Street. He writes in his autobiography that he was overjoyed at the sight of the restaurant as a small child would be on receiving a new toy! Before entering the restaurant he saw a book entitled '*Benefits of Vegetarianism*' by Henry Salt. He bought the book and proceeded to have his first hearty meal in London. After reading Henry Salt's book Gandhi was converted to the vegetarian cause for ever. He later became the secretary to the Bayswater branch of the vegetarian society and it became his first experience in addressing and conducting meetings. Gandhi's vegetarian ideal brought him in touch with many like minded people. He was introduced to the theosophical society and there he met Madame Blavastky and Mrs. Anne Besant – both of whom were leading lights of the time.

During that period only he happened to read the book called *'Light of Asia'*. He had read nothing of any religion in the world, nothing therefore of Hinduism. He knew of Hinduism what his parents had taught in his early child hood. He knew only about *Rama* whose name to take had been recommended by Rambha, his servant, at the time of any fear or problems. That was the only stock with which he sailed for England. Hence, when he found himself in possession of the *Light of Asia,* he devoured it. He went through the book page by page; he was really indifferent reader of literature, but he could not resist the temptation that each page afforded him and he closed the book with deep veneration for the expounding or teaching which has been so beautifully expressed by Sir Edwin Arnold. He said that,

"I read the book again when I had commenced the practice of my profession in South Africa. At that time, I had read something of the other great religions of the world, but the second study of that book did not diminish my veneration. Beyond that I have practically no acquaintance with Buddhism. I read some more literature in the Yeravada Jail, but I know that the reason why I am called upon to preside at such functions, whether they were in connection with Buddha or Mahavira, or even with Jesus Christ, is that I endeavour to follow to the best of my ability such of these masters teachings as my limited understanding enables me to appreciate."

(A Gandhi Reader, Pg. No. 73)

Conclusion: It is very less to encapsulate Gandhiji's experience in a couple of pages but it is hoped that the current information will be sufficient for the readers to understand the legendary character's diasporic experience. His three books give us immense idea about the family and societal impact on his ideology, his diasporic experience which has clearly been expressed in *"Hind Swaraj"* and *"Satyagraha in South Africa"* and his overall practical experience which has brought radical change in the Indian history.

References

Primary Sources:

1. Gandhi, Mohandas K. *The Story of My Experiment with Truth.* Ahmedabad:

   Navjivan Publishing House, 1927.

2. Gandhi, Mohandas K. *Indian Home Rule (Hind Swaraj).* Ahmedabad: Navjivan

   Publishing House, 1938.

3. Gandhi, Mohandas K. *Satyagraha in South Africa.* Ahmedabad: Navjivan

   Publishing House, 1928.

Secondary Sources:

1. Ahmed, Aizaz. *'In Theory: Classes Nations, Literatures'*. London: Verso, 1995.
2. Andrews, C.F. *To the Students*. Madras: S. Ganesan, 1921.
3. Andrews, C.F. *Mahatma Gandhi's Ideas.* London: Allen and Unwin, 1929.
4. Bhabha, Homi. *The Location of Culture*. London: Routledge, 1994.
5. Bhabha, Homi. *Nation and Narration.* London: Routledge, 1990.
6. Bhana, Surendra and Goolam Vahed. *The Making of a Political Reformer: Gandhi in South Africa, 1893–1914.* New Delhi: Manohar, 2005.
7. Cohen, Robin. *Global Diasporas: An Introduction.* London: UCL Press, 1997
8. Cohen, Robin. *Global Diasporas: An Introduction*. Seattle: University of Washington Press, 1997.
9. *'Commemorating the Centenary of Phoenix settlement'. – 1904-2004*
10. Gandhi, Mahatma. *The Collected Works of Mahatma Gandhi.* New Delhi: Publications Division, Ministry of Information and Broadcasting, Govt. of india, 1994.

11. Ghosh, Amitava. *'The Diaspora in Indian Culture' in The Imam and The Indian.* Delhi: Ravi Dayal and Permanent Books, 2002.
12. Ghosh, Amitava. *The Ghost of Mrs. Gandhi in The Imam and The Indian.* New Delhi: Ravi Dayal Publication, 2002.
13. Jain, Satish K. *Towards a Framework for understanding Gandhiji's critique of modernity in Hind Swaraj.* New Delhi, 2010.
14. Reddy, E. S. *"United Nations, India and South Africa's Liberation Struggle."* Asian Times, 1988.
15. S. Vertovec. *The Hindu Diaspora - Comparative Patterns.* London: Routledge, 2000.
16. Tolstoy, Leo. *From Recollections & Essays.* New York, Toronto: Oxford University Press, 1937.
17. Terchek, Ronald J. *Gandhi: Struggling for Autonomy.* United States of America: Rowman & Littlefield Publishes, Inc., 1998.
18. Trivedi, Harish and Meenakshi Mukherjee, eds. *Interrogative Post-Colonial:Theory, Text and Context.* Shimla: Indian Institute of Advanced Studies 1996.

Web-links

1. www.Sahistory.org:

   www.sahistory.org.za/pages/libraryresources/online%20books/phoenix/significance.htm

2. www.mahatma.com

   http://www.mahatma.com/php/showNews.php?newsid=39&linkid=10www.lifepositive.com

3. www.lifepositive.com

   http://www.lifepositive.com/spirit/masters/mahatmagandhi/gandhi.asp

4. en.wikipedia.org

   http://en.wikipedia.org/wiki/Mohandas_Karamchand_Gandhi

14

The Space of Identity: Chitra Banerjee Divakaruni's The Mistress of Spices

Ramesh P. Chavan

Assistant Professor in English

Shri. Shankar Arts & Commerce, College

Navalgund, 582208, Dist. Dharwad

rpchavan55@gmail.com

Chitra Banerjee Divakaruni is an award-winning author, poet and teacher. Her work has been published in over 50 magazines, including the Atlantic Monthly and The New Yorker, and her writing has been included in over 50 anthologies. Her books have been translated into 29 languages, including Dutch, Hebrew and Japanese.

Much of Divakaruni's works deal with the immigrant experience, an important theme in the mosaic of American society. Her book *Arranged Marriage*, winner of an American Book Award, is a collection of short stories about women from India caught between two worlds. In *The Mistress of Spices*, named one of the best books of the 20th Century by the San Francisco Chronicle, the heroine Tilo provides spices, not only for cooking, but also for the homesickness and alienation that the Indian immigrants in her shop experience. In *Sister of My Heart*, two cousins—one in America, the other in India, share details of their lives with each other and help each other solve problems that threaten their marriages. In *One Amazing Thing*, a group of strangers of varied backgrounds, trapped by an earthquake in an Indian visa office, discover what they have in common as they struggle to save themselves. Divakaruni writes to unite people. Her aims are to destroy myths and stereotypes. She hopes through her writing to dissolve boundaries between people of different backgrounds, communities and ages.

Chitra Banerjee Divakaruni presents multiple consciousnesses as an identity that is in between such oppositional states, characterized by being neither rather than both. In *The Mistress of Spices*, the process of self-perception is the foundation of identity formation for the central character Tilotamma (Tilo). As Tilo strives to define herself as South Asian and American, she develops multiple consciousnesses that manifest themselves in both her experiences and her subsequent relationships with her racial and sexual identities. While Tilo is living in America, she is incapable of pure self-perception, and can only see herself through the eyes of those around her, leaving her own self-seeing as a secondary and almost marginal perspective. Tilo views herself through the lens of her surrounding society, thereby leading to various and often conflicting simultaneous visions of her identity.

The Mistress of Spices is the story of Tilo, a young woman born in another time, in a faraway place, who is trained in the ancient art of spices and ordained as a mistress charged with special powers. Once fully initiated in a rite of fire, the now immortal Tilo—in the gnarled and arthritic body of an old woman—travels through time to Oakland, California, where she opens a shop from which she administers spices as curatives to her customers. An unexpected romance with a handsome stranger eventually forces her to choose between the supernatural life of an immortal and the vicissitudes of modern life. Spellbinding and hypnotizing, The Mistress of Spices is a tale of joy and sorrow and one special woman's magical powers.

Mistress of Spices is a story of a girl who is born to poor parents and regarded as a one who will again put her parents in misery as they will have to pay dowry. Little did they know at the time of her birth that she is born with supernatural powers of foreseeing future. As her fame spread, pirates hear about her and abducts her one day! However, she was powerful enough to overthrow the chief and became the queen of pirates. She was not satisfied and when in search of peace, she comes to an island where she is to become the Mistress of Spices under the rigorous training of First Mother.

The First Mother teaches her along with other girls all about the Spices. These spices are later to be used to cure other peoples' misery when given to them with the magical chants. Once she manages to learn all those Special Powers, she is to run a Spice Store in Oakland. She is given the name 'Tilo'. Tilo should never leave the store, she should never use the powers for herself but for others to help and last but not the least she should not make any physical contact with any human being. As the story progresses, readers find smaller stories intertwined where Tilo uses her powers to help others. While helping others, she is so taken into it that one after another she starts breaking the forbidden rules laid for Mistresses. Not only she breaks rules but she also allows herself to fall in love with a lonely American.

D. B Gavani comments: "For the second generation Indian like Geeta, the question about identity is differently poised. She challenges continuous identification with patriarchal traditions which she associates her grandfather. Tilo empathizes with Geeta, tries to assenge their pain and the novel tells us that she succeeds in restoring within the family" (Gavani, 79)

At first, Tilo allows these perceptions of herself as created by others to dominate her thinking, yet as she assimilates herself to American culture throughout the course of the text, Tilo comes to claim her own self-perception. The result of this knowledge is Tilo's recognition of her multiple consciousnesses, and although this tiplicity is replete with contradictions, Divakaruni nevertheless presents it as a possible solution for Tilo's dilemma of cross-cultural identity formation.

An older woman born with supernatural shaman-like abilities in a small village in India, Tilo's gift is her ability to elicit specific powers inherent in spices and use them to cure the maladies of those around her. In Tilo's preteen years, pirates storm into her home, murder her entire family and abduct Tilo, taking her on board their ship as a prisoner. Eventually, Tilo overthrows the pirate captain to become the pirate "queen, leading [her] pirates to fame and glory, so that bards sang their fearless exploits."(Divakaruni, 20)

But, Tilo abandons this exalted position when mystical sea serpents tell her about the existence of an island upon which she, and other women like her, can develop their supernatural talents to use them for a greater good. This isolated island is a haven for these women, who call themselves the "*Mistresses of Spices*" and are under the care of the First Mother, the eldest and wisest teacher of all the women. The women are trained in the art of listening and controlling the spices, and are then sent forth into the greater world to aid humanity. After Tilo learns all that she can, she is sent to Oakland, California, to a tiny Indian spice shop where she must begin her duties of healing the masses. Thus, she is thrust into the chaos of American life and the newness of a culture to which she must adapt. Although Tilo has already begun her diasporic journey, she does not feel the loss of a home, but rather a finding of many. Tilo sails upon a ship to the island of the Mistresses, a reference to the kalipani, or dark water, the term used in order to describe the journey made by indentured laborers and immigrants from the motherland of India to other foreign lands, creating what we today refer to as the "diaspora."

Already, Divakaruni presents Tilo as inextricably mired in the workings of the diaspora, and the entire notion of home becomes displaced, transformed into an intangible condition that is not based on a singular location but rather a movement among many places. When Tilo arrives on the Island, she and the other young girls like her are given new identities, indicating that the past is being relegated to memory and new personas are being forged. Tilo meets the First Mother, a figure who foreshadows the paradoxical identity that Tilo will soon find herself grappling with.

The First Mother is elderly and maternal, representing the traditionalist notion of the South Asian woman in the domestic sphere. Yet at the same time, she is outside the boundaries of conventional culture, for she lives on an isolated island, possesses magical powers and urges the young girls toward progression and change rather than the maintenance of the status quo. She is at once the old world and the new, a juxtaposition of differing geographical spaces, times and cultures. Upon their arrival, the First Mother tells the girls, "Daughters it is time for me to give you your new names. For when you came to this island you left your old names behind, and have remained nameless since."(Divakarun, 42)

D B Gavani commented: "Divakaruni is writing the script of women's rebellion against the pressure to suppress their desire and their bodies. The order of Mistresses clearly replicates patriarchal struggle and Tilo must be made to break free of them. She struggles with her own passions as she builds emotional relationship with Native American man, whom she calls, Raven. She transforms herself into a woman, feeling guilty about her self indulge, but decides to brave the retribution that she would have to face" (Gavani, 80)

Tilo, the mistress of spices takes her name from Tilottam, the divine danseuse in Indra's court. But she also brings another meaning to the name. She associates herself with till, the sesame seed. In this sense the divine and the earthly are united into Tilo. When she decides to give up the divine and restrict herself only to the human, she takes another name Maya, a name with profound mythological and philosophical associations. Maya, in Hindu philosophy is feminine and is the principle behind the entire material universe. The material universe is considered an allusion. When Tilo assumes the name Maya, she once again reasserts her earthly and feminine character.

Tilo receives her new name and identity, leaving her childhood in a village in India behind her, and assuming a temporary persona that is of the uncertain present rather than the definitive and historical past. Tilo spends decades learning the delicate art of the spices, but the moment arrives when she must leave the island and continue the diasporic journey she has begun. Before Tilo is sent to Oakland, the First Mother gives her a knife as a gift, the purpose of which Tilo believes is "...to cut my moorings from the past, the future. To keep me always rocking at sea" (Divakaruni, 53)

Tilo has entered a state of liminality, a space between the past and the future and without a precise knowledge of where the present. She is unmoored and treading the dark waters between the lands of her past and the lands of her future, a theme that will reappear throughout in the text's representations of the relationship between time and space.

The Island is the first diasporic space that we encounter, and while it exhibits the same liminality and ambiguity as America does, Divakaruni clearly genders the island differently than she later will America. The Island exudes femininity - specifically, Divakaruni constructs it as a maternal space with the figure of the First Mother and the presence of only females on the island. The Island nurtures Tilo, educating and preparing her for the next stage of life she will encounter when she leaves, and also imbuing Tilo with a sense of singularity of identity. While its women learn and grow, the Island itself never changes- the daily routines of the Mistresses remain the same and an ambiance of group unity amongst all females is fostered. Such community cohesion and support will later contrast sharply with the multiplicity and solitude that Divakaruni presents as indicative of the diasporic experience of America.

Tilo is transported to America by means of "Shampati's Fire," a giant bonfire into which she steps and disappears. The symbolism of fire is obvious in its action: the destruction of present physical form, and a reduction to ashes that are then scattered to the far corners of the globe. Divakaruni is again foreshadowing the process of Tilo's identity formation, using the fire as a metaphor for the recreation of the self and presenting identity as erratic rather than permanent. The actual word "Shampati" is a reference to the "bird of myth and memory who dived into conflagration and rose new from ash," or what can be considered an Eastern version of the phoenix.(Divakaruni,58)

Tilo's journey to America is a form rebirth; it is a literal recreation of the self. She emerges from the fire on a bed of ash, in a small spice store in Oakland that she will make her own. The presence of this ash serves as an ambiguous omen, for Tilo enters into her new life upon the remnants of her old, with life and death inextricably linked together just as they are for the phoenix. Once in America, Tilo is immediately placed in yet another interstitial space, unable to forget her history but still wanting to move forward with life. She lives in between, for the island of the past is no longer her home, while America is still too unfamiliar to describe as such. While Divakaruni had gendered the Island as female, America is now portrayed as an almost hermaphroditic space, as ambiguous and uncertain in its many identities as Tilo is in hers. When in America, Tilo interacts with all genders, identifying with both her male and female customers and friends alike. She experiences the sadness and anger of the young and confused adolescent Indian boy who is tormented at school while at the same time sympathizing with the pain of the newly-wed Indian bride who suffers from the terror of domestic abuse. Tilo's consciousness, like America, is in between genders, possessing the characteristics of both so she never has to choose one or the other. Even though she now lives in California, Tilo finds that she cannot let go of her time on the Island with the First Mother and the other Mistresses. The memories are with her night and day, reminders and warnings of the past stream into her thoughts, creating conflict in her present life. As her relationship with her lover Raven progresses, Tilo finds the past inescapable, for the possible admonitions of the First Mother constantly plague her present consciousness. "The spice's silence is like a stone in my heart, like ash on my tongue. Through it I can hear back to long ago, the Old One laughing bitter as bile. I know what she would say were she here."(Divakaruni, 136)

"Tilo often dreams of the island, and even engages in a silent mental dialogue with the First Mother across the expanses of space Time" (Divakarun, 121-22). There is a sense of simultaneous universes, or different spheres that exist at the same time and in the same place. As Tilo ponders one day, "First Mother, are you at this very moment singing the song of welcome, the song to help my soul through the layers, bone and steel and forbidding word, that separate the two worlds." (Divakaruni, 316)

The phrase at this very moment suggests a synchrony between the Island and America, rather than a divide between them that would relegate the Island to the past and America to the present. Tilo's past does not simply haunt her, but instead it is part of her current sphere, making it impossible for her to live simply in the present because the present does not exist by itself. This new sense of time is also expressed in the very structure of the text itself, for Mukherjee jumps from one temporal location to another with almost every chapter. By oscillating between Tilo's childhood, her time spent on the Island, and the various stages of her life in America, Mukherjee elicits a somatic reaction within readers, causing us to experience the same senses of temporal liminality and dislocation as Tilo herself feels. Tilo also feels unmoored spatially, for America is only a temporary place for her; it is her home only insofar as she is fulfilling her duty as a *Mistress of Spices.* The first time that Tilo exits the comfort of her store, she experiences an intense wave of longing for a place to call home:

"I run my hand over the door, which looks so alien in outdoor light, and I am struck by the sudden vertigo of homelessness" (Divakarun, 137). It does not have a home in the traditional and permanent sense, and America is simply one point in between her geographical migrations. Tilo has left the Island but knows that she will someday return to it, to that place that is still "in between" worlds, yet remains the only location in which she feels the comfort of belongingness. Tilo's emotions are an extreme version of the diasporic experience of space in which continents are separated not by miles but by universes, where home does not exist except in the space of idealizing memory. Frantz Fanon explores the impact of altered space upon one's consciousness in the colonial context, describing the experience of existing in such a luminal space as follows: "Consciousness of the body is solely a negating activity. It is a third-person consciousness. The body is surrounded by an atmosphere of certain uncertainty. A slow composition of myself as a body in the middle of a spatial and temporal world such seems to be the schema. It does not impose itself on me; it is, rather, a definitive structuring of the self and of the world - definitive because it creates a real dialectic between my body and the world."(Frantz Fanon, 110-1 11).

Tilo's understanding of time and space results in the creation of a schema in which her existence relates to these constructions through a dialectic of mentality and physicality, that is to say, time and space are no longer solely corporeal locations (past or present, continents or nations) but rather states of being that are intertwined with her consciousnesses, spanning numerous locations and incorporating the presence of various spheres simultaneously. Tilo's fluidity of identity also translates into a fluidity of identification, for Tilo's gift is her ability to read into the lives of all those who enter her store, seeing all of the problems they endure as they assimilate, feeling their daily sufferings and understanding even their most private thoughts and wishes. Ironically, she has the deepest vision for the innermost selves of all others, yet is still incapable of actually perceiving herself. In fact, Tilo is expressly forbidden to look in a mirror while she lives in Oakland and fulfills her duties as a Mistress of Spices, for "Once a Mistress has taken on her magic Mistress-body, she is never to look on her reflection again."(Divakaruni, p. 61)

This strict prohibition of mirrors is a metaphor for Tilo's inability to perceive herself through her own eyes; instead, she formulates her identity upon the vision of others, based upon the differing perceptions of herself as seen by friends, patrons and lovers. Tilo first confronts conflicting perceptions of herself through her experiences with race and class, both of which are inextricably linked together in South Asian formations of identity. She consistently sees the damaging effects of racism on the lower-class patrons of her store, the emergence of an Indian elite upper-middle class community, and the general displacement of South Asians in traditional American categorizations of race and class. As Vijay Prashad observes, South Asians have been "confusedly named and renamed both as 'whites' and as 'minorities7 throughout the twentieth century," for "white Americans have been unable to decide how to identify Asian Indians in terms of Race" (Vijay Prashad, p. 109). Rather than a singular approach to South Asian racial identity, there has only been an abundance of contradictions and paradoxes. As Tilo observes the manner in which South Asians are treated in America, she begins to formulate a conception of her place in the overall structure of American race relations. Tilo first encounters the brutality of racism when one of her working class patrons, Mohan, is brutally assaulted by two young white men one evening. As the men viciously beat Mohan, they scream, "Sonofabitch Indian, shoulda stayed in your own goddam country." (Divakaruni, p. 180)

The young men classify Mohan who has lived in the United States for over a decade in the same category as all immigrants in the United States, just another minority amongst many. In contrast, Mohan and his wife Veena see themselves as separate from other minority communities and wonder why they are the targets of racism. Tilo experiences Mohan's pain and Veena's suffering as if it were her own, crying out after her vision of the beating, "My limbs ache as after a long illness, my sari is damp with shiver-sweat, and in my heart I cannot tell where your pain ends and mine begins. For your story is the story of all those 1 have learned to love in this country, and to fear for."(Divakaruni, 182)

Another young South Asian patron of Tilo's is assaulted at school, taunted by white classmates who scream, "Talk English son of a bitch. Speak up nigger wetback asshole." (Divakaruni, **p.** 41). Tilo's patron sobs and tries to understand why the jeering must occur, wondering what it means to be called nigger, when he is not black but rather South Asian. "The experience of being discriminated against is one common to many South Asians living in America, and acts of violence against South Asian immigrants have only increased over the years"(Prashad, p. 87)

Prashad examines this rise in racist attacks in the United States and the impact that such attacks have upon the racial consciousness of ***desis:*** "Immigrants can work, but if they choose to enact their cultural resources, they may face anti-immigrant wrath. Since 1994 the National Asian Pacific American Legal Consortium's annual audit of violence has shown a gradual increase in the number of racist attacks.. .Though desis have faced the tyranny of white supremacy since the nineteenth century... the incident of the 'Dotbusters' reminded us of the threat to our existence.. .Some white youths in New Jersey fastened upon that 'dot'. ..dubbed themselves 'Dotbusters,' and issued a manifesto to the local press: 'We will go to any extreme to get Indians to move out of Jersey City,' they wrote."(Vijay Prashad, 87)

Regardless of the manner in which South Asians perceive themselves, they are still subject to the prejudices of racism that plague society, and when Tilo observes such discrimination, it influences her perception of her race in relation to greater American society. She now identifies with the experiences of other minority groups in the United States, groups that are constantly fighting for recognition and respect from the majority. Yet when Tilo observes a different class of South Asians, she sees the other side of South Asian racial identity. As opposed to the lower-class patrons described earlier, the rich Indians are protected from racism and disassociate themselves from the black community, identifying almost completely with the white-upper class.

"The rich Indians descend from hills that twinkle brighter than stars..

.

The car stops, the uniformed chauffeur jumps out to hold open the gold-handled door, and a foot in a gold sandal steps down. Soft and arched and almost white.. .the rich Indians rarely speak.. .Inside the store which they have entered only because friends said, " it's so quaint, you must go and see it at least once". . .The rich Indians crane their necks and lift their chins high because they have to be more always than other people, taller, handsomer, better dressed.. .[They] heave their bodies like moneybags out the door and into their satin cars.. .Other rich people send lists instead, because being a rich person is a busy job. Golf cruises charity luncheons in the Cornelian Room shopping for new Lamborghinis and cigar cases inlaid with Lapis Lazuli. Still others have forgotten to be Indian and eat caviar" (Divakaruni, p. 78-9)

The minority group described above differs greatly from the patrons who were terrorized by racism and prejudice, even though both groups are of South Asian descent. This difference serves to illustrate the fact that the marker of race changes in relation to South Asians- it is no longer skin colour only, but rather class, which possesses an immense influence over the creation of identity, resulting in distinctly different characterizations of the South Asian self. Because class is such a strong indicator of race, the very notion of race itself is transformed to the point where it is as changeable as one's job or financial security. Tilo soon realizes that the South Asian in America is considered neither white nor black in American society, but rather a race in-between, depending on one's particular class. Tilo's racial identity can be characterized as entailing a self that is seen as non white but not black, lower-class but in certain instances upper-class, part of an immigrant minority and an assimilated elite community. But the moment that money and upper class status enter into the equation, the South Asians in this text are considered almost white by themselves, other South Asians and even Americans. Nevertheless, these upper-class South Asians are still perceived (and perceive themselves) as an "Other," a mimicry of whiteness that lives on the border of almost passing. The knowledge of inescapable and indeterminate otherness causes the wealthy South Asians in this text to feel as though they must constantly prove themselves as legitimate, lifting their chins high "because they have to be more always than other people."(Divakaruni, 78-79)

Prashad captures the paradox of South Asian racial identity in his chapter on the complex consciousnesses of *desis,* presenting an interesting argument for why South Asians do not perceive themselves as black, even though they suffer many of the same experiences as African-Americans. Prashad claims that this disassociation is due to the desire for upward socio-economic mobility in a racist society: "Desis realize they are not 'white,' but there is certainly a strong sense among most desis that they are not 'black.' In a racist society, it is hard to expect people to opt for the most despised category. Desis came to the United States and denied their 'blackness' at least partly out of a desire for class mobility (something, in the main, denied to blacks). . . "(Prashad, p. 94)

Again, the notion of race as being redefined as class is clear from the manner in which South Asians perceive both themselves and other minorities groups. Tilo has observed what it means to be a South Asian living in America in terms of race relations, and the moment arrives when she herself experiences what it is like to be an American. When Tilo dons her first American outfit and walks out into the street on which her store is located, she makes the striking transition between states of mind and possesses a consciousness that she believes is that of an American but at the same time it is a foreign and "other" consciousness for her.

. . .I pull on my no-nonsense pants and polyester top, button my nondescript brown coat all the way to my calves. I lace my sturdy brown shoes, heft my brown umbrella in readiness. This new-clothed self, I and not-I, is woven of strands of brownness with only her young eyes and her bleached jute-hair for surprise. She tries a hesitant smile which resettles her wrinkles.. .Outside at a bus stop crowded with other strands of brown and white and black she will get into line, will marvel that no one even raises their eyes, suspicious at her moving through the air of America.. .She will finger in pleased wonder the collar of her coat, which is better even than a cloak of disappearing. And when the bus comes, she will surge at it with the others, her blending so successful that you standing across the street will no longer know who is who" (Divakaruni, p. 139-40)

Tilo's shift in consciousnesses is further suggested by the change in pronouns- moving from a narrative "I" to a third-person "she" when describing herself through the lens of an American. It is as if Tilo is a different person, yet she is cognizant of the fact that this new woman is still "herself." Tilo embraces the idea that she can blend in with America and be a part of it; as she waits at the bus stop, she relishes the fact that her difference is no longer the marker of her racial identity, for she can stand amongst a group of true Americans and exist as one herself, with no one being able to tell "who is who." This sense of betweeness is also inherent in Tilo's perception of her sexuality. Tilo observes some of her female patrons fulfilling the traditional submissive role of the South Asian housewife, with patriarchal dominance and instances of domestic abuse. Yet she also observes the young, sexualized and flirtatious patrons who come to her store, "all fizzy laughter and flutter lashes. In miniskirts their legs are long and tan, cocoabutter smooth. Their lips are dark and pouting. They toss back their crinkle-cut hair and glance around and laugh again.. .all sway and undulation" (Divakaruni, 270-271). These are the two extremes of sexuality of South Asian women that Tilo encounters, and she herself begins to fall into these contrasting (and stereotypical) roles in perceiving her own sexuality. Tilo's female patrons view her as a traditional older South Asian woman, unattractive in her age, sexless in terms of her desires and submissive to the will of others. Tilo begins to see herself as she believes others do: "a bent woman with skin the colour of old sand, behind a glass counter that hold.. .sweets of their childhoods. Out of their mothers' kitchens."(Divakaruni, 5)

Tilo describes herself as possessing an "old woman voice" and an "old woman body," covered in "creases and gnarls," and layers of wrinkles like "old snakeskin" *(Divakarunpi* 71, 114,.5,51)

"She is deferential to the elders who enter the store, referring to older men as "dada," a term of endearing respect(Divakaruni, 87). She is not seductive but rather matronly, repressing any sexual desire; she is silent in her opinions and offers advice only when asked. In her behavior in the store, Tilo typifies the traditional submissive Indian woman and she is perceived to be so by her various patrons. Yet Tilo's sense of passion and her ability to seduce are clearly evident in her relationship with Raven. Even in their initial encounters, Raven appeals to Tilo's sexual side, creating emotions in Tilo that she has never experienced before. During their first conversation, Tilo thinks to herself, "There is a Iurching inside me, like something stitched up tearing lose. O danger."(Divakaruni, 71)

Divakaruni uses to describe Tilo's sensations is replete with a sexual suggestiveness that grows more overt as the relationship between Raven and Tilo progresses. When they finally consummate their love, Tilo appears as a highly knowledgeable and sensual lover, and her sexuality is in stark contrast to the older asexual woman from the spice store. Strangely, there is a sense that this sexual knowledge was already there for Tilo, existing (though hidden) while she perceived herself as the asexual woman from the spice store. Divakaruni is subtly suggesting the possibility of simultaneous selves, as if Tilo had another younger and more sexualized identity that existed (albeit unexpressed) along with the asexual identity of the older woman.

The complexities of race in South Asian identity remerge in the formations of sexual identities, and racism and prejudice take the form of Orientalist fantasies and all that they imply. Tilo's American lover Raven sees her as a paradigmatic representation of Eastern beauty, an "authentic...Real Indian," and since Tilo is estranged from her own self-perceptions, she eventually comes to view herself as Raven's Orientalist fantasy, hyper-sexualized and representative of all that is seen as Indian in American culture. Suddenly, cultural categories such as Indian" (Divakaruni, 272-3)' and American, which may at first appear concrete, are subject to the biases and stereotypes of perception and self-perception, thereby changing the very meaning of what it means to even call oneself by those markers of nationality.

At first, Tilo is suspicious of her new sexualized perspective on herself (or rather, Raven's perspective on her which she adopts) and she muses, "My American Raven, how you have romanticized my land and my people. And most of all me.. ..." (Divakaruni, 226)

But soon she cannot help but view herself from this exoticized standpoint, as Raven7 s "mysterious Indian beauty." When Tilo perceives herself as Raven's idealized Indian fantasy, she becomes subject to a specific form of racism that gained much attention during the 201h century. "Orientalism," Edward Said says,

... is a style of thought based upon an ontological and epistemological distinction made between 'the Orient' and (most of the time) 'the Occident'. . .Orientalism can be discussed and analyzed as the corporate institution for dealing with the Orient- dealing with it by making statements about it, authorizing views of it, describing it.. . Orientalism is premised upon exteriority, that is, on the fact that the Orientalist.. .makes the Orient speak, describes the Orient, renders its mysteries plain for and to the West.." (Edward W. Said, p. 21-22)

In his relationship with Tilo, Raven falls prey to describing and categorizing her based upon his knowledge of her race but without a true understanding of her actual identity. Raven thus becomes the quintessential orientalist described by cultural scholar and writer Anwar Abdel Malek: "According to the traditional orientalist, an essence should exist-sometimes even clearly described in metaphysical terms- which constitutes the inalienable and common basis of all the beings considered.. . ..." (Anwar Abdel Malek, 107-8)

Evidence of Raven's tendency toward an Orientalist perspective is evident in the conversation that ensues when a group of beautiful young Indian women, whom Tilo terms the "bougainvilla girls," enter the spice store one day. He smiles, squeezes my hand. "Hey. You can do things these girls couldn't in a hundred years." The pinpricks begin to fade. "You're authentic in a way they'll never be," he adds, Authentic. A curious word to use. "What do you mean, authentic?" I ask. "You know, real, Real Indian." I know he means it as a compliment. Still, it bothers me. Raven, despite their fizzy laughter, their lipstick and lace, the bougainvilla girls are in their way as Indian as I. And who is to say which of us is more real" (Divakaruni, *309)*

Tilo bonds with the old one and the other women who were in the island training to be mistresses. There on the island she feels safe and secure. Once she lands in America in her spice store she is able to empathize with her woman customers better than with her male customers. Although she helps all who come to her store irrespective of their sex, she can feel the pain of women like Lalita, Ahuja and Geeta as her own. Her understanding of the women is expressed through the typically feminine metaphor of spices. Although she does reach out to male characters like raven, Haroun, Geeta's grandfather and Jagjit, she cannot relate to them in the same way. When Tilo talks about the lessons she learnt on the island she says:

"Most of all we learned to feel without word the sorrow of our sister, and without words to console them. In this way our lives were not Different from those of the girls we left behind in our home villages" (Divakaruni, 52)

They learn this lesson of bonding with other women by doing ordinary everyday chores like sweeping and stitching. When she says that their life on the island of spices was no different from that of the village girls, the implication is that women for generations have learnt to bond with one another while learning household chores. Female bonding, therefore, has always been indirect and Tilo learns it the same indirect way as women all over the world.

D.B.Gavani commented: : "Tilo or Tilotama, *The Mistress of Spices* is really a young woman who is required by the dictates of the order to disguise herself as an old woman, thus accentuating her a sexuality and inducing anonymity and restraint. She cannot be aware of her own body" (Gavani, 80)

Raven believes that Tilo possesses an intangible essence that makes her an authentic Indian as compared to the other young Indian women in the store. Tilo questions Raven's conferring of authenticity, for even using the term authentic suggests that there is a certain fundamental nature that is a prerequisite for true Indian identity, an essence that Raven gives himself the ability and power to judge as legitimate. In thinking about Raven, Tilo says, "You have loved me for the colour of my skin, the accent of my speaking, and the quaintness of my customs which promised you the magic you no longer found in the women of your own land. In your yearning you have made me into that which I am not."(Divakaruni, 309)

Just as her lower-class patrons suffered the taunts and jeers of racist slurs, Tilo suffers the feelings of objectification and exoticization that come from Raven's Orientalism. Yet Tilo herself falls prey to a sort of reverse Orientalism- she begins to view Raven as a representative of American culture. From the moment she meets him, she refers to him not by name, but rather as 'my American' and 'the American'. While Raven views her as his Eastern exotic fantasy, Tilo comes to see him as her token American lover. When Tilo realizes this, she thinks that the relationship must end because it was a love that "would never have lasted, for it was based upon fantasy of what it is to be Indian. To be American "(Divakaruni, P. *311)*

As Tilo moves through the maze of American culture, she desires even more to see herself, to view her life through her own eyes rather than the perspectives of others. Tilo's moment of "self-perception" occurs after she questions the prohibition of mirrors for Mistresses. "Here is a question I never thought to ask on the island: First Mother, why is it not allowed, what can be wrong with seeing yourself?"(Divakarun,. *151).* Before she looks at her reflection, Tilo decides to drink a special potion, a concoction whose power stems from the spice Makaradwaj, and is considered the "conqueror of time."(Divakaruni, *277)*

This potion will transform Tilo's body from that of the "old woman disguise" she has been wearing since she arrived in America, to a body of youthful beauty. Over the course of three days, Tilo's beauty increases as the layers of age peel away. "Now I am ready. I go to the back where [the mirror] hangs on the wall, remove the covering from it, I Tilo who have broken too many rules to count. How many lifetimes since I have looked into one. Mirror what will you reveal of myself" (Divakaruni, *297).* Tilo gazes into the mirror, but does not see some great truth about identity revealed to her. Instead, she sees " ... a face that gives away nothing, a goddess-face free of mortal blemish.. .Only the eyes are human, frail."(Divakaruni, p. *297)*

Tilo's physical transformation represents the illusion of the notion of a singular "true identity," for in the process of trying to reveal a real self, Tilo finds that she has lost all that was human about her. In her desire to see a unified identity free of the "mortal blemish" of contradiction, Tilo is faced with a reflection that is blank, the only hint of life residing in the eyes that stare back at her. The frailty and humanity of Tilo's eyes mirror her reading of this moment, for when Tilo looks for unity, all she sees is the reality of the human condition reflected in her eyes. The contradictions that Tilo believes make her frail are, paradoxically, the very foundations of her identity. Thus, Tilo realizes that in place of a unified identity she possesses an identity of multiplicity and ambiguity; she is comprised of many different and contradictory perceptions of the self, or else she is a blank. At this pivotal point in the text, Tilo realizes that self-perception is a matter of acknowledging the multiple processes and factors that influence the formation of identity, of embracing each of the contradictory characteristics and consciousnesses as legitimate identities. She describes this process of understanding in rather surreal terms: "I move as through deep water, I who have waited all my life- though I see it only now- for this brief moment blossoming like fireworks in a midnight sky. My whole body trembles, the desire and fear.. .." (Divakaruni, ***298)***

But Tilo's happiness is soon diminished, for she has a dream in which the First Mother tells her that she only has three more days in America, and on the third day she will have to enter once again into Shampati's Fire and return to the island. Yet when the moment arrives for the fire to consume her, Tilo is surprised to find that the flames do not envelop her as they did once long ago. Rather, she is transformed back into the body of the old woman, wrinkled with age and bereft of her youthful beauty. The transformation back into the body of the old woman further reinforces the notion that identity is not a question of cohesion, for when Tilo returns to the body with which she experienced the different perceptions of race and sexuality, she is in essence accepting her fragmented selves in place of a unified identity. The novel closes with Tilo renaming herself Maya, which "can mean many things. The Illusion, spell, enchantment, the power that keeps this imperfect world going day after day."(Divakaruni ***338)***

Dr. D. B Gavani asserts as : "The novel validates women's empowerment through articulation of their desire. As with her protagonists in the short stories, Divakaruni argues for recognition of women's full control of their bodies. Once Tilo is in touch with her own sexuality, she can no longer assuage others pains or even see in to the future, but she can live the live of the young woman. The Mistress has to extinguish herself in order that the woman find her voice, fellow her desire and search for an identity outside of that of a ministering angel. She must live her domain, the beautiful, organized spices store, in order to fulfil desire" (Gavani ,81)

Tilo chooses a name that can mean many things, a name that embodies the multiplicity of her identities, the many consciousnesses that lie within her. Interestingly, 'Maya' is also an ancient Sanskrit name, and the juxtaposition of a name so representative of a cultural past with Tilo's present power suggests that Tilo still lives in between spheres, with contradictory spaces and times comprising the rather ambiguous landscape of her existence. In naming herself, Tilo reveals that which she is made of: multiple consciousnesses that allow her to exist as not as South Asian or American only, but rather as everything in between, living a life that spans the endless boundaries of space and time and in which identity is filled with the promise of endless possibility and eternal evolution.

Worked Cited

- Chitra Banerjee Divakaruni, *The Mistress* of *Spices* (New York: Anchor Books, 1998)
- Frantz Fanon, *Black* Skin White *Masks* (New York: Grove Press, Inc.), 1967
- Vijay Prashad, "Crafting Solidarities," *A Part, Yet Apart: South Asians in Asian America* (Philadelphia: Temple University Press, 1998),
- Edward W. Said, *Orientalism* (New York: Random House, Inc., 1978),
- Dr D. B Gavani, Immigrant Indian Writers, Ravi Prakashan, Gadag, 2011
- Anwar Abdel Malek, "Orientalism in Crisis," *Diogenes* 44 (Winter 1963)

15

Diaspora Study of Bharati Mukherjee's Jasmine

Dixit Pushpa D.

Faculty in English

Swami Sahajanand College of Commerce & Management,

M.K.Bhavnagar University, Bhavnagar, Gujarat.

"On the margin of European culture, and alienated from his own, the 'coloured' [...person] is an artifact of colonial history, marginal man par excellence. He is a creature of two worlds, and of none. Thrown by a specific history, he remains stranded on its shores even as it recedes; and what he comes into is not so much a twilight world, as a world of false shadows and false light." (A. Sivanandan, *Alien Gods* 104-18)

Introduction

Diaspora literature has made a significant contribution to Indian Writing in English by its rich exposure to multiculturalism. The spirit of exile and alienation enriches the diasporic writers to seek rehabilitation in their writings and establish a permanent place in the mind of readers. Diasporic literature addresses issues such as identity, culture, hybridity, nationality, home, homelessness and binary categories like self/other, insider/outsider and margin/center.

The eminent writers of Indian Diaspora are Bharati Mukherjee, Rohinton Mistry, Salman Rushdie, V.S. Naipaul, Jumpa Lahiri, Uma Parameswaran and Vikram Seth. They have been discussing several issues concerning their homelands and the land in which they live in their works.

Migrations have both erased and re-inscribed patterns of being and belonging, producing a self with multiple and partial identification which is simultaneously both individualized and community oriented. Thus the diasporic writer occupies a space of exile and cultural solitude which can be called a hybrid location of antagonism, perpetual tension and pregnant chaos. Here the reality of the body, a material production of one local culture, and the abstraction of the mind, a cultural sub-text of a global experience, provide the intertwining threads of the diasporic existence of a writer.

In fact writing allows individuals to regain control over the self, the world and their own life story narrative. It provides a unique safe space in which new identities can be created and linguistic transitions accomplished. Therefore the writer begins by mapping the contours of their own transited identity that are in constant negotiation and transformation because of the interaction between the past and the present.

This metastasis is also seen in the novels of Bharati Mukherjee, who is one of the most celebrated writers of the Asian immigrant experience in America. Her writings are largely honed by the multiple dislocations of her personal biography, which itself has been described as a text in a kind of perennial immigration. Lying at the heart of Mukherjee's cultural poetics is her espousal of the immigrant aesthetics, integral to which is a rejection of fixed conceptions of national cultural identity.

In my view point, Mukherjee describes her narratives as "stories of broken identities and discarded languages" that nevertheless, represent her characters as fired by the "will to bond to a new community" (introduction *Darkness*). Discarding nostalgia, they are willing to be changed and open to the act of transformation, adopting new possibilities as offered by the narrative of assimilation. Thus we see her protagonist Jasmine, boldly asserting: "I changed because I wanted to. To bunker oneself inside nostalgia, to sheathe the heart in a bullet-proof vest, was to be a coward" (Jasmine, 185).

Bharati Mukherjee is one of the Indian diasporic writers whose most memorable works reflect her pride in her Indian heritage, but also her celebration of embracing America. As she said in an interview in the Massachusetts Review, "the immigrants in my stories go through extreme transformations in America and at the same time they alter the country's appearance and psychological make-up." (Carb, 645) In her own voice she tells the stories of her own experiences to show the changing shape of American society. She describes herself as unhyphenated American and not the hyphenated Indian-American title:

"I maintain that I am an American writer of Indian origin,not because I'm ashamed of my past, not because I'm betraying or distorting my past, but because my whole adult life has been lived here, and I write about the people who are immigrants going through the process of making a home here...." (Carb, 654)

Bharati Mukherjee considers herself a writer of the Indian Diaspora who cherishes the "melting pot" of America. Her main theme throughout her writing discusses the condition of Asian immigrants in North America, with particular awareness towards the changes taking place in South Asian women in a new world. Her protagonists are well-aware of the viciousness and hostility that environ them and are often made victims by various forms of social restraint; she characterizes them as survivors. The phenomenon of migration, the condition of new immigrants, and the sensitivity of estrangement and alienation often experienced by expatriates and the struggle of Indian women as immigrants are the major themes of her novels. According to Fakrul Alam:

"her own struggle with identity first as an exile from India, then an Indian expatriate in Canada, and finally as an immigrant in the United States has lead to her current contentment of being an immigrant in a country of immigrants." (Alam, 10).

Jasmine (1989) is a story that is the mixing of the East and West through the story telling of a seventeen-year-old Hindu woman who leaves India for the U.S. after her husband's murder. Her husband dies due to a religious attack in India. In her path she faces many problems including rape and eventually returned to the position of a health professional through a series of jobs. Here in this context the unity between the First and Third World is shown to be in the treatment of women as subordinate in both countries. The story expanded as a story of a young widow suddenly widowed at seventeen. She uproots herself from her life in India and re-roots herself in search of a new life and the image of America as well. It is a story of dislocation and relocation as the protagonist continually sheds lives to move into other roles, moving further westward. The author in some parts of this novel shows some agony to the third world as she shows that Jasmine needs to travel to America to make something significant in her life. And in the third world she faced only despair and loss.

Jasmine builds up the proposal of the amalgamation, combination and absorption of the East in the West with a story telling of a young Hindu woman who leaves India for the U.S. following her husband's assassination, merely to be raped and in the long run return to the understanding of a caregiver through a succession of jobs. Jasmine voluntarily undergoes transformation of the self from Jyoti to Jane to Jase to Jasmine. At every conversion of the personality she stands unyielding in resistance to her providence and destiny. It is not the uncertainties of the new continent that challenge her but the uncertainties of her life in an unknown terra ferma. Her journey to the New World is a sort of regeneration through violence and her ultimate realization in America "that it won't disintegrate' (Jasmine, 181).

The theme of *Jasmine* is an Indian Immigrant's encounter with the new world and her gradual transformation as she thoroughly imbibes the new culture. At every stage of her life Jasmine revolts against her fate and the path drawn for her. There is a shift of past and present and vice versa as the novel progresses. The present is her life as Jane in Iowa, where she is a live-in- companion to Bud Ripple Meyer, a small town banker. The past is Jyoti's childhood in the small village of Hasnapur, Punjab, her marriage to Prakash, the young ambitious city man, who always thrashed traditions. The American experience shocks Jane and she is disgusted many a time, she thinks:

This country has so many ways of humiliating, of disappointing .... There are no harmless, compassionate ways to remake one self. We murder who we were so we can rebirth ourselves in the images of dreams (Jasmine, 29).

Her journey through life leads Jasmine through many transformations. While she was in Manhattan for two years, she learns the ways of American family life, husband helping in the kitchen, wife working for longer hours outside and that the young couple could adopt a child and not wait for the natural child. She loves and admires the American world so well. She also understands that clinging on to one's own culture tenaciously while living in an immigrant locale does not help an immigrant in anyway. Though she becomes more Americanized, more confident of her proficiency in English, her instinctive Indian values do surface now and then. For instance, when she comes to know that Duff is not a natural child but an adopted one, her reactions are culturally revealing. "I could not imagine a non – genetic child .... Adoption was foreign to me as the idea of widow remarriage (Jasmine, 170).

The interaction between two cultures leads to a gradual transformation in the protagonist:

She walks American; she dresses American. She says; in this apartment of artificially maintained Indianness, I wanted to distance myself from everything Indian, everything Jyoti – like (Jasmine, 145).

Jasmine's every movement is a calculated step into her Americanization and with each development a vital change is marked in her personality. Jasmine's flight to Iowa and her renaming as Jane is indicative of a slow but steady immersion into the mainstream American culture. The Assimilation of Jasmine is not as smooth as it might appear on the surface.

Displacement from home: Jasmine experiences displacement within her very home. In Hasnapur, she suffers with the local configurations of gender relations which oppress her and turn her into an obedient and submissive woman. Even though she is offered the opportunity to build a better home with Prakash, her sudden widowhood takes her back to the old and oppressive home. That is why she escapes and moves to the United States. Even though her first impulse is still to play the widow role she learns about in India, the possibilities that living in that new location offers make Jasmine long to make her at home there. But the protagonist does not immediately belong to that place and still looks for one in which she does not feel an alien. She has a homing desire, but never a desire to return to her homeland. In spite of all suffering that she goes through in her new home, she has the opportunity to go beyond the role of an Indian widow she is destined to fulfill and acts differently from the way she is taught to be and behave. Jasmine is able to shape her subjectivity and to make the life choices that will offer her a sense of possibility. Agency for her is the ability to choose. Moving away from home gives her the possibility of subverting the gender relations that limited her life back home.

Although the diasporic women characters in *Jasmine* represent different relationships to home. Jasmine somehow is displaced within home as the gender roles and relations practiced in the public and private spheres of her homes in India oppress her and restrict her life options. In spite of the suffering and feelings of alienation associated with leaving home and placing oneself in a foreign land, the outcomes of such experience still seem to be positive ones. Moving away from home and putting down roots elsewhere provide them with the opportunity to transform their once believed stable identities and as a consequence open space for new subjectivities and for agency. Thus, Jasmine has reinvented herself and has forged a new identity in the country of adoption. This kind of tendency in Jasmine is the one that contributes wholly to the optimistic end of the novel. An immigrant is one who is reborn in the adopted culture. Jasmine's acculturation and assimilation into American culture is certainly better than bunkering in nostalgia on remaining torn between two worlds, two cultures, two ways of life and two faiths for a life time.

Even though I claim that all women characters are diasporic women who established gender relations, their experiences of migration are diverse and that they are not transgressive in the same way. Based on postcolonial, diaspora and feminist literary studies, I argue that gender, class, caste, education and social conditions in general are factors that differentiate each character's diasporic movement and influence their disruptive attitudes. While class, caste, education and social conditions place the women characters in privileged and unprivileged positions both in India and in the United States, gender, combined with those other factors, seems mostly to render them inferior, constricted and submissive. It is mainly the indoctrination of the characters to their gender roles in a patriarchal society, within their specific class and caste that triggers their impetus to subvert such roles and modify their subjectivities. Such disruptive attitudes can be referred to as the characters' assertion of agency, that is, the ability to act or perform action, which is made possible precisely by their physical and psychological displacements from home. Not surprisingly, the woman character who is capable of enacting the most radical destabilizations of gender relations is Jasmine.

The characters in Mukherjee's novel develop multiple consciousnesses, resulting in a self that is neither unified nor hybrid but rather fragmented. As the protagonists perceive both their race and sexuality through new and different lenses throughout the course of the text, they come to realize that the notion of a singular identity is a fallacy and the reality of the diasporic experience is the indeterminacy of multiplicity. This multiplicity at time becomes a significant plight for her characters and they are left uncertain as to the nature of their identities, not knowing where they fit in the American society. Finally they become capable of living in a world where individuals exist not as a unified One, but as many bounds by no borders and infinite in the possibility of inventing identities.

In Mukherjee's *Jasmine* the women characters are displaced from India and put down roots in the United States. My point, which I have demonstrated, is that, as a consequence of their diasporic movement, the women characters question the gender roles that they were taught to play in their homeland and suffer transformations in their subjectivities. Even though contemporary times are changing, and liberal ideas have been influencing the way women are treated and given opportunities in societies that are still patriarchal, it is mainly because of their displacement from home that Jasmine, the protagonist is given the chance to modify her gender relations so as to adapt to her new realities in the United States.

Conclusion: As I demonstrated, Jasmine is not interested in simply replacing the way gender roles are played in her home country. She does not simply assimilate the liberal behavior and feminist ideas that she encounters there. Instead, she questions both social constructions of gender relations and look for alternatives that apply to her realities. It can be said that all women characters are exposed to liberal and feminist attitudes in the United States, I state that they react to that cultural influence in the same way. Jasmine seems to be more open to adapt to American culture. She, however, presents disruptive behaviors as she plays the roles of sister, daughter, mother, wife, lover and widow in her new homes, which are quite different from the way she was taught to conduct herself in India. As I argue, the characters are in-between cultures, that is, they are cultural hybrids, and do not simply assimilate their host land culture. Instead, they keep a critical view of both the United States and India.

As a writer, Bharati Mukherjee is concerned about depicting her picture of Indian life intelligible and interesting to the American readers through her novels. But she is too good an artist to distort reality just to capture attention. She avoids stereotyped versions and sentimental exaggerations and tries to pack into her novels a rich resonance of meaning by the deft device of combining immigrant, feminist and existentialistic perspectives. She focuses her attention on the growing awareness of the dark spots in the lives of her characters, and their courageous efforts to discover areas of light. This search for light, for happiness and fulfillment is subtly linked in her fiction to her protagonists' struggle for self actualization.

References

- Alam, Fakrul. Bharati Mukherjee. New York: Twayne, 1996, pp. 10.
- Carb, Alison B. "An Interview with Bharati Mukherjee. "The Massachusetts Review 29.4 (1988): p.645, 654.
- Mukherjee, Bharati. *Jasmine*. New York: Fawcett Crest, 1989, pp.29,

  —, pp. 145.

  —, pp. 170.
- Mukherjee, Bharati. *Jasmine*. http://en.wikipedia.org/wiki/Jasmine_(novel) 8th April, 2013.
- Sivanandan, A. 'Alien Gods' (Ed.) Bhikhu Parekh. Colour, Culture and Counsiousness: Immigrant Intellectuals in Britain. London: George Allen and Unwin, 1974.

16

The Diasporic Elements in Bharati Mukherjee's Novels, The Tiger's Daughter, Wife, and Jasmine

Gogineni Naga Jyothi
Lecturer in English
Govt. Degree College
Morthad, A.P.

The term Diaspora is not a new word. It is as old as the genesis of human race. It originates from Greek language to denote the displacement of Jews. The term Diaspora originally used for dispersal from ones' own homeland but now it is used to expatriates, refugees and immigrants. Indian Diaspora is increasingly perceived as intrinsic part of humanities drifting towards globalization, transitional, economical and cultural flow and hybrid form of socio -cultural identity. Indian Diaspora constitutes a major study of the literature and other cultural texts related to it. The writers of Diaspora are the global paradigm shift; the challenges of postmodernism to overreaching narratives of power have gained ascendance and even found a current status of privilege. These shifts suggest domination, Diaspora, displacement with most enduring lessons for living and thinking.

Though the means of communication and transportation have, to some extent softened towards their idealized homeland. The cultural amnesia and uprootment from the native soil make them the feeling of alienation from the homeland, feeling of insecuriarity in the adopted land and drag the men to no man's Island. The characteristics of Diaspora writings are; the problem of identity, loneliness, alienation, multiculturalism and gender violence and discrimination.

Bharati Mukherjee is an Indian born novelist who is now as an American citizen. She occupies a unique position among the foremost chronicle of the multicultural new America. She has been widely acknowledged as a voice of expatriate immigrant sensibility. She was born in Calcutta .She completed M.A in English from the University of Baroda. Then she moved to United States of America. She was awarded a scholarship from the university of Iowa earned her M.F.A in creative writing and her Ph. D in English and comparative Literature. She married a Canadian student from Harvard, Clark Blaise who is also a writer. They have subsequently produced two books in collaboration. She took Canadian citizenship but the feeling of alienation haunts her always. As she says," In Canada I feel isolated, separated in the vastness of this under populated country. I have not yet learned the words of national anthem… In Canada I am bit too visible and too invisible. I am brown. I cannot disappear in a rush hour, montrial crowd" [Blaise and Mukherjee; 1997; 169]. This feeling is reflected in her novel *Tiger's daughter [1972], wife [1975] and Jasmine [1989].*

Bharati Muskherjee's creative career can be divided into three phases. The first phase contains two novels *The Tiger's Daughter* in 1972 and *Wife in* 1975 which were written during her stay in Canada. The second phase consists of two short story collections *Darkness in 1985* and *The Middle man and the other stories* in 1988.This was the transitional stage of her career when she moved to U.S. The third phase is the fictional output which contains the three novels *Jasmine* in 1989, The Holder of the World in 1993 and Leave It to Me in 1997 that were brought out during this period.

In my paper I would like to focus on the diasporic characteristics in Bharati *Muskherjee's The Tiger's Daughter, Wife and Jasmine. The Tiger's daughter* is a story about a young girl named Tara; the protagonist embraces the American way of life in an act of total rejection of Indian pseudo values and hypocrasies. Tara is rich industrialist's pampered daughter who returns to Calcutta "in search of Indian dream"[1.] After seven years in U.S .She is unable to fit into the culture of Calcutta where she grew up, she finds that she is as much of an alien at home as she was abroad. Ironically, Tara accuses her friends of lacking depth which is clearly absent in her too. Tara thinks of her friends as being,

Sharing's of her personality. She fed their tone, their
Omissions, their aristocratic oneness. They had asked
Her about the things that she had brought back and had
Admired her valours jumpsuit and electric-shaver, but
Not once had they asked about her husband.[2]

American experience has isolated her from Indian life and culture. Tara wonders; ''How does the foreignness of the spirit begin?''[3]for even the familiar David now appears unfamiliar to her. All through her childhood, Tara has been unknown to the reality of Calcutta life. When she is travelling by train to Calcutta she finds a Marwari and Nepali detestable creatures. . Even when she is surrounded by friends and relatives, she is totally isolated and completely alone. By not being able to fit back into Calcutta society, Tara realizes that she is totally misfit at both places .In Calcutta, people call her" our lone America walli "[4].Since the life journey of Tara parallels that of Bharati Mukherjee, it can be called a semi - autobiographical novel. Tara can neither embrace her old Indian self nor did her newly discover American self .David fails to understand many aspects of her life. Being married a foreigner Tara does not change immediately. In failing to understand her, David shows the distance that has still to be covered between two cultures. By reading books on India, he cannot comprehend her country .In *The Tiger's Daughter B*harati Mukherjee describes Indian traditional marriage in very unflattering ,unromantic terms like bargaining ,rape on flower decked bed, etc.

Tara's journey to India which is her native land ironically proves frustrating which led her to realm of illusion, depression and finally meets her tragic end. She became a victim of her tragic end in her native soil-her home which she had longed to see since migration to New York and where she comes to seek solace. Her desire to find a place to love and security which she missed in New York ends ironically in frustration. From being a dutiful daughter to Bengal tiger, she wants to become a dutiful wife in the traditional mould. She wants to be appreciated by David and is most wary of his comments or criticism. Her experience with Tuntunwala embitters her to a great extent and makes her decide to return to David, like a child running back into the arms of an adult. Her father in childhood and husband in later life are essential protectors. Her homesickness, which is one of the diasporic elements, is glaringly visible in the novel. Tara's identity crisis is evidenced in the novel which is diasporic character.

The other novel of Bharati Mukherjee also reflects diasporic characters. The *Wife is* the story of Dimple Das Gupta whose was an arranged marriage. Her husband is Amity Basu an engineer. Her intention is to marry a neuro-surgeon but she obeyed her father's decision and married Amit. They move to U.S and experience culture shock and loneliness .As the frustration becomes expressed as abuse, the tale turns tragedy. She wished that her husband who is infallible, and God like. The gap between her anticipation and reality becomes very vast. She is aching with disorder complex and contemplates that she is unable to win her husband's love and affection.

Dimple shows dilemma of cultures which is domino effect of her phobic condition. Two incidents from the novel, one her enforced self abortion and other, her atrocious assassination of her husband are emblematic expressions. Amity could only visualize the external changes in Dimple and explains it as a case of 'cultural shock'. He even promises her to take her to Calcutta. This does not console her. Dimple starts contemplating the murder of her husband. The outside violence turns inside. She now fails to differentiate between what she views on television and what she contemplates. The idea of murdering her husband fascinates her. She thinks she could kill Amit and hide his body in the refrigerator, similar to American T.V serials. The major theme of this novel are cultural dilemmas, alienation, and unfriendliness with her neighbors, marriage, fantasy and psychological fatigue. The story is an upsetting account of conflict between the Western and Indian cultures.

In leisure hours she tries to dream about her husband, Amit but failed to do so. When she was at Queens she used to share her private feelings with Mena Sen. But at Greenwich she is isolated. Her depression manifests in different ways. Generally every wife after marriage, shares her inmost heart with her husband. But she cannot do that she used to bear everything in mind and try to adjust there in America. When loneliness becomes unbearable she contemplates as many as seven ways of committing suicide. Amity may also be blamed for his ignorance of female psychology .He thinks that providing comforts is enough and hardly bothers for her emotional needs. He takes her out of four walls very rarely. He goes on saying that ''You must go out, make friends, do something constructive, not stay at home and think about Calcutta''.[5] The obligation of husband is ignored by him towards her genuine feelings which leads her to isolation. To be fair to Dimple, it can be said that she is unable to communicate with the neighbors due to language problem. That's must go out, make friends, do something constructive, not stay at home and think about Calcutta''.[5] The obligation of husband is ignored by him towards her genuine feelings which leads her to isolation. To be fair to Dimple, it can be said that she is unable to communicate with the neighbors due to language problem. That's why she is gripped by a sense of nostalgia: 'How could she live in a country where every other woman was a stranger, where she felt different, ignorant exposed to ridicule in the elevator? ''.[6]Her whole world is limited to four walls of the apartment and media. Media is only her friend. Dimple's crazy ideas formed through the television and American magazines. ''Everything she saw on T.V was about love, even murder and death with love gone awry. But all she read in the news papers was about death, the scary, ugly kind of death random and poorly timid. Dimple much preferred to watch T.V than read .And she gave up trying to make friends with children ''.[7]Dimple feels confused as the T.V programmers prevent her from realizing the sense of reality. She also finds much difficulty in distinguishing her husband from the men on T.V. Dimple set on a long journey of unreal meaningless and morbid existence. Dimple is preparing to leave for America. Dimple induces miscarriage by skipping rope. Dimple believes that pregnancy is inconvenience .In anticipation of new experiences in the United States; she cannot adjust to the foreign and violent environment of New York City. She feels as if she converses with a character of television, Jyoti about the murder. She falls an easy prey to the glamorous way in such violence is depicted. It culminates in her imaginary killing of her husband over his breakfast table. The title of the novel is significant. Temperamentally she is ill suited to play the role of wife. Her wavering to identity between the two cultures reflects in the novel which is an ingredient of diasporic literature.

Jasmine is the story of Punjabi peasant girl. In this novel the protagonist Jasmine reinvents herself in the western world. The novel is narrated in flashback from Jasmine's comfortable life that is twenty four years old. The village astrologer under a banyan tree foretells Jasmine's widowhood and exile life. Astrologer's prediction becomes true in the life of Jasmine. From the beginning Jyoti rebels against her cultural inscriptions. She could not comprehend astrologer's predication .when she boldly challenged the astrologer's prophecy his anger soars. In order to escape the anger of the astrologer, she runs and fell .She received a star-like wound on her forehead. Her sister was worried because the wound may hinder the prospect of her marriage. But Jasmine is not worried and said it was her ''third eye.'' She proclaims herself a sage, rewriting her position from passive object to empowered seer. Jasmine leads the life of many transformations such as, Jyothi, Jasmine, Jase, and Jane. At every step she revolts against her fate. The narrative shuttles between the past and the present life. Jasmine is the name given by her husband Prakash. Identities of Jyoti and Jasmine are different, though they are one. Jasmine lost her husband in a bomb explosion in shop. Then she goes to U.S.A by arranging forged documents. Jasmine's first sight of America is painted .There was no one to receive her .The captain raped her. Jasmine attempted to kill herself but she decided that her mission was not fulfilled so she continues her existence .Later she met Taylor and Buds. She tries to establish a new cultural identity by incorporating new desires, skills, and habits. She married a Du and becomes an American.

The Tiger's Daughter Tara is as much of an alien at home as she was abroad when she returns to her homeland. *Wife* deals with the pre- and post- marital experiences of Dimple Das Gupta an ordinary middle class girl who fed on film magazines and T.V serials. Moving to New York only makes matters worse and her psychotic nature finds a final answer in the gruesome murder of her husband, after planning suicide in a dozen different ways. *Jasmine* is the story of an uneducated, simple but courageous Punjabi girl Jasmine, who travels from an inconspicuous village in Punjab to U.S to fulfill a farfetched dream. Her determination and resilience help her in the new land. The beauties as well as the brutality of America are encapsulated in the experiences of Jasmine who changes names and identities with equal ease. The first two are unable to come out of their alien status and become an integral part of their new milieu while Jasmine succeeds in experiencing life to the full with all the exuberance of immigration.

Bharati Mukherjee has personally experienced both negative hatred and positive welcome in the country of immigration. Her experiences in the two countries were widely different .Her three protagonists emigrate for three different reasons. Tara is sent abroad for a degree by her father. Though the desire to become a part of new milieu is strong, her attempts appear very superficial. She lacks the capacity to accept the merits of both or one and then accept the necessary changes. Dimple emigrates after a seemingly long wait, when she prays and hopes that America would welcome them early as she wants to start a new life. Though she imagines that moving to the U.S will bring about a sea change in her life she soon realizes that her bitterness and loneliness only increase in the U.S. The protagonist, Jasmine is very different from the other two protagonists and her reason for emigrating and her experiences too very different. Moving to the U.S. as an illegal immigrant with forged papers, with little or no knowledge of American life, only with the address of Prof. Adhere whom she had never met. Jasmine's entry into the U.S. is fraught with dangers and pitfalls. The re – moulding of self in America and search for identity, for immigrants in general, women in particular, is an odyssey which requires sacrifices on the part of those who aspire for it. This re-moulding of self is realized by facing number of physical and mental problems. This is revealed in the novels of Bharati Mukherjee.

Referenc

1. Shinde, Shoba."Cross-cultural crisis in Bharati Muskherjee's *'Jasmine' and 'The tiger's Daughter',* Commonwealth writing: A study in Expatriate Experienced ed.R.K.Dhavan and L.S.K.Krishna satyr (New Delhi: Prestige, 1994) p.55.
2. Mukherjee, Bharati.The *tiger's daughter.1971* (India: Penguine, 1990) p.45
3. Ibid., p.151.
4. Mukhrjee, Bharati.Wife *(New Delhi; Penguin books, 1990) p.3.*
5. *Ibid., p.112.*
6. Ibid., p.73.
7. Mukherjee, Bharati.Jasmine.New *York: Grover press, 1989.*

17

Redefining Diasporic Discourse: Cultural Assertions and Alienation Voiced from The Main Stream

Vishwas Joshi

Government Engineering College,
Patan

The recent years in the field of literary creation and criticism three major terms have emerged: postcolonialism, postmodernism and diasporic writings. It may be argued that these phenomena are different from one another. But it is an undeniable fact that these three theories hinge on aspect of culture. If we begin to focus on culture or cultural representation, we start confronting with a number of issues. On one hand, the cultural boundaries are dissipating and therefore it has become impossible to talk of cultures as self-contained and authentic wholes. On the other hand the Post-colonial discourse has put this liberal concept into a margin and postulated a new paradigm on cultural encounters. On the same line, diasporic writings also tend to make watertight compartments between the 'native culture' and the 'host culture'. It is interesting to note that most of the 'native cultures' which are being asserted by the diasporic writers had been colonized in the past. Therefore diasporic emersions cannot be void of 'counter discourse', an essential element of post-colonial writings. Central to the postcolonial writing is the longing to reclaim an identity and through narrative voice to counter centuries of denial and misrepresentation; central to much of diasporic writing is the longing to retrieve a 'home', however symbolically. Both are marked by psychological and ethical dimensions of the notion of nostalgia and reclamation of identity. Nostalgia here should not be misinterpreted as 'home sicknesses' or 'longing for the past'. The diasporic theory also addresses the questions of recall, homeland, ancient past, the urge to return and the impossibility of return. One of the key themes in postcolonial theory is the concern with 'place and displacement'. Here the dislocation is a probable result of migration and the consequent sense of loss is again related to diasporic writing.

Among the writers who write on Indian diasporic experiences, Gita Mehta occupies a unique place. She was born in India and now she stays in the USA and England. Generally a diasporic experience is of being positioned as an outsider to the main stream society. It is an experience of a person who never qualifies a s a norm; someone who is not authorized to speak but is always spoken of. But the two cardinal aspects of diasporic writings, alienation and up-rootedness are missing in Gita Mehta's works. She enjoys good status in those two countries and thereby she has qualified as a norm. Her financial and social status allows her to visit the motherland at her will. Therefore the longing to be with the motherland or the sense of being up-rooted is also not discernible in her works. On the contrary, she makes an attempt to justify the Indian cultural, social, religious and political aspects to the western audience. Because of migration, globalization and multi-nationalism culture has become a shared aspect. Gita Mehta finds this 'shared status' precarious to Indian culture (as she says in a publisher's party, " Karma isn't what is has cracked up to be.")

Gita Mehta has written two novels- Raj and A River Sutra- , one non-fiction- Karma Cola- and one collection of short essays- Snakes and Ladders. Her last book Ganesha explains a Hindu deity Ganesha. These works cannot be immediately put into the category of diasporic writings. But they are diasporic in more than one ways. These works are diasporic in innovative ways. They are not dominated by the traditional diasporic patterns of marginalization, identity politics and ethnicity. On the contrary, they have evolved different narration techniques. These techniques do convey the notion of 'otherness' with a faint flavor of irony. The ironic tone is directed towards the peculiarities of both, the motherland and the foreign land. Another technique is of self-appraisal. Her works have a tendency to revisit and re-vision the past but it does not come out of longing. Rather than creating an imaginative motherland to subdue up rootedness, there are conscious efforts to preserve the indigenous identity of home culture and to show the right image of India. In Karma Cola

Gita Mehta laughs at both, the western gullibility and contemporary Indian pseudo spirituality. In A River Sutra, the focus is on Indian mythology and cultural life which existed in past and up to certain extent does persist. In Raj, the interrogation is into the nature of Indian Kingship, Rajniti and social matrix. In Snakes and Ladders, Mehta returns to the homeland and highlights the multicolored picture of contradictions which prevails in her homeland. The author's relationship with the motherland operates in very subtle manner as she looks back in awe and wonder, amusement and skepticism.

There is a broad categorization under which new diasporic writings can be studied to understand the author's relationship with the motherland. These categories are: exotica, history, fantasy, collusion and use of third space. These categories explain that the diasporic writer's situation is always on the flux and one has to constantly reinvent himself and work out new strategies to relate to his acute experiences. When we look at Gita Mehta's works in the light of above mentioned categories, we find that each book fits into a specific category. In A River Sutra, the author looks at the homeland from a distance in time and space. It creates a world of myths and an exotic ambience. Thus it can be categorized as exotica and fantasy. In Raj she attempts to revisit the past and thus revision the history. Snakes and Ladders is again a work of collusion and history. It makes an honest attempt to look back at India as she was. What adds to this book is the author's bemused look as an outsider or at least a look from distance. Indian aspects are described in a manner that it becomes 'assault on the senses' and 'assault of the senses'. In Raj, the author has tried to form a self-definition by creating and recreating the colonial past. In Karma Cola, cultural conspiracy and complexity are at work. In all her works, Gita Mehta has ruled out the possibility of return to the homeland. But at latent level, at unconscious level of mind, there persists an urge of the unfulfilled desire. In her specific case, she is well set in the USA and England in social as well as economic terms. Therefore more than the urge to return to the homeland, it is her urge to uphold the homeland in the eyes of the host country.

If we assess Gita Mehta's works as a whole, there is always a forward movement. It vindicates the argument that the author is not caught between the two opposing worlds. It is not the existence of contradictions but of dynamic existence. For her, interrelationship of the host country and motherland produces a satisfactory self-image. In her interview, she herself has made it clear that the experience of living in three different continents is enriching:

"There is a tremendous richness of living on three continents. The magic of America is the can-doism, it gives me the belief that anything is possible. Each time I finish a book and I think I'll never write another. America makes me think, 'Yeah, I'll have another shot'. London's great virtue is that, as the capital of an empire, its libraries have staggering material on India. And because of the British reticence, it's easy to be alone and write there. My heart is in India- it's home- so when I'm there I don't write. I just let it all seep through in my prose." (Gita Mehta: Making India Accessible, p.53-54)

This expression of her ease, comfort, social status and economic stability immediately puts her works in different category. A general diasporic experience is in sharp contrast with her experience. For example, Bharti Mukherjee's character, Jasmine, remarks:

"The country has so many ways of humiliating, of disappointing. There are no harmless, compassionate ways to remake oneself. We murder who we were so we can rebirth ourselves in the image of dreams." (Jasmine, p. 21)

Thus Gita Mehta's acknowledged status in the 'foreign land' allows her to derive her material boldly from Indian culture, history, mythology and religiosity. Homi Bhabha's remark about a common state of diasporic mind makes it clear that Gita Mehta's personal experiences and her works represent the diaspora in a redefining manner:

However, I do want to make graphic what it means to survive, to produce, to labor and to create, within a world-system whose major economic impulses and cultural investments are pointed in a direction away from you, your country or your people. Such neglect can be deeply negating experience, oppressive and exclusionary....(The Location of Culture, p. xi)

Gita Mehta displays a tendency to glorify her motherland. In order to achieve this goal she also creates an imaginary motherland. Among all her works, A River Sutra is the best example of this tendency. The long descriptive passages and themes of certain stories have been questioned. For example, the story of the courtesan's daughter has glorified the life of a courtesan. There is a romanticized description of exotic romance in the Haveli life and justification of their importance in the name of store house of courtesy. They are described as versatile ladies who claim to be the most learned women of India. They were supposed to know about everything: sixty four arts from architecture to zoology, painting, flower arrangements, music language, philosophy, jewelry, literature, mathematic and so on.

There are passages after passages that celebrate the significance, learning and expertise of courtesans. The author is at pains to use the courtesan as a mouthpiece to convey to the readers the efficiency of their lives. It is an attempt to take out the stigma attached to the profession:

To give such a compliment is one of the things we taught these princes. But to teach a prince the subtle grading of color or the microtones of melody, to educate a young man's palate so he becomes an epicure, to introduce him to the alchemy of scents- this was the most demanding part of our education. You see, we were forbidden to voice our instructions. (A River Sutra, p. 202)

Even such description is not enough. Mehta weaves other impressive images of the courtesans to drive the nail into the minds of readers that they were not mere dancing girls. They were socially useful and highly respected. The courtesan's grandmother was an expert in dance and music.

We come across one more exotica in the form of the Executive's story. It is not a simple tale of aberration of love. It goes beyond love and shows how life had been for the colonial estate managers. Nitin Bose himself was aware of the 'Englishness' of the place. He describes it as the realm of the British fantasy untouched by the modern India. The temporal setting of Nitin Bose's life is postcolonial time but his life carries the colors of the colonial masters. When he reaches the tea estate, he assumes the role of a 'Pukka Sahib'. It is clearly suggestive of the colonial dominance. He vehemently gives orders to servants. It proves the point that colonialism does not end with the colonial rule. The two aspects of colonization, of being dominated and of domination in post-colonial time do persist for a long time. Reading in-between the lines informs us that Bose's article on tribal life and rituals carries an echo of colonial attitude. From another perspective, the elite class of independent India carries the look of superiority to the tribal. So the tribal are still in a state of colonization even in free democratic country. It suggests a very deep impact of colonized psychology. Once a race is colonized, the traces of colonial psychology are almost everlasting. As an unconventional diasporic writer Gita Mehta boldly put forth the aftermath of colonization.

The musician's daughter with ugly appearance creates an enchanting world of music with musical notes and her veena. There is pages long description of musical note found in the nature. The correlation between the musical notes of the instruments and the natural revelations of the same code is exotic. Birds, animals and trees teach the rudiments of music to his daughter. It is suggested that music, when learnt in this passion and dedication, leads one to salvation. But statements like the following can reinforce the western romanticism of the East, "The Vedas say that by playing veena, with the correct rhythm, keeping its notes and characters intact, a man can hear the sound and attain salvation." (A River Sutra, p. 207).

In A River Sutra in particular, Gita Mehta's efforts are to impart subtle delicacy of Indian culture through various stories. She does not lack knowledge of music and her authenticity is beyond doubt. But there are experts who opine that while writing for the western audience she has missed the essential flavor. She is criticized for not having the scent and sound of the land. Usha Bande writes:

It is generated because of her diasporic situation in which she tends to look at the land and look at it from distance in time and space. It could be because she reflects on the issue of identity when confronted with otherness, and the process of reflection-evocation, using the prop of memory, helps in visualizing beauty and richness in retrospect. (Gita Mehta: Writing Home/ Creating Homeland, p. 37)).

Her works are set in India. They speak for India, her culture, mythology, rich traditions and religiosity. Even in single work, the tone varies. Sometimes it is ironical; sometimes it is serious; more often it is the tone of demystifying of cultural concepts that the West generally associates with India.

Snakes and Ladders is another significant work from the point of view of diasporic writing. Though in the very preface, Gita Mehta clarifies that the essays are written to explain India to herself, we can say that they are for the western audience as well. The first three parts are written with no sparing sarcasm and criticism of the post independent India. The book seems to be her statement that India people lack in proper governance. As a piece of diasporic writer, it may also be a kind of justification of the western approach to India as a corrupt country. However, the later part of the book reveals another tendency of diaspora; to glorify the mother land. She praises the vividness of Indian life and praises the contradictions. In the last essay, "The Leisure Time", she evokes a 'romantic' atmosphere with the help of myriad of indigenous sounds and smells which are indispensible elements of common Indian life. Even here, the description lacks the original touch. It seems that what she describes is at the level of 'seeing' and not 'feeling'. In other words, India is seen through binoculars. In this way only colors can be captured, not the essence. The following are few lines from this essay:

The scent of parched earth in the monsoon rains

When peacocks fan their tails to dance.

The green sweep of parakeets crossing the sunset.

The popping of water lilies, the snarling of pi-dogs,

The koyal bird crying for rain

Glass Bengals sold by lantern light, fragile color fracturing the dark

(Snakes and Ladders, p. 286-287)

In her works, Gita Mehta shows India's attractions and projects an Indian world-vie. Her approach is neither of self-denigration nor of mere self-appraisal. In this context the basic diasporic elements like rootlessness, marginalization, alienation and longing for home are not clearly traceable. As mentioned earlier, there is a constant movement in her work. Snakes and Ladders has an autobiographical element in the initial essays. But what is a bit strange is the impersonal tone in autobiographic description. She does not mention her home. Her parents are not named. Her uncle who was sent to Kalapani is not named either. Thus there are no psychological implications of diasporic writing. After the first chapter, the essays are on people, leaders, politics, places and so on.

The psychological aspect of colonization is brilliantly portrayed in Raj. How the dominance of the colonizing culture deeply affects the native psychology and the notions of superiority and inferiority become an integral part of collective unconscious is portrayed with confident stroke. People like Prince Pratap, Tikka and Victor suffer from duality of culture and since they are in powerful position, they make others suffer as well.

A common diasporic attempt is to strive for survival and sustenance; economic survival and social sustenance. But Gita Mehta does not need to be worried about these aspects. It imparts her boldness to bluntly canvas the British hypocrisy, colonial cruelty and the notion of superiority:

The sovereignty of the British crown is supreme in India, and therefore no ruler of an Indian State can justifiably claim to negotiate with the British Government on an equal footing. Our supremacy is based not only upon treaties but exists independently of them.

The Angrez are worse than money lenders. They steal everything we have and still say we are in their debt. (Raj, p. 395)

The depiction of characters like Maharajah Jai Singh and Maharajah Dungra, the author gives a vivid picture of Indian Kinship and principles of Rajniti. Through assertions of the Raj Guru and Jai Singh we realize that those principles were not least inferior to those of democracy.

In A River Sutra, the narrator is nameless and homeless. No biographical information is available except he was a bureaucratic and after his retirement he comes to Narmada Guest House for peace and tranquility. Karma Cola has numerous faceless wonderers. In Raj, Jaya is twice displaced. Once when she gets married and enters into a world completely alien to her; second time, when she is rejected by her husband. Being uprooted from Balmer in the north-west to Sirpur in north-east is a kind of internal diaspora. (Even in Snakes and Ladders, a gentleman from Chennai tells Gita Mehta that he was living abroad, in Delhi) There is one more up-rootedness in Jaya's character. She is uprooted from her culture when the Maharajah asks her to get rid of her native culture and adopt the British culture.

Thus, as a diasporic writer, Gita Mehta attempts to depict India. On one hand there is a tendency to uphold the native culture; to demystify and thereby to justify it; to describe the damage done by the prolonged period of colonization. On the other hand, she herself brings out the weaknesses, issues of caste and gender discrimination boldly. It seems that while portraying present India, she simultaneously shows what she was and what she could have been.

References

- Bande Usha. Gita Mehta: Writing Home /Creating Homeland. Rawat Publication; Jaipur: 2008.

- Bhabha, Homi. The Location of Culture. Routledge; New York: 2004.
- Jain, Jasbir. "Post-Colonial Realities: Women Writing History." *Interrogating Postcolonialism.* Eds. Harish Trivedi and Meenakshee Mukherjee. Shimla: IIAS, 1996.
- Mehta, Gita. A River Sutra. N.A. Talese; New York: 1993.
- Mehta, Gita. Ganesha. The Vendom Press; New York: 2006
- Mehta, Gita. Karma Cola. Simon &Schuster; New York: 1979.
- Mehta, Gita. Raj. Simon & Schuster: New York: 1989.
- Mehta, Gita. Snakes and Ladders. N.A. Talese; New York: 1997.
- Mukherjee, Bharti. Jasmine. Penguin Books; New Delhi: 1989.
- Smith, Wendy. "Gita Mehta: Making India Accessible". Publisher's Weekly.

18

Voicing The Unvoiced: Women, Alienation and Trauma in *What The Body Remembers*

Priyanka Yadav

lecturer at Jecrc Udml College of Eng. Jaipur.

Migration and immigration have directly or indirectly affected several generations of contemporary writers in English, engendering hybridism and culture complexity within them to grapple with multiple cultures and countries and tensions between them.

South Asian women writers are the most rapidly emerging group on the North American literary scene. Ramabai Espinet,Jhupma Lahiri, Amulya Malladi,Bharati Mukherjee,Uma Parmeswaran, Kirin Narayan, Anita Rau Badami, Shauna Singh Baldwin are some of them. These diasporic writers are not merely assimilating to their host cultures but they are also actively reshaping them through their own new voices bringing new definitions of identity. Their works signal an engagement with a matrix of diversity, of cultures, languages, histories, people, places and times.The diasporic community is varied and complex. As Bhikhu Parekh also puts:

The diasporic Indian is like the Banayan tree, the traditional symbol of the Indian way of life, he spreads out his roots in several soils, drawing nourishment from one when the rest dry up. Far from being homeless, he has increasingly come to feel at home in the world. (106)

Yet this multiplicity of 'homes' does not bridge the gap between 'home'——the culture of origin and 'world'——the culture of adoption.

The immigrant writer 'writes' his sense of belonging and this is worked out through retellings of the past in various different ways and thus the pre occupation with the past, the lost homeland and the lost identity is always there. It is through these retellings that inner conflicts are worked out and resolved, a renegotiation takes place with the self and a voice is found for self assertion. When writers frame their realities and look for parallels elsewhere, the connections are being made between the remembered, the experienced, the collected and the desired. The past remains a part of the 'self', conscious of inhabiting different worlds. Their imagined communities do not substitute old ones; rather create new marginalities, hybridities and dependencies, resulting in multiple marginalizations and hyphenizations.

The sense of an identity is very crucial for an individual both as an independent entity and social relationships. It is defined through environment, past experiences, collective memories and in this process the space occupied by the place it is located in, is crucial to the construction of the self. The past always lingers back in the mind and have a tendency to surface either through recognition or memory or collectivity. The role of imagination is also a crucial one in this whole process, culture; history and memory interact with multiple dimensions. Women writers, who migrated to different countries have always recalled their past, showing the inevitability of forgetting. They write their identities, negotiating the memories of inherited past and female projections of duties and rights.

For centuries, India has been a patrilineal and patriarchal society where the role of women has been highly marginalized and her status constantly reduced. From this standpoint, when we look at the Indian diasporic women writers in Canada, we find an attempt on the part of these writers to transcend societal restrictions and renegotiating or relocating the 'self' in another culture. Relocation in another culture, leads to the re-examination of gender roles. The 'adopted land' with a different culture and seemingly an entirely different set of norms gives them an opportunity to redefine gender roles. They cast off the parameters lined for women in the patriarchal set up. But we need to study the experiences of the female protagonists to see how far they try to emerge out of the 'other'.

Novel has been one of the prime genres of literary expression, a torchbearer in the realm of women's emancipation. Women writers abound in themes that relate to the plight of women and their struggle to seek recognition and rightful place in family and society. Celebration of women has a long tradition in Indian ethos and literature which recognize the Shakti (power) of women. However, empowering them in real life always legged behind the declared myths.

Women writers those in India and those of the Indian diaspora have portrayed real protagonists who are peculiar in their relationships to their surroundings, society, and their families or so on. And the narrative fiction became a canvas to challenge the hegemonic practices of gender biased society.

Shauna Singh Baldwin, born in Montreal and brought up in India, is one of the prolific writers of Indo-Canadian women diaspora. She is the author of *English Lessons and Other Stories* and her short fiction, poetry and essays have been published in various literary magazines in U.S.A., Canada and India.Her first novel *What the Body Remembers* published in the year 1999 has remained the receipient of Commonwealth Writers' Prize for Canada/ Caribbean region (2000). The idea for this novel was born out of a short story titled 'satya' which won the 1997 Canadian Literary Award. With the partition milieu, *What the Body Remembers* is the story of a polygamous marriage and three characters, Saradarji, his first wife Satya and her archenemy Roop, the young girl whom Sardarji, a wealthy person, Rawalpindi born,UK educated with a degree in engineering, is a man caught up in the midest of transition on more than one front. Baldwin has drawn Roop's character, her desires, her fears, her valour and most crucially her patience and altruism,with great detail and minuteness. Satya and Roop, the two women married to Sardarji who are so different in their personality and temperament, live under the same fear of the fragility of their security. From different levels of prosperity and status they see each other and with clarity the ease with their lives can be blown all away at the slightest show of free will or disobedience. It is a story lived by many women, all across the world.

The writer, Shauna Singh Baldwin, herself commented upon the agenda behind the novel:

My challenge to myself was not to tell the story of the Sikhs from the standpoint of the men——there a few non-fiction books that cover their story——but from the perspective of the Sikh Women. This quickly became very frustrating because books on Sikh history are usually written by men. As a member of one of the few religions in the world that actually says women and men are equal, and demands that a Sikh woman be called 'princess' to show how valuable she is, I found my research running up against the difference between theory and practice".(Shauna Singh Baldwin)

Most of the history is male written but here we have two women- Roop and Satya- symbolically-Beauty and Truth, expressing and recording their experiences as being the members or representing thousands of 'other' women, who suffered silently at every turn of history.Virginia Woolf argues in *A Room of One's Own*: "Women are simultaneously victims of themselves as well as victims of men and upholders of society by acting as mirrors to men". (35)

This novel begins mainly in Punjab————Pari Darvaza————the doorway of fairies———a small village where Roop takes birth. The historical frame work for the events in the protagonists' lives is 1937 to 1947. Deputy Bachan Singh, Roop's father, is a man of genuine standing in the village but of modest means. Roop, born into a Sikh family of dependents and servants, receives the benefit of a school education and some religious training but sees that it's a men's world and it's on her brother that her father's all ambitions are concentrated. Being brought up in a household which has more women than men, she is pampered as well, perhaps because she is more beautiful than her sister. In her household, a variance is found in women characters- her mother—Deputy Bachan Singh's 'Purdah' woman, who could never see anything outside in the world other than the house she lived, Revati Bhua—who after being widowed in a young age, is condemned to live in Singh's house, carrying all of his orders, Gujri, who was sent with Roop's mother as an alley in a very young age and the two daughters Madni and Roop. Roop stands in sharp contrast with Madni, her elder sister, rather plain looking but Roop, so self aware of her beauty, always made herself believe, "I am Dipty Bachan Singh's daughter and have good kismat".(79)

Stunningly beautiful, Roop is a free spirit child who hates all sorts of restrictions. But it's right from her childhood that she, alongwith her sister Madni is being brought up and conditioned keeping in light woman's typical roles and responsibilities. Here famous lines of Simone de Beauvoir click into mind: "One is not born, rather becomes a woman". (Introduction, the Second Sex)

Roop sees how her mother happened to be so ill all the time and delivering yet another child for Papaji and here we see how women themselves are the very perpetuators of so-called 'femininty' in their own sex, marginalizing them doubly. We see how Roop's Nani highly objects to the very idea of Roop's mother being taken to hospital because for Roop's Nani, her daughter is not more than a 'body' which must not be shown to stranger men. Even if she is dying, a male doctor cannot see her body and cure the ailment. She is just a machine for 'producing sons'. Here we feel compelled to ask ourselves: What is a woman? Teta Mulier gives the answer that woman is a womb. Nani infuses the significance of only these roles for women in her coming generations also, teaching such lessons to her granddaughters at the time of Roop's mother's delivery as, "Ay, learn learn what we women are for" (32).

Roop sees her mother, suffering endlessly and ultimately dying after the pursuit of her goal to give birth to one more son to the house, the house which clinged to her like her 'Purdah', crossing its boundaries only to embrace death. But it turns up into a highly ironical situation where Roop's father comes out with an altogether different interpretation of the causes of his wife's death. He rather superstitiously blames Revati Bhua's practices of Hindu religion for all misfortunes and evils upon his house and one more time proving that, "Men see women from the corner of each eye, like a horse, never seeing what directly lies before them". One more poor victim of patriarchal hegemony, Revati Bhua suffers silently and little Roop learns one more lesson of 'Proposed, imposed and forced womanhood'. She learns how men control women lives and that too in such a closed way as to even decide the Guru and God for them to follow.

Deputy Bachan Singh who works on the fields of Sardar Kaushal Singh is the father of two girls. Elder one Madni is a 'sweet-sweet, good-good girl', destined to do all household chores, bear children and after living and dying unacknowledged. But 'women don't die of pain——— it turns into children' (85) is what they have been taught right from childhood and this reminds Shirley Chilscholem's words that the emotional, sexual and psychological stereotyping of female begins from the moment when the doctor says 'It's a girl'. Little girls are being nurtured and conditioned within their families by such 'torch bearers' of womanhood like Lajo Bhua who in themselves are the biggest stereotyping agencies. Madni and Roop travel to Bhua's place to learn how to become 'good-good, sweet-sweet girls'. Here they are given a distinctive code of conduct to follow. Rule No.1: "You want to make a good marriage, you must be more graceful, more pleasing to your elders. I want to hear only 'Achchaji', 'Haanji', and 'yes ji' from you. Never 'Nahinji' or No-ji" (76). Rule No.2 "Speak softly, always softly" (76). Rule No.3 "Never feel angry, never, never. No matter what happens, or what your husband says, feel angry. You might be hurt, but never feel angry" (77).

Here, we see how 'woman' is made, produced or manufactured in such stereotyping agencies. I again, feel like quoting Simone de Beauvoir's too irresistible lines "One is not born rather becomes a woman". And in our story, Roop is the perfect specimen of this sort of 'becoming'. We witness the transformation of our little Princess Roop, from a self-centred, precocious, ambitious, rather proud child into a 'sweet-sweet, good good girl'. She forgets the taste of eggs and chicken, no longer a quarrelsome girl; she learns when to be quiet. She expects things only she truly needs. She is no longer adventurous, having learnt the fear of unrelated men. She has, at last learnt how to please Bachan Singh as Madni did, as Kusum does in turn, covering her head, being silent and obedient all the time. We, the readers witness ourselves how this whole process of perpetuation of womanhood has been going on relentlessly from generation to generation since those times and how this has become a commonly inherited code of conduct now for women to follow all around. And the irony of the situation lies in the fact that women simply do not know what they have been doing by bringing up, modeling their daughters like this. They are not the makers of these codes but over obedient executors. Such constraints and social constructs and relationships within their own gender complicate the whole discourse of gender rights and equality.

Simone de Beauvoir asks this question in *The Second Sex*, 'What is a woman'? Woman, she realizes is always perceived as 'other'. She is defined and differentiated with references to man and not he with references to her. In this book and her essay 'Woman: Myth and Reality', De Beauvoir anticipates Betty Friedan in seeking to demythologize the male concept of women: *"A myth invented by men to confine women to their oppressed state. For women it is not a question of asserting themselves as women but of becoming full scale human beings"(20).* Men only created this myth called women and they were women themselves who lived, highlighted and immortalized this myth. After her elder sister Madni's marriage, Roop almost desperately waits for her own marriage, feeling claustrophobic in her father's house and suffocating under his endless restrictions. But Roop's marriage is not going to be an easy affair for Bachan Singh. Despite the beauty part on her favour, a dowry less girl is not at all a desired match. Here, Sardar Kaushal Singh enters on the scene with the match of his brother-in law for Roop, a man in his forties, already having a wife though barren. Sixteen years old beautiful Roop gets ready to marry a man almost thrice of her age and already married because she thinks that it will enable her to leave the poverty and restrictions of her father's house. She sees the future prospects of being a rich landlord's wife, with all amenities at her disposal and sees 'Sardarji' (as he is mentioned in the whole novel) as her 'liberator'. Though initially Bachan Singh could not reconcile himself with this decision of Roop but 'a manglik girl, with one deaf ear, also ambitious, slightly vain, lazily intelligent and above all dowry less and Bachan Singh excuses himself saying "the girl's kismat will take care of her" (100).

Carrying a sort of self assurance and her Papaji's words "Above all give no trouble", in her heart, Roop reaches to Rawalpindi after marriage with the hope that Satya(first wife) will be an old friend like a sister or even a substitute for the mother she lost as a young girl. But Roop only finds more trouble in the form of 'Satya'. Satya, married to Sardarji, is in her forties in the year 1937. She hails from a reputed family, excels in all duties at home and takes care of all Sardarji's business. But her doting position is threatened because of her barrenness, of her inability to produce a son for Sardarji's house. Sardarji, always a man with a strong sense of 'Dharma' feels persuaded to marry for a second time because of his duty towards the preservation and promulgation of his family. He uses Satya's barrenness as well as her impatience with her sharp tongue as excuses for marrying a second wife. Satya who would have welcomed Roop as her daughter will not welcome her as a competing wife and on the contrary of Roop's all hopes begins a subtle campaign to destroy Roop. She could never bare the thought of Sardarji's continuing favour and love for Roop. She could not reconcile herself to the thought of Roop's body thickening to ripeness—two children proof of her fertility and Satya's failure.

Satya puts the umbilical cord of Roop's son on fire-full of hatred-not letting earth produce more sons to Roop. Even after taking Roop's children, Satya is not generous to Roop. Her haughty face knows no peace. In her grey eyes there is only fear, fear turning to hate, hate that radiates to Roop. But Lajo Bhua's rule no. three is so stuck with Roop that how can she get angry with Satya? She remains hungry but fear from Satya eats on Roop and she finds herself in danger. She writes to her father and ultimately returns to Pari Darvaza. But on return she finds that her father's home no longer belongs to her and for her Papaji, it's a matter of disgrace and ingratitude that she has returned from her husband's place, without his permission, whatever is the reason. Roop is being told that death is preferable to dishonour for good-good Sikh girls and Roop realizes the limits of her sky where she could only flutter her wings but cannot fly as her sky is in the Patriarchal territory. At one place, Joseph Conrad appropriately remarks that being a woman is a terribly difficult task since they have to principally deal with men.

On the part of Sardarji also, Roop's step is betrayal, bestowed on him as a return of his generosity. He thinks that she should have communicated her fears to him but without informing, leaving his children behind and going all alone to her father's house could not be justified in any way, in Sardarji's point of view. And men as always only have their versions of 'Rights':

If Roop is going to get his protection, his name and live like a little rani in his home, she is going to have to give something. Whatever possible, sons, for one thing, not just one son, and that too a sickly little chap. Yes, sons *and loyalty. These are his rights. He is within his rights, by Jove, within his rights (272).*

Here Jane Fonda comes in mind, "*A man has every season while a woman only has the right to spring" (*25). But here, when Roop with her small daughter and son takes refuge with her father and her brother, the traditional protectors of women, Sardarji is forced to agree that Roop, the mother of his son, will be the wife who will live with him wherever he is posted as an engineer. Roop becomes the 'official' wife while Satya, the woman who has no males to protect her against her husband, is left without her husband or Roop's children she had laid claim to earlier.

But Shauna Singh Baldwin's constant references to Draupadi and Sita transform the personal struggle between Satya and Roop(of course, Truth and Beauty) into a struggle between two different strategies used by two different woman to secure their positions in a world hostile, or at least indifferent to women. Satya, who refuses to lower her voice or to stop speaking the truth about her personal life, about the effects of colonialization on her husband and her country and about the events taking place in India, is Draupadi. Roop on the other hand, chooses to learn from her brother's wife, Kusum, the art of seemingly acquiescing to everything she is supposed to do as a traditional, dutiful wife, Sita of the popular imagination. But at the end of the novel, Baldwin complicates the simple equation. Satya refuses to live her life as the solitary first wife and decides to choose her own death, her self-selected disappearance from the life of her husband. When she deliberately kisses and breathes in her own death from her cousion who is dying of tuberculosis, the author does not let the reader forget that Sita in the end also selected her own path, her exit from Rama's life, one needs to keep in mind that Satya's suicide is text of a one life/ one death belief system. She knows that she will be reborn to continue her struggle and her story.

Satya refuses to live a life where her positions as the first wife and the desires and needs of her woman's body have been usurped by her husband's second wife.

Margaret Sanger says: "No woman can call herself free who does not control her own body" (45).And seeing Satya, we get the feeling of watching a warrior choosing her own death, rather than staying alive as a conquered pitied, subservient woman. Satya's suicide raises many complex issues and questions that are not easy to explain. It is a difficult act to accept. But it is certainly not an unfamiliar act in the women history. In *The Second Neurotic's Notebook*, Mignon McLaughlin puts: "Many *beautiful women might have been made happy by their own beauty, but no intelligent woman has ever been made happy by her own intelligence*" (37).

Satya dies, being an intelligent woman. But we wonder, seeing this equation of Sita and Draupadi, where would Baldwin place Kusum? Kusum dies, facing a ritual slaughter at the hands of her father-in-law, who kills her in order to save the 'izzat', the honour of the family and the community as the violence between Hindus, Muslims and Sikhs escalates. Is this a continuation of the stories repeated throughout the India about women who voluntarily and involuntarily jump into pyres and into wells to escape rape and mutilation in order to save their men's sense of honour? It is a sense of honour constructed as dependent on women's bodies, on women's behavior and on women's fate. And this has increased the agony of the whole plot. Elaine Booster's words define woman's plight aptly that she is just a person, trapped inside a woman's body. The protection of women's bodies or the killing or the subjugation, lies within men's hands. Women do not possess their own bodies.

Their bodies are like instruments rather than ornaments. And men are the players of these 'instruments', but not always without the complicity on the part of women. But as it is evident from the novel that this complicity on the part of women is born out of the need to survive in a patriarchal society. But this novel does not lack strong women also. When Roop briefly faces the possibility of a life without a protecting male, she calls upon the dead Satya and conjures up Satya's strength to help her. This blending of Draupadi and Sita in Satya's death is reversed at the end of the novel when Roop feels that she and Satya have become 'one woman'.

The core of the narrative is death and divison, during partition. The demand for the birth of a son visited upon Satya and Roop subjects both women to emotional violence and one of them to suicide. Baldwin, very well makes the two women and their story, her main focus, rather than the history of events leading to partition and independence. This narrative about fathers estranged from daughters, mothers from sons, husbands from wives, becomes a metaphor for the historical turmoil and flux. Though it's these three characters Roop, Satya and Sardarji and their movement towards reconciliation that rivets the story. The canvas of *What the Body Remembers* also takes the sweep of history from 1895 to 1948, but what makes the novel striking is the fact that *What the Body Remembers* is one of those very few books where the history of partition is solely told from the point of view of Sikh women. And so, this novel is not just about a disposed and displaced community within community (women) and their struggle. The violent birth and division of India are here played out onto the bodies and lives of women.

Writers like Bapsi Sidhwa and Amrita Pritam have portrayed the destruction of women's bodies and lives as tangible. Baldwin's challenge in writing this book lies in the fact that there were only a few books which narrated the story of partition from the perspective of Sikh women. *What the Body Remembers* is a very feminist text so to say if one defines feminism as the radical notion that a woman is a person and it depends on how accustomed you are to women having rights as people, including the right to own their own bodies. It comments on woman power relations, surrogate motherhood, and the two strains of feminism-strident and persuasive, that we have in operation today.

At the end, last but not the least, it is about the division of India, the sorrows of patrichay, the trauma and alienation and marginalization women face due to it and women's role in the emerging nation state and their ongoing struggle. In the epilogue 'Satya' is born again. Once again a girl with her eyes wide open and once again kicking and screaming. Her last words to the reader are:

———I know because my body remembers without the benefit of words, that men who do not welcome girl-babies will not treasure me as I grow to woman—though he calls me princess just because the Gurus told him to, I have come so far, I have borne so much pain and emptiness! But men have not yet changed (471).

References

- Baldwin, Shauna Singh. *What the Body Remembers.* Toronto: Knopf, 1999.
- Beauvoir, Simone De. *The Second Sex* (1952). Tran and ed. H.M.Parshley, New York: Vintage Books, 1989.
- Davidson, Bill. *Jane Fonda: An Intimate Biography.* New American Library, 1991.
- Hoard, Walter B. ed. *Quotations and Sayings of People of Color.* Uni.of Michigan:R& R Research Associates, 1973.
- Mclaughin, Mignon. *The Second Neurotic's Notebook.* Castle Books, 1981.
- Parekh, Bhikhu."Some Reflections on the Indian Diaspora". *Journal of Contemporary Thought.* 34.2 (2003).
- Sanger, Margaret. *Woman and the New Race.* New York: Brentanos Publishers, 1920.
- Woolf, Virginia. *A Room of One's Own.* (1929). Flamingo: Harper Collins Publishers, 1994.

19

Multicultural Accommodation of Diverse 'Desires' in Chitra Banerjee Divakaruni's *The Mistress of Spices*

Dr Deepali Rajshekhar Patil

Appasaheb Jedhe College

Pune

Diaspora writing fosters multiculturalism. The diaspora writers are usually ensnared by two worlds physically, mentally and experientially. Such writings demonstrate a transitional phase, a movement from one cultural scenario to another, striving to integrate with their new environment yet attached to their ancestral customs, traditions, languages and religions. Characteristically diaspora writers reveal a negotiation between their identity and a hyphenated space. The arena of multicultural experience is explored through a focus on the discrimination, differentiation, injustices and inequalities that feature the life of every immigrant. This treatment of life compels them to become nostalgic about the homeland. Operating through multicultural space enables the author to inhabit the dual worlds and grants them an opportunity to de-stress by dwelling in an imaginary world that is magical, poetic and fable-like. Such an interpretation of the present ruptures from the recalled past. Shobita Jain aptly describes the diaspora women:

> Just as diaspora settings of Indians living abroad provide a window to understanding process of social transformation I India, we may say that looking at diaspora Indian women may give us an insight into situations of our own fast changing social fabric in India (qtd in Sahu 2007: xxiv)

It reveals that in current usage, the term 'diaspora' is moving into a broad semantic realm, liberating itself from all political domains and major religious and ethnic groups o the past. The present endeavour therefore focuses on *The Mistress of Spices* as a conscious effort on the part of Chitra Banerjee Divakaruni to enliven and convey a linguistic and multicultural heritage as a part of personal and collective memory.

Multiculturalism dwells in a plane space, not a hierarchical space. This can be explained in the light of postmodern theory. Postmodern theory, in theorizing plane space, challenges foundational theory, or essentialist philosophy, that supports mono-culturalism. Francois Lyotard defines, postmodernism as "incredulity towards metanarrative" that displaces the discourse of metanarrative or grand narrative and argues for cultural space that is populated by little narratives (1993: 3). These narratives are governed by their own constituting rules and are not dependent on extra-narrational foundational rules for articulation. Such discursive forms are not arranged in a hierarchical order; they are allowed to flourish in conjunction with each other, on a plane space of cultural autonomy. Another term Lyotard has coined is *differend*, which denotes "a case of conflict between two parties that can not be resolved for lack of a rule of judgment applicable to both arguments" (1988:xi).

To illustrate postmodern multicultural space Gilles Deleuze and Felix Guattari develop the concept of *rhizome*. A rhizome is any plant (like grass) whose root system spreads horizontally on the ground; as the plant grows outward and across it can grow to cover the whole land mass. It is a figure of non- hierarchical, structureless, open system. It is apposed to the *aborescent*, the tree, which suggests the image of a root that grounds textual (and cultural) complexes in a foundational matrix in order to uphold a unified, centered and hierarchical system that characterizes the narratives of modernity.

In keeping with this description is the fiction of Chitra Banerjee Divakaruni who born in India now resides at San Francisco with her family. An author of several award winning volumes of poetry, and several novels to her credit including *The Mistress of Spices, Sister of My Heart, The Vine of Desire, The Couch Bearer and Queen of Dreams*, she won the most coveted PEN Oakland Josephine Miles Prize for fiction and also the Bay Area Book Reviewers Award for fiction. *The Mistress of Spices* (1997) is a spectacular blend of myth and romance, social critique and poetry. Tilo abbreviation for Tillotama, an immigrant from India, is the sole proprietor of a spice shop in Oakland, California. Her brief interaction with her customers, as she supplies the ingredients for curries and kormas, allows her the insight into their lives and she then readily assists them to gain a more precious commodity: *desires*, whatever they desperately yearn for... For Tilo is a Mistress of Spices, a priestess of the secret magical powers of spices. Through those who visit and revisit her shop, she catches glimpses of the life of the local Indian expatriate community. To each, Tilo offers wisdom and the appropriate spice, for the restoration of sight, the cleansing of evil, the pain of rejection. In *Imaginary Homelands* (1991), Salman Rushdie states that "the Indian writer who writes roam outside India... is obliged to deal with broken mirrors, some of whose fragments have been irretrievably lost" and he "will create fictions, not actual cities or villages, but invisible ones, imaginary homelands, Indias of the mind" (10-11). Tilo has stepped into the heart of Shampati's fire to awaken at in Oakland as the aged Tillotama with "the store already hardening its protective shell around her, the spices on their shelves meticulous and waiting" (58). Tilo's life that has almost become captivated under the spell of her spices finds a new breath on the arrival of an American. When the Lonely American ventures into the store, a distressed Tilo cannot find the correct spice to soothe his desires, for he has enkindled in her heart a flame she had long buried- her forbidden desires... that if she follows will obliterate her magical powers. These encounters with desires of different kinds create a space for multicultural exchanges. The book is superbly orchestrated with fifteen chapters, each entitled with a different spice excluding the first and the last. At the outset the novel reveals that a land enriched with immense wealth of spices and enchanted powers seems to be too impoverished for the birth of a girl child. The midwife cried out a 'veiny purple cowl', the fortune-teller shook his head sorrowfully and though the parents name her Nayan Tara, Star of the Eye, their faces are heavy with fallen hope, in their mute perception... "What does she bring to the family except a dowry debt" (1997: 7). She nearly escapes infanticide for they whisper "Wrap her in old cloth, lay her face down on the floor" (7). However she is no ordinary child but a blessed one who soon brings fame and riches to her family as the 'seer' gifted with magical powers who can ward off evil and offer help and advice. She narrates the event of her wishful thinking that transformed her at once from Nayan Tara to Bhagyavati after she was abducted by the pirates. She is filled with guilt and remorse at the thought of invoking the calamity and ruining the village.

The entire text provides glimpses into the lives of interesting characters instead of a single metanarrative. Haroun, who drives the Rolls Royce for Mrs. Kapadia visits Tilo's shop with hopes and expectations. She lends him a listening ear and a helping hand to mitigate his pains in the far off country. Haroun quits his job for the need of his stomach cannot be fulfilled at the cost of his self-esteem. "All these rich people, they think they're still in India. Treat you like janwaars, animals. Order this, order that, no end to it, and after you wear out your soles running around for them, not even a nod in thanks" (28-9). Haroun carries the poignant memories of his long lost relatives and devastated village, where rebels rode down the mountain passes of his Kashmiri village with machine guns and tried to take young men. The red silk of the *shikaras* is redder with pools of blood. Haroun migrates to America, the new land in search of riches and happiness that he lost in his land. Fortunately Mujibar, a man from his uncle's village is in America and willing to appoint him as a taxi driver. Later Tilo senses his need for company and steps beyond her world of spices to go around with him. She is able to anticipate the danger that lurks in the future and wishes to warn him but is unable to stop the chain of events. As fate would have it, Haroun is attacked by a pack of miscreants, left wounded, bleeding profusely and gains consciousness in a hospital room. He complains "Yes, always smile, even when people say 'Bastard, foreigner taking over the country stealing our jobs' (62). This encounter shows the ugly side of America, where despite his readiness to part with all his belongings, the goons abuse him as an Indian and unleash their hatred.

Mohan, who runs *Mohan Indian foods* is attacked unexpectedly by some white teenagers, who start abusing and thrashing him "Sonofabitch Indian, should a stayed in your own goddamn country"(170). He is mercilessly beaten up only because he denies to open the shop once closed for them. They kick him in the groin, 'head yanked up, and dragged through the gravel, so that he almost loses his consciousness and cries "bachao, bachao" only to gain his senses on the hospital bed, aware of his unbearable pain. He is shocked beyond words so that there are questions rattling in his skull box- "will I walk again, how will I make a living now, the right eye, is it totally gone, Veena so young and pretty left with a crippled scarred husband. And over and over those two haramis, did the police get them, may they rot in jail" (171). The severe pain and suffering is aggravated and he becomes hysteric when the culprits are acquitted by law. He brings down his crutches on dishes, furniture even the stereo that has been purchased with all his savings, so that poor Veena has to seek the help of her neighbours to bring him under control.

Tilo gloomily remarks "O Mohan broken in body, broken in mind by America, I come back from your story in pieces, find myself at last on the chill floor of the shop. My limbs ache as after illness, my sari is damp with shivering sweat, and in my heart I cannot tell where your pain ends and mine begins. For your story is the story of all those I have learned to love in this country, and to fear for (171). All night I will whisper into air purifying prayers for the maimed, for each lost limb, each crushed tongue. Each silenced heart (172).

To this list of the sufferers is added the name of Jagjit who also finds himself victimized as an Indian in America. Jagjit finds it difficult to unlearn his Punjabi and get adapted to English in the schools and becomes an easy target for ridicule, so that the only word he knows in English is 'Idiot, Idiot and Idiot'. The girls pull his pants and the poor child protests "Choddo meinu" to which he is told "Talk English sonofabitch (39). He is humiliated, jeered at, mocked by others for being slow witted. Tilo realises his potential and offers cinnamon to him which is a spice for making friends. Jagjit falls in bad company trying to assert his individuality but gradually learns and turns to the right track. Later Tilo willingly parts with all her money to allow him a fresh start.

Another victim of this American dream is Lalita married to the man Ahuja settled in America. Like many Indian parents falling for the glitzy America, the Chowdharies fix the match without verifying the facts so that the man who reaches India for the marriage is a pot-bellied, bald man much older than the photograph taken many years before. Poor Lalita has to get married but is unable to accept the match at heart for the feeling of being cheated and the hypocrisies of the man create a divide between them.

"Silence and tears, silence and tears all the way to America....Here in America maybe we could start again, away from those eyes, those mouths always telling us how a man should act, what is a woman's duty. But ah the voices, we carried them all the way inside our heads' (102-3).

Shamelessly the man exploits his own wife and on being opposed manhandles her every day. The poor, forlorn woman desires to have a child and undergoes tests which to her misfortune reveal that the problem lies with her husband. Unable to face the facts he harasses her further even more mercilessly. Tilo seems to be her only confidante in the strange land. Tilo offers her Fennel that would grant her the mental strength and freshen her breath besides being an aid to digestion. Lalita is scared to reveal the detestable truth about her conjugal relationship that is falling apart. Her deeply ingrained Indian values dissuade her to seek the help from the American helpline but finally she overcomes her fears and anxieties. The sense of repulsion and contempt for the marriage in tethers is snapped when she moves out to join many others in the care of the American agency. She has an opportunity to begin her own tailoring shop or even file a case against her husband but Lalita finds the atmosphere suffocating and even more depressing. She feels ill at ease and is nostalgic about the lavish gifts and attention that her husband pampered her with. After considerable efforts Lalita manages to gather herself and firmly assert "I tell myself, I deserve dignity, I deserve happiness" (272).

Another bead woven in this chain of events is Geeta, a young and charming girl whose grand-father is a regular customer at Tilo's shop. He highly disapproves about the changes in the family that he witnesses across the years and also across his land. He is indignant at the late night work of Geeta and the lax discipline in which she is brought up.

"May be OK for these *firingi* women in this country, but you tell me yourself *didi*, if a young girl should work late- late in the office with other men and come home only after dark and sometimes in their car too? *Chee Chee,* back in Jamshedpur they would have smeared dung on our faces for that. And who would ever marry her" (85).

He is highly critical of the amount of make-up she uses or her mannerisms; moreover he is vexed by the negligence of Geeta's parents. However a greater cultural shock lies in store for them when Geeta's decision to marry a white man is announced. Helpless to convince her family members Geeta leaves the house and it is Tilo's timely intervention that settles the things to the normal. Tilo's own journey of exploring and establishing her own identity caught between two worlds finds expression in the conflicts faced by other women. As grandfather remarks, "Even from birth a girl's real home is with her future husband's family only"

(88) an opinion reiterated by Sudhir Kakar's observation that a girl is regarded "as a guest in her own home...Her 'real' family is her husband's family. Whatever her future fortunes, when she marries, an Indian girl knows that, in a psychological sense, she can never go home again" (*Inner* 73). Same is the destiny of Lalita. Moreover, the ideals or role-models who mould, inform, and define an Indian woman's sensibility and her sense of identity are Sita, Draupadi, Savitri, Shakuntala almost all archetypal exiles. Tilo not only administers her knowledge of the proper spices to restore the relations but also tries to resolve the misconceptions of the family members so that Geeta is accepted back warm heartedly into her family, that is overwhelmed to know that Geeta did not consent to live in relationship but sought refuge at her friend's house till the issues were sorted out. The family certainly undergoes a revolutionary change so that they agree to meet her white man. Tilo is successful in restoring peace and enkindling hope in their lives.

The form and the content of the novel are inextricably interwoven to form a continuous fluidity between the outer and inner worlds, physical and psychological, past and present, reality and fantasy, the I that asserts and dissolves or fades away. As Sonya Domergue aptly points out "Tilo, like her customers, is caught up in the flux of being and becoming- that inevitable space and time zone through which all immigrants must transit before redefining a new self and a new identity" (qtd in Mcleod, 2000:68). This conflict accelerates towards its climax and gathers momentum with Raven, the American who trespasses the well-guarded precipices of Tilo's world and persuasively reveals his own story. Raven becomes the defining other for Tilo. In order to break her freefall through the "vertigo of homelessness" (128), Tilo is forced to choose between her grander, mythic destiny of spice-mistress and that of ordinary mortal. She does so when she meets Raven, the nurturing other, the only person who "sees through and through [her] old woman body" (109). Their romantic attachment deviates phenomenally from the traditional Indian concept of mythic, male-female complementarity as embodied in the Rama-Sita story. Raven a younger man woos Tilo, a woman older than him. It is he, in a complete role reversal, who decides to follow her in her exile. Tilo not only proves to be a rebel but can firmly assert herself, as she has learned to say "No, that word so hard for Indian woman" (81). Tilo's metamorphosed self would always be marked by her cultural inheritance, just as Raven's will carry the stigmata of the legacy of which he has been deprived. He remains the invisible immigrant born and brought up in the United States by an American-Indian mother who totally cut herself and her family off from her origins. Conversely Tilo is the visible immigrant, both being Indians but moving from the polarities of East and West towards the precarious balance of being American. As Jerome Bruner terms, exile blurs "range of metaphoric identity" (357), that the Indian woman has accessed to define herself. Both, Tilo and Raven personify the Janus –face of exile and what Salman Rushdie calls "the Indian talent for non- stop self-regeneration" (16).

The earthquake becomes a divine force of retribution and the spatial equivalent of the psychological upheaval that Tilo survived. In a completely stunning turn-around she decides to go back instead of pursuing the earthly paradise that she and Raven hoped to find. By turning back Tilo has annexed the freedom to go back. She feels she is responsible for the calamity, "I made it happen" (313) but ultimately Raven convinces her that it is not so. The climactic enigma serves to bring out the dual nature of the exile and immigration. There seems to be reciprocity, as the landscape of the immigrant mind has been altered by the new homeland, the immigrant dramatically alters or modifies the landscape of the new country.

It cannot be overlooked that multiculturalism is a site that offers recognition to the hitherto marginalized voices of the oppressed and grants empowerment to them. The present text is singularly characteristic of the empowered women who have either been neglected or silenced. Every single woman like Lalita, Geeta with Tilo at the lead aspire for liberation and rebel in their own ways. Incidentally a girl forsaken at birth and left to die alone becomes the saviour of many and the foreseer of the future. Lalita with her determination, Geeta with her moral righteousness, Tilo with her unflinching faith in service to humanity are emblems of a true multicultural spirit and undying conviction to initiate the journey towards self-discovery without abandoning their originality in the new socio-cultural scenario. Even a minor Jagjit seeks to assert his individuality and Haroun who feels marginalized is able to carve a niche for himself in the new system of America. The oppressed are able to shed off the shackles of confinement and fight for their rights. The diverse desires are not thwarted despite many struggles and hurdles in the path and signify a optimistic vision. The novel significantly brings out a crucial aspect of pluralism that these expatriates do not desire to dissolve their identities into enforced homogeneity but have a quest for retaining their identities in the New land.

Thus the multicultural hues of the diaspora weave it together into a beautiful aesthetic and artistic experience. The strange encounter with myths and magic interspersed with hard core realities serve as the *rhizome,* an outgrowth that pervades the entire landscape of the new land and offers insights into the lives of various characters. It successfully illustrates how multiculturalism is one of the systems that adapts itself to social milieu and culture. Multiculturalism ensures flexibility in the culture and the outlook to accommodate the changes in times and space. With the countries and states already at cross-roads in the global scenario, diaspora and multiculturalism stand for building bridges rather than erecting walls of differences. The diverse voices are able to articulate their desires and seek fulfilment through the catalytic presence of Tilo, who finally rises from the ashes like a phoenix to be *The Mistress of Spices.*

Works Cited

- Bruner, J., Spring 1959. "Myths and Identity", *Daedalus*, 355-62.
- Deleuze, G. and F. Guattari. 1983. *A Thousand Plateaus: Capitalism and Schizophrenia.* Trans. R. Hurley, M. Seem and H. R Lane. Minneapolis: University of Minnesota Press.
- Divakaruni, Chitra Banerjee. 1997. *The Mistress of Spices.* London: Black Swan.
- Domergue, Sonya 2000. "The Mistress of Spices: Falling through a Hole in the Earth". In *The Literature of Indian Diaspora.* Ed. A.L. Mcleod. New Delhi: Sterling Publishers.
- Kakar, Sudhir. 1992. *The Inner World: a Psychoanalytic Study of Childhood and Society in India.* Delhi: Oxford University Press.
- Lyotard, J.F.1993 (1984). *The Postmodern Condition: A Report on Knowledge.* Trans.G. Bennington and B. Massumi. Minneapolis: University of Minnesota Press.
- Lyotard, J.F. 1988. *The Differend: Phrases in Dispute.* Trans. G. Van Abele. Minneapolis: University of Minnesota Press.
- Rushdie, Salman. 1991. *Imaginary Homelands.* London: Granta Publications.
- Sahu, Nandini. 2007 (ed.). *The Post-Colonial Space: Writing the Self and the Nation.* Delhi: Atlantic publishers.

20

Indian Diasporas : We Lost our Expression, Mother Tongue (1880-2000)

Dr.Vinay Kumar Pandey

Associate Professor

Dept.of English

VTHT, Dr.RR.Dr.SR.Engineering College,Avadi, Chennai

In the nineteenth century, trade between South Asia and East Africawas constrained by the rhythm of the monsoons. From November to March, the famous, beautiful dhows sailed from West India to East Africa and between April and October, they made the return journey. The trade in cotton textiles, ivory, and spices was profitable but dangerous. Many traders did not return home safely. Rough seas, pirates, and various diseases took the lives of many traders and early adventurers.

The first generation of Hindu Lohanas in East Africa were born between 1880 and 1920 in Gujarat, western India. Most of them received at least their primary educations in their homeland. They were able toread, write, and speak Gujarati and some had a little knowledge of English when they arrived in East Africa. The names of the informants have been changed for reasons of privacy.

Contact between Asians, Africans, and Europeans in East Africa has a long history and was largely influenced by the economics and politics of colonisation and the emergence of nation-states.2 This long-standing relationship resulted in a particular 'East African Asian culture' in which Gujarati (Indian), Swahili (East African) and European cultures were adapted, transformed, and re-invented. The migration of Asians from one continent to another, where they became a minority, resulted in the development of various strategies of adaptation, with the group adopting new socio-cultural values while maintaining some of their original values. Despite the information we have on the number of migrants, their religious backgrounds and their reasons for migration, we know very little about the 'cultural baggage' of these migrants and even less about how and why this changed after their migration.3 This cultural change was not a natural, harmonious process; rather there were many conflicts, which required painful decisions to be made. One such decision was the exchange of the Gujarati language in favour of the Swahili and English languages.

The first generation of Gujaratis in East Africa knew how to read, write, and speak Gujarati, whereas the third-generation migrants may speak Gujarati with their parents but prefer to use English among themselves and they also do not know how to read or write Gujarati. This exchange of Gujarati in favour of English was the result of individual and community-based decisions. It should not be seen as a simplified process of a minority community adapting to 'globalisation', or 'westernisation' by instrumentally choosing the more 'global' language, the language of the business elite. On the contrary, as we will see, the colonial state promoted English and German education in a period when the Gujaratis successfully supported and sponsored their own Indian schools, using Gujarati as the vernacular language. The Germans in Tanganyika and the Britishin Uganda and Kenya were not able to implement their education systems because Gujaratis refused to support the interests of colonial states. They followed their own cultural and economical agenda. Interestingly, the Gujaratis themselves promoted the English language when the independent East African nations started to promote Swahili, the vernacular East African language. This was the consequence of intended and unintended Government policies and the realisation by Gujaratis that their future did not lay in India but in Africa and the West. This struggle over the 'teaching language' is one of the most important variables of ethnic identity. Together with religion, food and dress habits, and a shared history [real or imagined], 'language' is among the key variables of most definitions and descriptions of 'ethnicity'. The maintenance of aspects of Indian culture(s), in the form of the reproduction of language, is seen as a key element in many definitions of diaspora. In the book's introduction, I have shown that there is a tendency to 'unify' the South Asian diaspora in the diaspora debate. In this article, I emphasise that migrants make their own adaptations to local circumstances. The consequence may well be that they do not identify with their ancestors' culture 'back home'. It is therefore intriguing to see how the shift in identity and the choice of language occurred among the Gujarati businessmen of East Africa. The choice of the 'teaching language' was instrumentally made. The Indian/Gujarati community had an active and successful lobby in this matter.

In this article, I use the image of 'three generations' of Hindu Lohanas in Tanzania:

(1) the pioneers (born 1880-1920), who decided to settle with their families in East Africa;

(2) the Asian East Africans (born 1920-1960), who made East Africa their home;

(3) the internationalists (born 1960-2000), whose 'roots' are as Asian East Africans, but who are economically oriented towards the west and culturally towards both west and east.

This typology reflects the change in identity from one oriented towards the Gujarat region to an 'international' orientation. The Lohanas lost a part of their primary 'Gujarati' identity and gained an 'international' identity. This change was, however, not welcomed by all of the community's members. Some expressed their concern about the loss of 'the gift of expression'.

In this article, I focus solely on Hindu Lohana families. The research was based on the history of twenty Hindu Lohana families who have lived in East Africa for three or more generations.

My argumentation is divided into five sections.

1. We introduce the general migration history of South Asians in East Africa. Here the main focus .will be on the absence of Hindu women in East Africa.
2. Looks at the life histories of early Lohana migrants who settled in East Africa between 1880 and 1920. Here, the main aim is to show the emphasis on their knowledge of reading and writing Gujarati.

3. Highlights the second-generation Lohanas' efforts to establish 'Indian Schools' that would teach Indian languages.
4. Dramatic shift in the colonial history of East Africa.
5. The consequences of these findings in relation to the discourses around the diaspora concept.

These five above mentioned points related to the migration and settlement of South Asians in East Africa In the nineteenth century, trade between South Asia and East Africa was constrained by the rhythm of the monsoons. From November to March, the famous, beautiful dhows sailed from West India to East Africa and between April and October, they made the return journey. The trade in cotton textiles, ivory, and spices was profitable but dangerous. Many traders did not return home safely. Rough seas, pirates, and various diseases took the lives of many traders and early adventure.

We Lost our Gift of Expression

It was only in the late nineteenth century that some South Asian traders started to settle in Zanzibar and on the East African coast. These early South Asian settlers are nowadays seen as the pioneers of many South Asian family business houses in East Africa, such as that of Nanji Damordas, who at the age of ten, accompanied by his father, came to look after some business in Zanzibar. Most of these early migrants were asked to join the flourishing family businesses or to assist in the businesses of community members. Initially, they travelled back and forth to India, but slowly they settled in East Africa and invited their brothers and sisters, wives, and children to join them. The general migration history of Asian East Africans is well documented. Long before East Africa was 'discovered' by Europeans, Zanzibar and the East African coast were well-known trading destinations for Arabs and South Asians. Trading relations were strengthened with the establishment of the British Empire in East Africa. In the period between 1880 and 1920, the number of South Asians in East Africa grew from about 6,000 to 54,000. These included Hindus (among them well-known business communities like Patels, Lohanas, and Shahs), Muslims (especially Ithnasheries, Bohras, Ismailis), Sikhs, Goans, and others. The various Asian business communities that arrived in the late nineteenth century developed far more intimate social and economic relationships with each other than they did in India. These linkages resulted in new business habits, marriage policies and forms of capital accumulation. Their shared knowledge of the Gujarati language and their minority status (never more than 2 per cent of the total population in East Africa, somewhat higher in the main trading ports) in a new society played an important role in this process. Despite the development of intimate social economic links, inter-caste marriages and marriages between Hindus and Muslims were still uncommon. The Muslims settled earlier with their families than Hindus owingto the Hindu taboo on travel overseas. Upper-caste Hindu men considered Africa to be 'alien' and 'unsafe' for women, and believed that women would be better off if they stayed behind in their own extended households in India. Owing to economic and social uncertainty in East Africa, Hindu women often remained behind in India to look after their parents-in-law, children and property, and to take care of their children's education. The unmarried Hindu men generally went back to India to marry, and their wives stayed behind from the outset, with the men making frequent trips back and forth. In other cases, the women came to the East African coast for a few years, returning to India to give birth, where they then generally remained for the next 10 to 20 years, until their children finished their educations.

In this article, I focus solely on Hindu Lohana families. The research was based on the history of twenty Hindu Lohana families who have lived in East Africa for three or more generations. The results of this research are particularly accurate for Dares Salaam and the Coastal Region, where most of the interviews were conducted. Wherever relevant, I discuss the variation among and within the various families and relate these families to the more ideal type of family. Furthermore, archival material has been added, especially data related to the educational and language policies of the German and British colonial governments. In general, the development of Indian education in East Africa is a much-neglected area of research. At best, it is hinted at in general histories on Asians in East Africa. Moreover, the use of sometimes very valuable German sources in the Tanganyika National Archives (TNA) is rare because of the language problems faced by many English- and/or Swahili-speaking scholars.

This article is the first attempt to fill this gap. I also argue that there is a need to study language adaptation as a local 'bottom-up' process; local, in the sense of a well-defined geographical and historical area and 'bottom-up' in the sense that we choose to take the perspective of the 'agent', the one who accepts, refuses or mixes new language opportunities. By pursuing this perspective, we may gather a view of how the 'range of choices' is defined by the actors of change themselves. This may provide us with insights into the economic and cultural agendas of individuals as well as groups in a fast changing economic and cultural environment. My argumentation is divided into five sections. First, we introduce the general migration history of South Asians in East Africa. Here the main focus will be on the absence of Hindu women in East Africa. The second section looks at the life histories of early Lohana migrants who settled in East Africa between 1880 and 1920. Here, the main aim is to show the emphasis on their knowledge of reading and writing Gujarati. The third section highlights the second-generation Lohanas' efforts to establish 'Indian Schools' that would teach Indian languages. The fourth section coincides with a dramatic shift in the colonial history of East Africa, when the East African colonies became the independent countries of Uganda, Tanzania, and Kenya. These countries no longer subsidised Indian schools, so this option was no longer available. Hindu Lohanas opted for English-language education, and the third generation eventually 'forgot' how to read and write Gujarati. In the fifth and final section, I emphasise the consequences of these findings in relation to the discourses around the diaspora concept. Migration and Settlement of South Asians in East Africa In the nineteenth century, trade between South Asia and East Africa was constrained by the rhythm of the monsoons. From November to March, the famous, beautiful dhows sailed from West India to East Africa and between April and October, they made the return journey. The trade in cotton textiles, ivory, and spices was profitable but dangerous. Many traders did not return home safely. Rough seas, pirates, and various diseases took the lives of many traders and early adventurers.

The First Generation: Reading, Writing, and Speaking Gujarati

The first generation of Hindu Lohanas in East Africa were born between 1880 and 1920 in Gujarat, western India. Most of them received at least their primary educations in their homeland. They were able to read, write, and speak Gujarati and some had a little knowledge of English when they arrived in East Africa. Others travelled as young boys with their fathers and received some primary education in East Africa. An example is Sunderjibhai Damordas, a ninety-nine year old Hindu Lohana.

The migration history of Sunderjibhai follows the familiar pattern of his community to East Africa. In 1916, at the age of ten,he arrived in Zanzibar together with his father, Nanjibhai Damordar. They were asked to look after the shop of a relative, Kesawji Dewanji, whose sons didn't want to settle in East Africa and returned to India.

Formal and informal education played an important role in the lives of the pioneers. Most respondents recalled their primary and secondary schools. As might be expected, some received part of their education in India, whereas others were educated in East Africa exclusively. Sunderjibhai recalls that he had just finished King Readers II when he left school in Mombassa, i.e., his English was very poor at that time. However, he already knew how to read and write Gujarati, having learned it in Gujarat.

The Christian missionaries in East Africa had little interest in South Asians. Nevertheless, they could not afford to let them remain uneducated. They were middlemen between the economy of the West and the Swahili farmers. They therefore took a great interest in educating their children and started their own schools from the moment Gujaratis settled in East Africa.20 During the colonial period, Sunderji and most other South Asians in East Africa went to so-called 'Indian schools', where they were taught to read and write their 'own' languages. Though many schools were intended for certain communities or founded by religious institutions, others served a wide range of students of various backgrounds.21 Most of my respondents remembered that they had attended 'Indian schools' where Hindus and Muslims sat together. Many of these schools were (partly) financed by the prosperous South Asian business community and colonial governments. The colonial governments welcomed such initiatives by South Asians wholeheartedly.

One may here record a tribute of appreciation to the voluntary efforts that the Indian community has made throughout the Territory to provide some form of education, however poor, for its children. It is a tribute to their sense of responsibility towards the rising generation. In India people are well accustomed to the principle of providing at their own cost some kind of education for their children.......

It is difficult to judge the accusations of irregularities and illegal business practices, because most of the evidence comes from colonial officials who, generally, supported European interests. For example,

It is the opinion of the Europeans entrusted with Indian business relations that 30 per cent of the Indians of Kilwa and Mohorro become bankrupt as soon as accounting becomes obligatory (...). They always receive new credit from their fellow believers. Scarcely a month passes when Indians do not come forth to declare themselves bankrupt in one or other city of our colony. They gladly pay 200 rupees of the establishment tax.

Whether this is true or not, these accusations played a major role in the development of colonial policies towards the use of Gujarati account books and the teaching of Gujarati, English, and German in primary and secondary schools.

Meanwhile, the new Indian Association had taken up the 'language matter'. The secretary of the Indian Association reminded the British Chief Secretary in Dar es Salaam, Tanganyika, that,

My Association has also taken the trouble of making enquiries in Uganda regarding the matter and we are informed that even there it is permissible to keep such books in Gujarati amongst other languages.

In my view, the South Asian businessmen used the 'language' argument instrumentally in order to minimise colonial government interference. Tax avoidance and the misuse of trading licenses were just a small part of this. More importantly, I assume, was the desire to keep the 'social distance' between the legislators and the traders at a level that would allow them to outplay the legislators. Most of my informants in Dar es Salaam do not hesitate to state that they made 'fair deals' with the South Asian clerks regarding taxes without ever showing any of their accounting books. At the same time, raising taxes and checking accounting books was only an excuse by the colonial government to defend the interests of European firms in the area. This seems to have been the major reason behind proposed legislation, particularly during the German colonial period in Tanganyika.

In short, and as expected, the first generation of Hindu Lohana Gujarati businessmen could already read, write, and speak Gujarati when they arrived in East Africa. They kept their business records in Gujarati, except for a few larger firms, which kept them in English. The first-generation South Asians started to build educational institutions where the vernacular language would be Gujarati. Nevertheless, this was challenged in the following period by the colonial rulers who succeeded in making English the most important subject in the curriculum.

The Second Generation: Speaking and Reading Gujarati

The second-generation Hindu Lohanas in East Africa were born in East Africa in the period between 1920 and 1960. Manilal Sunderji Damordar is the third son of Sunderjibhai. He speaks fluent Gujarati, is able to read Gujarati but has difficulties in writing it. He was born in Dar es Salaam and had his primary and secondary educations there. He went to London in the 1960s to study for his university degree in commerce. He is fluent in English. Most of this generation learned to read and write Gujarati and English in the colony's 'Indian schools'.

As the British could not provide the education they wished to in the territories, they were happy with South Asian initiatives to build schools throughout the country. In general, the level of Indian education was sufficient and could easily bear comparison with most missionary schools. However, the colonial government was unhappy with the fact that in most Indian schools, the vernacular language remained Gujarat, while English was only treated as a subject. While the government was willing to promote the education of Indians in the colony, one important condition was that the vernacular language be English as well. In the words of R. Smith, the Director of Education in Dar es Salaam,

The medium of elementary education is the language of the country, but as the Indian Communities wish to maintain their identity by continuing to encourage the use of Gujarati for commercial purposes I warned them that it is not improbable that Government will decide to assist only in schools where English is taught.

In 1925, the Colonial Government was still arguing that the Gujarati language was mainly used for commercial purposes among South Asian traders and that the government therefore should not support Indian education unconditionally. Nevertheless, this reasoning lost out in favor of a new argument. The Colonial Government started to emphasize that their main interest was the development of the country, especially the Africans. Therefore, the education of Indians was not at the top of their agendas. Nevertheless, they were willing to support other groups as well. A remarkable conflict of interests between the colonial government and the South Asian settlers emerged. The colonial government demanded that education to be either in English or Swahili (or even in German, in German Tanganyika), whereas the settlers again opted for their own language. This conflict of interests was particularly intense during periods when there was a shortage of funds on both sides.

However, before this request could be granted, the British colonial officials had to develop their own educational priorities, conditions for funding, and legislation. The following topics and questions appeared in formal and informal correspondence:

- whether special education for Indians was desirable at all. Were not large numbers of South Asians returning to India anyway? In other words, 'African' tax money should not be wasted on temporary migrants;
- legislation that accounting should be kept in Roman alphabet with Arabic numbers in
- other words, not in Gujarati;
- whether the quality of the buildings, educational materials, and the teachers were adequate, and
- whether the colonial government should support education in the Gujarati language and, if so, up to what level?

The Lok Tilak Memorial School was lucky until the early 1930s to receive some ad-hoc funding from the government. The grants never amounted to more than fifty per cent of the total operating costs, however. The main source of income came from the parents of the children and generous contributions from the South Asian business community. This period of financial uncertainty would not end until a definite education policy was developed in 1937.

On the question of language, the general feeling among colonial officials was well formulated by the General Governor of Tanganyika, Donald Cameron, in a confidential letter to L.C.N.C. Amery (Member of the British Parliament):

I am in favor of grants-in-aid being made to Indian schools under a grant-code when it is prepared, but only in respect of education imparted in English. The teaching of Gujarati to Indian children is not to the general benefit of Tanganyika and for that reason I consider that assistance to it from public funds is not justified.

Nevertheless, teaching in Gujarati was an important issue for the Gujarati community. The language became an instrumental symbol for

Gujarati culture in the case of the Kitui Indian School in Moshi. This school was so small that the Education Officer opted for amalgamation with the Arab School. The South Asians were furious and argued fiercely that the:

Kitui Indian School is a Gujarati Primary School, running up to standard V. Its main language is Gujarati and all the subjects is being taught in Gujarati…. The Indian Community is not willing at all to enroll Arab boys in their Gujarati Primary School and is also unwilling to have a combined school for there is a vast difference in Indians and Arabs culture and behavior.

From the correspondence it is not clear what is meant by the 'vast difference in South Asian and Arab culture', though some hints are made elsewhere that the differences are related to the unwillingness of South Asians to have combined classes (South Asians and Arabs), especially with regard to South Asian girls.

This is confirmed by some figures, however sketchy, from the 1931 census report, which stated that more than one-fifth of the Tanganyika South Asians were able to speak English, whereas more than 75 per cent stated that they could not (the remaining 5 per cent did not answer the question on language). Furthermore, the report stated that about half of the South Asian population was able to read and write Gujarati, whereas only 5 per cent could read and write English. However, competency in the English language grew rapidly in the years to come.

In 2000, although Manilal Sunderji Damordar spoke and read Gujarati, he had difficulty with writing it. He did not show the same interest in Gujarati newspapers as his father had. He had not subscribed to any of the Gujarati newspapers or magazines. His English was fluent and he kept his business correspondence in English. Sometimes, however, when he wrote his father, he made an effort to formulate at least a few sentences in Gujarati. With other Gujarati businessmen of his generation he spoke Gujarati, sometimes mixing in a few English words. At home, he spoke Gujarati with his wife and children; and while his wife would respond in Gujarati, his children usually responded in English.

The Third Generation: Speaking Gujarati

Third-generation Hindu Lohanas were raised in East Africa in the period 1960-2000. One day, I was invited to a Gujarati dinner at the

Damordar house. There I noticed that Gujarati was being spoken. Manilal Sunderji Damordar spoke Gujarati with his wife and his son, (22 years old) and daughter Shrutti (20 years). They responded to their father in Gujarati; however, Jivraj and Shrutti spoke English with each other and immediately admitted that they could neither read nor write Gujarati. Jivraj even admitted that he was unable to follow Gujarati lecture sat the temple. His mother was especially concerned about this.

Jivraj and Shrutti were born after the independence of the East African nations (Uganda, Kenya and Tanganyika in 1961-1962). By this time, there were no longer any 'Indian schools' that could provide the basic knowledge required for writing and reading Gujarati. In Kenya and Uganda, they would have been taught in English; while in Tanzania, Swahili became the language used in schools. Interestingly, the South Asian business community did not attempt to provide their community with language classes. They must have realised that their economic outlook was 'international' and not 'South Asian'. This was a consequence of their economic re-orientation towards the UK and the West in general, and the political events of the early 1960s (independence) and early 1970s (expulsion of Asians by Idi Amin). Theseevents made them realise that the English language had become a necessity. However, some religious institutions advocated separate religious classes. In this context, most Hindu Lohanas chose to send their children to schools in which English was the chief language or – if they could afford it – to the International School in Dar es Salaam.

Jivraj and Shrutti attended the International School in Dar es Salaam. Their English was perfect and their pronunciation was almost 'Oxford English', without the typical 'Indian' accent. Both of them admitted that they only ever spoke Gujarati at home with their parents, grandparents, or other elderly relations. Sometimes they used it as a secret language on school playgrounds when they did not want others to overhear what they were talking about. For them, knowledge of Gujarati was not an important part of their identity, although they did state that they felt 'Indian'. This feeling of being 'Indian' was reflected in their food and dress habits, but not in their language use. It is interesting to note that a part of this 'Indianness' was related to the Hindi language, because both of them liked to listen to Hindi Music and watch Hindi movies, which they could actually barely understand.

After interviewing them several times, we started corresponding via e-mail. They were studying in the UK and I was interested in their choice of food and their dress habits while they were abroad. During this correspondence, they began thinking more about their identities and background. One day, I asked them about their dress habits in the UK, Shrutti wrote:

Turning to Indian wear ... i [sic] do wear a simple salwaar (don't know how to spell it!!! how shameful! around the house. I find it comfortable and easy to wash and wear. The only time I would wear Indian out of the house in uk is when there is a special Indian occasion or ball (which is about once-twice a year).

Many members of the Lohana community in East Africa realise that knowledge of Gujarati is fading. Therefore, they encourage Gujarati language lessons on temple premises. Some (grand)parents try to teach their (grand)children Gujarati by introducing private tutors and extra language lessons. Nevertheless, I did not come across a single person of this generation who was born and/or lived in East Africa who could read and write in Gujarati. The knowledge of Gujarati is fading fast and is being replaced by English. Jivraj notes that:

My parents are proud of us when we know all the religious functions, despite the fact that we went to the International School. So we stayed in touch with our culture. They feel sorry that we are not able to read and write our language anymore. Because it would enable us to attend more lectures from the Gurus from India

Therefore, they agree that English should be the language used in school. Despite of all this, however, Gujarati is still considered the mother tongue by this third generation, and it plays an important role in the construction of identity. The question remains how many more generations it will take before this language is lost and English is accepted as the 'mother tongue'.

Conclusion

In this study, I have investigated the loss of the ability to read, write, and speak Gujarati among the Hindu Lohana community in East Africa and the increased importance of English among the various generations. The first generation of Hindu Lohanas in East Africa still speaks, writes, and reads Gujarati fluently; the second generation speaks and reads

Gujarati ,while the third generation may speak Gujarati at home with the (grand)parents, they are unable to read or write it. This youngest generation has developed a preference for English. This development occurred despite massive state intervention. Colonial officials needed the Asians to read and write in English in order to present their accounting books. The Hindu Lohanas successfully refused to do so. Nevertheless, the Lohanas developed the habit of reading and writing English just prior to the independence of the East African nations, in the period when not English, but Swahili was being promoted. This shows that the Gujaratis have had control over their 'identity' creation. This 'identity' creation was not a desire to 'hold onto tradition' and 'maintain the traditional language', nor was it part of the 'assimilation' into the local – i.e., Swahili – culture. These Hindu Lohana businessmen chose to become 'international' and opted for the English language.

Despite the concerns of elderly members of the community, Gujarati was replaced by English. One Hindu religious leader suggested that 'we may have lost our gift of expression', but many businessmen would reply 'but we gained a more international outlook'. Previously, I have described the development of an Asian African identity among Hindu Lohanas in East Africa, which was based on changing food and drinking habits in particular.51 The conclusions of that article are confirmed here. After three generations, the Hindu Lohana community in East Africa has developed a unique, self-determined combination of Swahili, European, and South Asian elements. This community does not identify with the Indian diaspora nor with the culture of their ancestors in India.52 Their home is Africa and their outlook is 'international'. In other words, the diaspora concept, with its emphasis on 'rootedness, the homeland, the reproduction of Indian culture abroad,' cannot help us to understand the history of the Lohana community in East Africa. Therefore, I again emphasize there is a further need to study these communities from a 'local bottom-up' angle.

References

1. The 'cultural baggage' of Asians in East Africa is: C. Salvadori, Through open Doors: A view of Asian Cultures in Kenya, Nairobi 1983.
2. W. Safran, 'Diasporas in modern societies: myths of homeland and return', Diasporas (1) 1991, 83- 99, S. Vertovec, The Hindu Diaspora: Comparative Patterns, London: Routledge 200

3. Hindu Lohanas in East Africa come from the rural districts of Cutch and Kathiawar (Gujarat, western India). They were traditionally laborers, masons, husbandmen, shopkeepers, and traders. Their history is related to that of one of the Kshatria (warrior) castes, which in ancient times was called Lavan. The plural form of this was Lavanam and, over a period of time, it changed first to Lavana and finally to Lohana. In the nineteenth century, many turned to weaving and textile trading. Those in Kathiawar were especially well established as maritime traders and many were doing business in Oman. When the Sultan of Oman moved his headquarters from Musquat to Zanzibar (1832), Lohana traders quickly followed him and set up shops there. From there, they spread to the mainland from 1885 onwards.

4. Robert G. Gregory, Quest for Equality: Asian Politics in East Africa, 1900-1967, New Delhi 1993, p. 13.

5. C. Voigt-Graf, Asian Communities in Tanzania: A Journey Through Past and Present Times, Hamburg 1998, p. 53.

6. The migration history of Asian East Africans is well documented. In general, it is suggested that there is a long history of trading relations between East Africa and South Asia. Long before East Africa was 'discovered' by Europeans, Zanzibar, Mombassa, and Kilwa were well-known trading ports for Arabs and South Asians. These trading relations were strengthened during the establishment of the British Empire in East Africa. A number of Indian indentured laborers supplemented the trading diaspora. In the period between 1880 and 1920, the number of South Asians in East Africa grew from about 6,000 to 54,000. These included Hindus (among them wellknown business communities like Patels, Lohanas, and Shahs), Muslims, Sikhs, Goans, and others. R. Gregory, South Asians in East Africa; R. Gregory.

7. The Indian Association to Chief Secretary in Dar es Salaam, 5 April 1933, TNA 11.660 p. 244

8. Dar es Salaam report cited in G. Hornsby, 'German Educational Achievement in East Africa', in Tanganyika Notes and Records (62) 1964, p. 86.

9. Third-generation Hindus in the Netherlands like and watch Hindi movies, but have established a preference for the Dutch language. Avoird, Determining language, p. 162.

10. Several authors reveal that, in Britain, Gujaratis from East Africa (who arrived in the 1960s and early 1970s) were more educated than those who had migrated directly from Gujarat. This may be attributed to their class background and their access to better education. T. Van der Avoird, Determining Language Vitality: The Language use of Hindu communities in the Netherlands and the United Kingdom, Tilburg 2001, p3. H.S. Morris, The Indians in Uganda, London 1968, p. 19.

11. G. Oonk, 'The Changing Culture of the Hindu Lohana community in East Africa,' Contemporary South Asia 13 (1) 2004, 7-23.

12. G. Oonk, 'After Shaking his Hand Start Counting Your Fingers.' Trust and Images in Indian Business Networks, East Africa 1900-2000, Itinerario XXVIII (3) 2004, 70-88.

21

History and The Unvoiced Struggl from The Margin: Rohinton Mistry's Appeal for a Fine Balance

Ambarish Sen

Assistant Professor of English

Barasat Govt. College

The concept of Indian Diaspora has its concomitant origin with the emerging post-colonial literature in India as well as abroad. Since 1980s the Indian diasporic writers started writing of their motherland from exile and expressed their own feelings, response and concern with divergent issues of Indian society, politics, culture and religion. Their aim is to portray the motherland in their own way within the broader socio-cultural background of emerging global scenario. So the nomenclature Diaspora does have its historical, cultural as well as political connotation.

The post independent Indian society has its own problems originating from cultural, political or religious differences. The problems in the villages are much more terrible and grave than its urban counterpart. In the villages casteism makes the life of poor marginals or the working class miserable. Mistry's sympathetic depiction of the tragic cycle of Dukhi Mochi's family reinforces the fact further that India can never reach its goal unless caste hatred or caste tension is abolished. The movement that has been launched by Dr. Babasaheb Vimrao Ambedkar still continues and has not been fulfilled after 30 yrs of independence.

Rohinton Mistry is a representative voice of contemporary Indian Diaspora and a glowing star in the cosmos of Indo-Anglican fiction. In the post *Midnight's Children* era Mistry along with a few other leading novelists emerged with their attempt to explore the leading trends of Indian society within the subjectivity of their diasporic consciousness. The problematics of diasporic writing consist of the novelists' vision of alienation, rootlessness and socio-political marginalization in the mother land as well as in the exile society or the country they inhabit. Rohinton Mistry like Salman Rushdie, Amitav Ghosh or V.S.Naipaul foregrounds into their fiction the agonized voice of such social, intellectual, cultural and political alienation. Their works result from a profound melancholy and a sense of nostalgia for the homeland as well as a quest for identity within the dominant social structure. Often they aim at revisiting history of their native land and render fictionalized account of the past through recollections or personal response. Unlike Rushdie, Rohinton Mistry aims at revisiting Indian society projecting into the center of his narratives several maladies and problems that are prevalent down the ages. As a post-colonial Indo-Anglican novelist Mistry delves deep into the composite nature of Indian society in order to give a fictionalized rendering of its major problems, evils and anti-progressive factors.

In this paper I would like to concentrate upon Mistry's depiction of Indian society and his projection of the story of struggling marginals – his recreation and sympathetic projection of their misery, disempowerment and untold sufferings. Mistry provides a humanistic treatment to the poor marginals – their ceaseless struggle against the parochial, anti-humanitarian trends in the rural as well as urban society. His is a subject that remains ever beyond the official archive of elitist construct of social history. My aim is to deal with the story of the struggling marginals who receive heart rending and sensitive treatment in Mistry's stories. My central aim in this paper will be to isolate several episodes of Mistry's novels that will be helpful to substantiate my point. In order to restrict my discussion within a limited compass I would like to keep confined within a critical study of his second and perhaps the most representative novel *A Fine Balance.* Although, Mistry's central thematic concern is the alienation of Parsi community within the Indian society and their marginalization across the generation, yet in *A Fine Balance* he broadens his canvass and encompasses the problem of a larger Indian society – it's inhuman caste hatred, poverty and arbitrary political design that make a thousand, homeless wanderers and victims of fate.

Rohinton Mistry was born in 1952 in Mumbai, India. He earned a BA in Mathematics and Economics at the University of Mumbai. He emigrated to Canada with his wife in 1975, settling in Toronto where he studied at the University of Toronto and received a BA in English and Philosophy. The first important writing of his career is the *Tales from Firozsha Baag,* which was published in 1989. When his second book, the novel *Such a Long Journey*, was published in 1991, it won the Governor General's Award, the Commonwealth for Best Book, and the W.H. Smith/Books in Canada First Novel Award. It was shortlisted for the prestigious Booker Prize and for the Trillium Award. The next important land mark in his writing career is *A Fine Balance* published in the year 1995 and won the second annual Giller Prize in 1995 and was shortlisted for the 1996 Booker prize. His next important novel *Family Matters* was published around May 2002. In his works Mistry deals with the alienation of Parsi community in the Indian society, particularly in the Western region and their age old marginalization. He also explores the social imbalances created by poverty, oppression, casteism and several other problems.

His novels demonstrate through the stories of alien individuals or community, the age old oppression and struggle of the disempowered marginals due to ethnic, economic, social, political and cultural exploitation. The empathetic concern for the oppressed, exploited and miserable section of the society recur in his works. His novels are imbued with intense human significance. He feels himself to be struggling for identity both in his motherland as well as in the immigrant country. He thinks himself to be doubly marginalized as a member of Parsi community and as a marginalized immigrant intellectuals struggling hard under the pangs of existential dilemma and identity crisis. P. Selvam in the book *Humanism in the Novels of Rohinto Mistry* writes – " As a Parsi and then as an immigrant in Canada, he sees himself as a symbol of double displacement. And this sense of displacement is a recurrent theme in his literary works" (p.18).

He projects his own melancholia and ceaseless quest for identity into the persona of his protagonists who represent similar struggle to combat with existing social oppression and ethnic or cultural alienation. Thus Mistry aims at articulating and legitimizing the voice of the oppressed and substantiates their claim for inclusion into mainstream life through his novels. In my view Mistry's novels are patterned around empowerment in a world that denies individual voices. They bring into foreground parental authority, class hierarchies, personal betrayal, political supremacy, and corruption. His fiction also depicts superstition and physical or mental limitations. He is more interested in revealing the problems of the untouchables, the poor people who stand at the bottom of the society and their suppressed condition by the class, upper caste, and the politicians, through fiction.

In the life of my above thematic observation let me now concentrate upon a fine balance which deals with and exposes most of the above thematic aspects in a comprehensive and plausibly realistic way. In this novel he powerfully articulates the agony of the oppressed sections who are denied their legitimate human dignity as the members of oppressed marginals in the society.

A Fine Balance is set in India in the mid-1970s. It tells how the lives of four ordinary people are overturned by the Emergency, a period of political turmoil and violence. Initially the book focuses on Dina Shroff, who was raised by her strict brother after her father died. She discovers a series of concerts, where she meets Rustom Dalal. The couple fall in love and marry, but on their third wedding anniversary Rustom is killed in a bicycle accident, leaving Dina alone. Rustom's aunt teaches Dina to sew, but her eyesight begins to fail, so she is forced to find another way to make money. Her friend Zenobia introduces her to Mrs Gupta, who offers her some tailoring piece work. She hires Ishvar Darji and his nephew Omprakash, originally from a small village, to do the work.

Ishvar's father was of a low Hindu caste, doing dirty leather work, and he suffered horrendous caste violence. He wanted a better life for his sons and so sent them to a neighbouring town to learn to be tailors. They became the apprentices of Muslim tailor Ashraf. But when Ishvar was seventeen, racial hatred of Muslims reached boiling point and any homes or shops belonging to Muslims were burnt to the ground. Ishvar and his brother Narayan saved Ashraf's shop by claiming it belonged to them, leaving Ashraf forever in their debt. Narayan returned to the village and set up a successful tailor business for lower caste people, refusing to serve those of higher caste. He married and had a son, Omprakash, and two daughters. His business was very successful and it gave him enough money to build a proper house. All was going well until Narayan discovered that the elections were being fixed by Thakur Dharamsi, a powerful land owner. Narayan confronted Thakur, who had him tortured. Not satisfied with just killing Narayan, Thakur decided to punish his whole family. Narayan's wife, daughters and parents were tied up and burnt alive in their home. Omprakesh and Ishvar were the only ones to escape. Shocked but safe, they continued working in their tailor shop, but were forced out of business when a ready-made clothing shop opened in the town.

The fourth central character is Maneck. He grew up in a mountain village, where his father was the proud owner of the local village store and inventor of a popular drink, Kohlah Cola. Maneck was sent to college. Due to various problems faced by Maneck in the college hostel and the declaration of Emergency Maneck had to shift to Dina dalal's rented flat as a paying guest arranged by his mother who was a school friend of Dina. The four characters are thus united in Dina's house and start living together through thick and thin. They are quite happy for almost a year, but then the Emergency starts to impact their lives. The tailor's shack is demolished in a government beautification program, forcing them to live on the streets. The tailors are then rounded up by the police and sold to a labour camp. After two months they bribe their way out and persuade Dina to let them move in with her. Ishvar decides it is time for Om to find a wife, so they return to Ashraf's town. There they bump into Thakur, who recognises the pair. He arranges for them to be rounded up by the Family Planning Centre. Ashraf is beaten to death and Ishvar and Om are given compulsory vasectomies. Thakur visits them as they are recovering from the operation and arranges on a medical pretext to have Om's testicles removed. Ishvar's legs become infected and have to be amputated. Maneck finishes his college course and returns home. His father's business is failing due to cheap imports of commercial soda, and Maneck decides to leave, taking a job in the Middle East. Dina finds herself all alone. A Beggarmaster who had been protecting her from her landlord's bailiffs is murdered, leaving her vulnerable; she reluctantly returns to live with her brother. Eight years later, Maneck returns home for his father's funeral. Riots are taking place and Sikhs are being persecuted because the Prime Minister was assassinated by one of her Sikh bodyguards. Maneck reads some old newspapers and discovers that his intimate college friend and a political activist Avinash was found dead by the side of a railway track and Avinash's three teenage sisters hanged themselves because their parents could not afford their wedding dowries.

Distraught, Maneck decides to visit Dina. She explains that Ishvar lost his legs and that the tailors are now beggars. Horrified, Maneck leaves Dina's house, pretending not to recognize the tailors in the street, and heads for the railway station where he steps in front of a train. The book ends with the tailors having an up-beat conversation with Dina. Thus the aspiring journey for the four central characters brings them down to utter disaster and the narrative closes on a bitter tragic note. It is the mechanism of the inscrutable destiny that all the four characters end their voyage either in complete obliteration through death or a life in death existence with complete psychophysical collapse.

The story in *A Fine Balance,* revolves around the small mobile widow living alone in the city of Bombay. The three threads of the narrative involving the upward journey of three other principal characters, develop side by side and are woven together and united when Maneck and the two tailors take shelter at Dina's rented flat. Maneck comes to city to study refrigeration from a hill station in northern India and becomes Dina's paying guest while Ishrer and Omprakash start working as her tailors. The four starts living together and are united on a common platform of humanity. The problems of urban life and rising political turmoil bring down complication to their otherwise peaceful coexistence. They are the four innocents crabbed in the smashing gears of history in *A Fine Balance.*

The story is set against the political backdrop of notorious Emergency of 1975 that brings a sweeping transformation in the socio-political and economic structure of the country. In the face of this sociopolitical upheaval Mistry tells the story of these four hapless protagonists who are uprooted and swept apart by this sweeping socio-political cataclysm. During the internal Emergency of 1975 when Prime Minister Mrs Gandhi suspends the civic rights and constitutional facilities of common man in order to save her narrow political interest. It brings unforeseen torture and sadness to millions of ordinary Indians. Here Mistry presents shards of history and the callousness and corruption before, during and immediately after the Emergency.

The novel offers a wonderful intermingling of history and the personal lives of the marginalized persons. He deals with the stories of the ordinary individuals against the complex backdrop of history and does so from his immigrant and diasporic consciousness. In the process of telling the stories of four ordinary individuals, Mistry offers a critic of the socio-political turmoil that makes their lives miserable. The four principal characters represent four different worlds or cross sections of society and the novelist skillfully interlinks them. The first is the middle class, urban world of Dina Dalal, a pretty widow in her forties. Then, there is a glimpse into rural India provided by Ishvar Darji and his nephew Omprakash. There is another world symbolized by Maneck Kohlah, a sensitive Parsi boy from mountains of the North. Mistry observes the dominant trends and alarming problems of contemporary Indian society in its totality. The two tailors' world is the world of rural India, harassed and disturbed by age old caste system, poverty, exploitation, and oppression. Maneck and Dina on the other hand, represent the maladies of urban life and the growing tension in the lives of emerging middle class.

Ishvar and Omprakash are from poor chammars –the accursed untouchables in the village life. Ishvar's father Dukhi and his wife Roopa had to undergo tremendous psychophysical torture in the hands of upper-class Zamindars and village heads like Thakur Dharamsi. Poverty joined hands to social exploitation to multiply their misery. The members of untouchable section were engaged by the village Zamindars to work in their lands or household at a vary meager wages. They took full advantage of their landlessness and poverty. If the poor labourer failed to finish the assigned task within the given time, they were denied the wages and sometimes even were tortured and exploited in various ways. Mistry depicts such inhuman treatment upon the poor villagers with penetrating appeal and poignant human significance. The passage that I am going to site here is worth quoting in this context –

The Thakur's wife was watching from the kitchen window, Oiee, my husband! Come quick! She screamed. "The chamar donkey has destroyed our mortar". What have you done, you witless animal! Is this what I hired you for? "I swear on the heads of my children", begged Dukhi, "I was only pounding chillies, as I have done all day. Look Thakurji, the sack is almost empty, the work_". Get up! Leave my land at once! I never want to see you again!..."But, Thakurji, the work_"...He hit Dukhi across the back with his stick. "Get up, I said! And get out!...Thakurji, have pity, there has been no work for days, I don't_"...Listen, you stinking dog! You have destroyed my property, yet I am letting you off! If I wasn't such a soft hearted fool, I would hand you to the police for your crime. Now get out!(Mistry, Rohinton. *A Fine Balance*.p.104).

Mistry powerfully depicts their struggle and bitter experience in the light of humanity. Their son Ishver and grandson Omprakash, two rural untouchables struggle to rise above their designated caste roles and better themselves by becoming tailors. They have to endure the atrocities of the so-called high class people and their future is bleak.

Dukhi Mochi takes the decision of sending his two sons Ishvar and Narayan to the town to be apprenticed to tailoring. The decision Dukhi takes is to save his sons from the humiliation in the village life. It is an act of silent rebellion against the curse of untouchability and is symbolic of a transgression from age old social and professional discrimination. This progressive attitude from an illiterate village Chammar also symbolizes the radical transformation of the society and a shift in the attitude. Through this, Mistry hints at the silent resistance of the subaltern against the age old social structure and the repressive caste hatred.

The aim behind this radical decision of changing the profession is to ameliorate their plight and to provide a better future for the subsequent generations. It is symbolic of those myriad underprivileged Indians who, due to economic and social reasons, are disempowered and displaced from their familiar world. Even after they become fully qualified tailors and return to their village, they cannot extricate themselves from the brutal tyranny of class or caste prejudice. The untouchables were not allowed to cast their vote rightfully in those days. After being literate, Ishvar's brother Narayan protests against this repressive system and wants to cast his legitimate vote. He along with a few of his neighbours goes to the election camp and demand to be allowed to exercise their basic right. This infuriated Thakur Dharamasi and he employs his ruffians to destroy Narayan and his family. The offence that Dukhi Moachi did by stepping out of his predestined profession has multiplied by Isvar and Narayan's success as tailors and their strong resistance to the repressive whims of upper-class villagers which even goes to the extent of denying the poor illiterates their basic constitutional writes.

One dark night Thakur's Gundas stormed into Narayan's house and inhuman brutality was perpetrated on the family. With specific instruction the Hooligans tortured Narayan, his old parents Dukhi and Roopa and even his wife and children. At last they burnt them alive by setting their small house on fire. Mistry's poignant description of this terrible episode goes as –

Two are missing, said Thakur Dharmasi. "Son and grandson"...well, never mind, these five will do. Only by the red birthmark on his chest could they recognize Narayan. A long howl broke from Radha. But the sound of grief soon mingled with the family's death agony; the house was set alight. The first flames licked at the bound flesh. The dry winds, furiously fanning the fire, showed the only spark of mercy during this night. The blaze swiftly enfolded all six of them. (p.147)

The journey of the two struggling tailors from village to town then to city correspond to the gradual development of human society from rural to urban :- from village to town and then to city. In the town and city life the tailors confront new set of bitter sweet experiences. Their struggle becomes tougher and rigorous as they have to move in search of a roof under their head. They are overwhelmed to see the callousness, inhumanity and selfishness of the city people. Through the chapters depicting their life in the slum (jhaopatti), Mistry suggests the poor living condition, the lack of health and hygiene in the densely populated city slum and the terrible face of poverty. His sociological concern and commitment to humanity is evident in his depiction of the tailors multiplying misery and the indifference of the city dwellers towards their rootless village counterparts. Ishvar and Omprakash have to move from door to door in search of a shelter and employment before they meet Dina Dalal. Their quest takes a new turn on their first days in Bombay. Mistry's stories depict his birth place Bombay with its dense population, problems of urbanization and similar other sociopolitical tensions of modern metropolis. The city serves as an appropriate symbolic backdrop to his tales of human sufferings and his pictures are plausibly realistic.

In the midst of inhumanity of city dwellers and selfish indifference of the city dwellers blossom the flower of love and solidarity in the figure of Asraf Chacha their mentor, Dina, Maneck and to some extent the beggar master. Asraf looked after them as his own sons, gave them food and shelter and taught them the skill of tailoring to earn their bread in the city. The tailors always remembered his generosity and saved him and his wife at the risk of their own lives when communal riot broke out. Mistry suggests a note of communal harmony and human solidarity in the face of confusion, riot and anarchy. In spite of their religious difference Ishvar and Om regards Asraf as their guardian and respects him next to his father. The novelist's message is clear that humanity and fraternity proves victorious against narrow fundamentalism and sectarian or communal prejudices –

Listen, smart boy. If you are lying, I will myself skrew you on the three points of my trishul. Why should I lie? Said Ishvar. I'm the same as you. You think I want to die to save a muslim?...step on the pavement and remove your pyjamas, said the leader. Both of you. What?...There was general agreement that the fore skins were intact…What's going on? Why are you harassing Hindu boys? Have you run out of Muslims? (p.129-130)

The portrayal of Asraf, Dina Dalal and Maneck Kohola offer a sharp contrast to the general callousness, inhumanity and lack of warmth in the hearts of the city people. One may counter my argument of Dina Dalal's generosity towards the tailors as she employs them for her business purpose and during the early days of their acquaintance the relation was that of a master slave. Yet I would strongly establish the point that Dina gradually softens, and develops an emotional bond with them. She even does not hesitate to acquaint Ishvar as her husband and Om as her son to the outsiders. The one year that Ishvar, Om, Maneck and Dina spend together is the most redeeming episode of the book as well as in their lives. Mistry draws this section with genial spirit and his superb art of storytelling records graphically the trivial gossip and light hearted humour among the four. Dina Dalal is the central figure around whom the other three revolves. It is she whose indefatigable struggle against adverse socio-economic condition inspires the rests to weave the dream.

Mistry revives the remnants of his early days in Bombay the overcrowded city with filth, squalor and dirty slums with innumerable shacks and processions of half starved necked children, poverty and misery. Mistry emigrated to Canada in his youth for a better living condition and prospective future. Yet the memory of motherland in general and Bombay in particular remain vivid in his disporic consciousness. The alienation, crisis and quest for identity of his protagonists thus have symbolic reflection on the author's alienation and marginalization in the exile country/society. A sense of loss and a hunting quest motive recur in Mistry's novels and invest them with a sense of isolated struggle and futile quest. This is the leading motive behind the symbolic journey of all the four protagonists in *A Fine Balance.* Mistry's depiction of Bombay and its inhabitants against rapid socio-economic transformation echoes a similar portrayal of city life by Charles Dickens. Dickens depicts the city London against the radical sociopolitical transformation caused by the transition from Victorian to modern era. So is Mistry depicting Bombay with Dickensian reformistic enthusiasm. The tailors are caught in the complex maze of modern metropolis and its degenerated humanity. Their unadulterated soul is broken by the inhuman face of modern politics and arbitrary designs in the name of development. Mistry's criticism of emergency, and its associated governmental programs like family planning, sterilization etc. is sharp, penetrating and full of ironic innuendoes.

In the novel Mistry depicts certain diabolic and inhuman practices prevalent in the modern metropolis. They are often done to fulfill the narrow business interests of certain reach people. The beggar master runs a business with deformed beggars and earns a lot of their begging. He collects the poor street dwellers, amputates their legs, hands or eyes and leaves them on the street for begging. Mistry is poignantly critical of these diabolic practices, yet this beggar master protects Dina from the rent collector and under goes a mental change after the death of Sankar who in fact is his half brother.

The four principal characters of the novel are exposed in the centre of complex city life and their challenged is to assert their stable identity and extricate themselves from the subjugations or marginality. The readers may find my point relevant to Ishvar and Om as they are from lowest untouchables and marginalized by indigenous social structure. But I find it necessary to spend a few words on Maneck and Dina's story whose origin and background poles apart from the two tailors.

A close scrutiny of Dina Dalal's development in the novel reveals that she is doubly marginalized. Firstly, her marginalization results from the fact that that she belongs to the alien Parsi community and secondly, within the patriarchal social convention. She belongs to a well to do Parsi Family where she is repressed by her elder brother Nuswan's oppressive tyranny. She refutes her brother's objection to her marriage and goes out in search of emancipation. But it is the ironic design of destiny that she becomes a widow within three years of her marriage. She finds herself crushed under tremendous economic pressure yet she continues her honest struggle to live independently beyond the control of patriarchal authority. Her days become tougher and tougher and she finds the two tailors and

Maneck joining hands in her struggle. Her independent will and bold resistance to male domination collapses at the end of the novel as she is ruined by her ill luck. Things have changed. She is found with weak eyesight engaged in the household work at her brother's house. The "wheel of tragic cycle is full". The youthful independent Dina Dalal ends her ironic quest exactly at the point she has begun. Only connection with her struggling past remains in her humanistic bond with the two tailors turned beggars, one is legless deformed while other is castrated. The novel ends with Dina talking to the two beggars (Ishvar and Om) and feeding them secretly with warmth of heart for her defeated compatriot.

Maneck Kohola represents the idealistic youth growing in similar gusto with the young nation weaving bright dreams for future. He comes to the city to build his career as a refrigeration specialist. He symbolizes the emancipated modern youth, free from all superstations, prejudices and deadly values and customs. He gets his first emotional jolt to confront his intimate friend Avinash's active involvement in politics which ultimately proves tragically deceptive for himself as well as his family. Maneck develops an intimate relation with Om and Ishvar Darji. They eat and dream together and pass happy moments along with them and his 'Dina aunty'. He gives farewell to Dina and the two tailors and goes to Dubai to join a lucrative job. When he returns, India is undergoing a tremendous political crisis that results from the assassination of Prime Minister Mrs. Gandhi in 1984. Maneck attempts to meet Dina and his two friends but are terribly shocked and overwhelmed to see the three in great distress. He receives another blow as learns the arrest of his former friend Avinash and the suicide of his three younger sisters under dire poverty.

Maneck's end is no less disastrous than the rests. His suicide under a running train is poignant and sounds a note of defeat – "Now the express could be seen in the distance,...When the first compartment had entered the station, he stepped off the platform and onto the gleaming silver tracks....The elderly woman in dark glasses was the first to scream. Then the shriek of the pneumatic brakes drowned all other sounds. The fast train took several hundred yards to stop....Maneck's last thought was that he still had Avinash's chessmen." (p.612). His tragic end symbolizes the collapse of youthful hope and aspiration in the face of chaos, confusion, degeneration and disorder. It is the moral defeat and a psychological collapse of budding youth before the sweeping change of globalization. The narrative encompasses a brief time span of around nine years, though brief yet remarkable for the decisive political twist and turns and radical socio-economic transformation. It is the period of our recent history, marked by unrest, tension, violence and large scale urbanization. Mistry's saga opens when the country was at the threshold of a political crisis resulted from state Emergency of 1975, and it ends when the nation is also on fire immediately after the assassination of Mrs. Indira Gandhi (1984). Anti Sikh agitation and protest broke out in the major provinces, the glimpse of which we see through Maneck eyes. The novelist becomes critical of such militant activities and denounces this terrible episode as a stigma to the history of the nation – "Sikhs are the ones being massacred in the riots. For three days they have been burning Sikh shops and homes, chopping up Sikh boys and men and the police are just running about here and there, pretending to protect the neighbourhoods…our best soilders, the BSF, First line of defence against enemy invasion. Now they must guard borderlines within our cities. How shameful for the whole country"(p.570). Mistry's protagonists are exposed against the sweeping transformation of political and social milieu or against such critical juncture of history. They find themselves tangled in a subtle and complex dilemma that results from their existential search for identity and stability. Their struggle is never ending as they are helpless marginals or marginalized somehow against a broader and more comprehensive trauma of history. The two tailors are born marginals because of their lower caste origin while the other two (Dina and Maneck) are marginalized because of their involvement to a different set off socio economic values.

In the European literary tradition, novelists like Dickens, Tolstoy and many others set their narratives against major historical backdrop that affect millions of individuals. They emerged with some reformistic enthusiasm and with the objective of amelioration of certain social ills. This tendency is evident in recent Indo-Anglican writings or the fictions of Indian Diaspora. The contemporary novelists incorporate into their narratives the history of the nation in its comprehensive totality. The stories of the individuals are powerfully interwoven with massive historical upheavals. The partition novels established itself as a distinctive literary genre, poignantly depicting the trauma of partition and the subsequent turmoil. Mistry follows the tradition and attempts to render the complex episode of state Emergency and its aftermath in connection with the life of his central characters. So history is a major force behind Mistry's novels as the Indo-Pak war of 1971 (*Such a Long Journey*) and Emergency (*A Fine Balance*). He projects his central characters in the midst of great socio-historical changes to which they are the victims.

Ishvar and Om are the worst sufferer of the projects like 'City beautification', clearing of slum and sterilization for 'Family planning'. Their shacks are broken; they are evicted and taken into a distant irrigation project to work as labourers along with a thousand of helpless pavement dwellers. In the camp they are treated like beasts and after backbreaking labour, Ishvar and Om fell ill. Mistry's criticism of the then Government and its arbitrary projects is evident through the plight of the tailors. Dina and Maneck though from different origin, are also harassed by the then sociopolitical turmoil. Their life is in tune with that of the tailors and their problem unsettles Dina and Maneck emotionally. So Dina's apparent indifference to approaching Emergency and its simultaneous ripples proves to be ironic. At the end of the story we see the four suffering the same tragic blow of fate and disastrous consequences. The four begins their journey with a quest for 'a fine balance' between hope and despair, struggle and fulfillment, aspiration and contentment but they all fail. This disastrous failure leads their journey to its tragic denouement.

Mistry's narrative raises another debating issue regarding the importance of oppressed marginals in the main stream political and historical scenario of the country. The socially marginal sections are the instruments in the hands of political power. The leaders and parties use them to fulfill their narrow ends, though vary little development occurs in the lives of poor marginals. They (political party) sometimes make them the vehicle for propagating their own message and dominant political ideology and sometimes come into power with the deceptive agenda of improving the condition of the poor. This tendency has been prevalent since antiquity and in this way the history in the annals of colonial power has marginalized the indigenous culture, native tradition, customs and demands.

Mistry critically denounces such inhuman political tendencies and objectives. One of the poignant scenes in *A Fine Balance* describes crowd renting for political purposes. The poor people who were all living in the Jhopdipatis were compelled to board the bus which took them to the Prime Minister's rally. They were not forced by the party men alone but the police also joined hands with them. The Government buses were used for transporting them. The poor people had been assured of some meal and a meager amount which was less than some of the people's income for a day. The two poor tailors also happened to be a part of the crowd and they lost their one day wages unwillingly. Here Mistry shows the corrupt political scenario of India. Mistry conveys his own moral attitudes and liberal views through characters. Various episodes in the novel reveal Mistry's sympathy for the oppressed and his bitter criticism at the excesses during the period of Emergency. The nexus between the police and the established hierarchy make the life of the poor rootless miserable. They join hands together and perpetrated ruthless torture to the helpless marginals. Various arbitrary acts like MISA led to the arrest of helpless innocents without any sufficient reason.

Countless marginals such as workers, beggars and slum-dwellers are dragged out of their ramshackle dwellings under the pretext of 'City Beautification'. The upper class people notice a semblance of order during the time of Emergency. For the bourgeoisie like Mrs. Gupta Emergency means "No more strikes and morchas and silly disturbances". (p.73) Business executives like Nusswan talk of eliminating two hundred million people surplus in the country. Nusswan proclaims: "with the Emergency, people can freely speak their minds. That's another good thing about it". (p.373)

This is how Mistry attempts to explore a fine balance between his contemporary political scenario in India and its impact in the lives of disempowered marginals. His protagonists are the worst victims of the repressive National Emergency: a politically and historically sensitive episode serving as a backdrop to *A Fine Balance.* Mistry projects his own search of identity against a destabilized global network and his protagonists are the embodiments of his own quest. The novelists own diasporic alienation and nostalgic reminiscences of his homeland is ever present in the background. The struggling quest of Ishvar and Om and Maneck and Dina represents their own search for identity on the one hand, the author's on the other. Mistry offers a diagnostic exploration of the evils of Indian society mid 1970s. He un ambiguously conveys his massage that, the country cannot become a modern welfare nation state, in the true sense of the term, unless the society is redeemed of its age old caste prejudice, superstation and narrow political interest. The untimely withering of the young buds like Maneck and Omprakash suggests the utter west of human potentials. The tragedy of Ishvar and Om symbolizes the terrible fate of rootless subalterns in the face of great social, historical or political upheavals.

The novelist offers his comprehensive attitude to life. The voice, through which the author speaks, is Mr. Vasantrao Valmik, the Proof. Reader. Valmik emerges as one of many finely rounded supporting characters. He puts forth his Yeatsian theory: "You can not draw lines and compartments. You have to maintain a fine balance between hope and despair. (p.231) Valmik suggests, "the secret of survival is to embrace change, and to adopt". (p.230) one has to use failures as stepping stones to success to maintain *A Fine Balance* between hope and despair. Valmik believes that "there is always hope – hope enough to balance our despair or we would be lost". (p.563) His is the wise and sane voice sobered by the experience of life: "our lives are but a sequence of accidents – a clanking chain of chance events. A string of choices, causal or deliberate, which add up to that one big calamity we call life." (p.564)

The journey motive in this novel continues from beginning to end encompassing the quest and aspiration of four principle characters whose aspiring journey ends in disillusionment, despair and nothingness. All the four characters sensitive and aspiring, lost out in their failure to maintain 'a fine balance between hope and despair'. The narrative opens with a train journey and concludes with "Epilogue: 1984", putting a seal to the aspiring voyage of the four as well as to the steal of suffering, misery and exploitation on the one hand, and blooming humanity on the other.

The separate stories of aspiration and failure involving the fate of the four characters are interwoven in Mistry's dexterous handling of the plot. The quilt that Dina weaves metaphorically suggests the interwoven pattern of their tales. In my closer analysis of Mistry's narrative the quilt metaphor seems to me to be the most powerful in the text that holds the several story lines together. A review by Patricia Goldblatt arrests my attention and I agree with its concluding comment – "And life, Mistry seems to say, is like a quilt, each piece separate, unique, but the odd one colourful, bright, standing out, holding together the many dull, frayed and monotonous ones. In the final scenes of the story, the quilt that was to be Om's wedding present serves as a kind of cushion for Ishvar to rest his body upon: a comfort and a support, a visual patchwork of a life, filled with many sorrows and few joys". (Goldblatt, Patricia. "Tailors Struggle in India." *English Journal 86,* no.2 (February 1997): 94.

Nonetheless Mistry's text gives rise to a complex critical debate as to whether the trauma within and without Indian society can ever be subdued or can the marginalized will ever be granted a legitimate voice in social history? The answer will of course be ambiguous and for a better understanding, we have to look forward with dumb expectancy to Mistry's later creations and the similar sensitive texts in the Indian Diaspora.

Work cited

1. Mistry, Rohinton. *A Fine Balance.* London : Faber and faber, 1996.
2. Selvam, P. *Humanism in the novels of Rohinton Mistry.* New Delhi : Creative Books, 2009.
3. Batra, Jagdish. *Rohinton Mistry Identity, Values and Other Sociological Concerns.* New Delhi : Prestige Books, 2008.
4. Morey, Peter. *Rohinton Mistry.* Published by Manchester University Press, 2004.
5. Dodiya, Jaydip Singh. *The Fiction of Rohinton Mistry.* New Delhi : Prestige Books, 1998.
6. Roy, Anjali Gera. T Pillai, Meena. *Rohinton Mistry An Anthology of Recent Criticism.* Delhi : Pencraft International,

22

Role of New Women in Bharati Mukherjee's with reference to *Jasmine and Wife*

Dr. Nagraj G. Holeyannavar
Assistant Professor of English
University of Horticultural Sciences
Bagalkot

Bharati Mukherjee is an expatriate writer and she has written about life of Indian women in America. She has portrayed the life of 'new women' struggling in alien world and in search of their identities and finding their selves as they are being trapped in identity crises. She has glorified the concept 'New Woman' with the help of her female characters. They are: "the emotional segregation of women and man, which brought about and led to the development of a specifically female world" (Gupta 154) i.e., the self-identity which is mostly needed in modern era for a woman. Her works reveal the actual position of women in the Indian society and the treatment they are subjected with all diversities in the guise of 'Unity'. However, she has written about the urban middle class people, the segment of the society they know the best. In most of her writings, she discusses the views concerning post colonialism, multiculturalism, identity, globalization, struggle of women, appose of outdated traditions etc.

Considering herself as an American writer, she expresses, "I totally consider myself an American writer, and that has been my big battle: to get to realize that my roots as a writer are no longer, if they ever were, among Indian writers, but that I am writing about the territory, about the feelings, of a new kind of pioneer here in America" (Tandon 135).Therefore, to understand the mindset of her writings. I have chosen two novels Jasmine and Wife. These are portrayed on culture differences and how they try to adjust or assimilate over there in an alien culture. How the difference in their thinking and approach changes the perception of understanding. *Jasmine* deals with in which the protagonist shows a strong oppose against the feudal traditions and superstitions in an attempt to find a prestigious and independent existence. And her novel *Wife* speaks about the life of traditional girl whose life gets disillusioned and she changes with circumstances.

In *Jasmine* Bharati Mukherjee depicts by setting up situation in present world about a young Indian woman in the United States who, trying to adapt to the American way of life to survive, changes identities several times. There in, this context the unity between the First and Third World is shown in the treatment of women as subordinate to men in both countries. She uproots herself from her life in India and re-roots herself in search of a new life and the image of America as well. It is a story of dislocation and relocation as the protagonist continually sheds lives to move into other roles, moving further westward. The author in parts of the novel shows some agony to the third world as she shows that Jasmine needs to travel to America to make something significant in her life. And in the third world she faced only despair and loss. The complex journey of immigration and the hardships immigrants undergo are common themes in Bharati Mukherjee's writings. The author, an immigrant herself, tries to show the darker side of immigration, especially for Hindu women, that is not often portrayed in other immigrant narratives. In the novel, *Jasmine* Mukherjee uses three types of immigrants to show how different the hardships of adhering to life in an adopted country can be. Her main immigrant characters fall mainly into three categories: the refugee, the hyphenated immigrant, and the chameleon. In response to her insecurities, Prakash says, "You're Jasmine now. You cannot jump into wells". Prakash believes that the new *Jasmine* that he has helped emerge is capable of living on her own and being independent. Even though many of Prakash's actions are controlling, Jasmine realizes that she has changed in many ways due to Prakash. She narrates, "My life before Prakash, the girl I had been, the village, were like a dream from another life". After Prakash dies by a radio bomb meant for Jyoti, she emerges as Jasmine.

In her path Jasmine faces many problems, including rape, eventually returning to the position of health professional through a series of jobs. There, in this context the unity between the First and Third World is shown in the treatment of women as subordinate to men in both countries. The story expanded as a story of a young girl suddenly widowed at seventeen. She uproots herself from her life in India and reroots herself in search of a new life and the image of America as well. It is a story of dislocation and relocation as the protagonist continually sheds lives to move into other roles, moving further westward. The author in parts of the novel shows some agony to the third world as she shows that Jasmine needs to travel to America to make something significant in her life. And in the third world she faced only despair and loss.

The complex journey of immigration and the hardship of immigrants undergo are common themes in Bharati Mukherjee's writings. The author, an immigrant herself, tries to show the darker side of immigration, especially for Hindu women, that is not often portrayed in other immigrant narratives. In the novel *Jasmine,* Mukherjee uses three types of immigrants to show how different the hardships of adhering to life in an adopted country can be. Her main immigrant characters fall mainly into three categories: the refugee, the hyphenated immigrant, and the chameleon. In response to her insecurities, Prakash says, "You're Jasmine now. You cannot jump into wells". Prakash believes that the new Jasmine he has helped emerge is capable of living on her own and being independent. Even though many of Prakash's actions are controlling, Jasmine realizes that she has changed in many ways due to Prakash. She narrates, "My life before Prakash, the girl I had been, the village, were like a dream from another life". After Prakash dies by a radio bomb meant for Jyoti, she emerges as Jasmine. Later, she becomes Jase for Taylor and Jane for bud and Half-Face for Kali.

The sexual freedom is revealed by the protagonist reflects the breaking up with traditional codes. She describes her decision to join Taylor

> I'm not choosing men. I am caught between the promise of America and old world dutifulness ... It isn t guilting that I feel, its relief. I realize I have already stopped thinking of myself as Jane. Adventure, risk, transformation: the frontier is pushing indoors through un-caulked windows. Watch me reposition the stars (Jasmine 240).

Jasmine does not have a consistency of life. She has to face many odds in life. Thus, She adopts and adapts according to her situations. The sense of movement is portrayed throughout the novel as it projects the necessity of change and transformation nevertheless the surviving aids for existence. In her journey Jasmine is assigned various names- Jyoti, Jasmine, Jane, Jase, finally renewing her as an independent woman who decides to live with the man whom she loves. The freedom of choice that she made gives new definitions to her inner self- a great fighter and survivor. Jasmine articulates her distinct identities throughout the novel in which she herself defines the changes happened to her both in physical and psychological levels. There is no consistency, as the protagonist is carried through various space dimensions, there happens an incarnation of her innate self, which in a way reflects her multiplicity of consciousness. Jasmine fights against every challenge in her quest to live. There is always a passion for life, an urge to move on. The feeling of displacement is overcome by the desire to settle down by capturing the present. The novel may be called as a series of struggle for living in alien soil and culture which turned a mere village girl to a strong and independent Americanized woman

In *Wife* Mukherjee has the element of transformation in most of her novels. Dimple, protagonist of the novel Wife plays different roles how Dimple undergoes transformation from a simple girl in Ballygunge to Amit Basu's wife. Dimple as the wife of Amit Basu wants to change herself in an effort to please her husband. She makes several efforts like dressing up differently, trying with new hairstyles etc. to please her husband. Dimple takes to wearing bright colours: red, oranges and purples. Amit even compliments her on the different looks. And Dimple begins to feel that her arranged marriage to Amit Basu leaves her disappointed and disillusioned. She hates her subservient role. She becomes pregnant expresses to be aborted. She spends more time alone in the apartment by sleeping, watching, television and reading magazines. Further, watching television made her that she is more psychic as she is exposed to daily serials and violence on television warps her values and distorts her sense of reality. And also she always used to get the thoughts like rape and feel like somebody breaking the window and coming into her room. She frequently plunges into moods of depression, fantasizing about different ways of committing suicide or inflicting pain on her husband.

However, the novel proceeds we find lot of change in Dimple's behaviour. She started going out with Ina and Milt a foreigner. She adopts western outfit, wears purple coloured tinted sunglasses. Each and every encounter of Dimple with Milt brought them closer. She does not find love in her arranged marriage; she has an affair with Milt Glasser, an all-American boy. She started extra marital affair with Milt. "The purple tinted sunglasses are perhaps the most typical index of American culture. For Dimple, they are a disguise, borrowed from the west, just like Marsha's clothes and the apartment in which she is living". This relation makes her neurotic and fails to differentiate between the real life and the picture depicted on Television. She also becomes alienated. Dimple started feeling gloomier day by day. "Her life was slow, full of miscalculations" (Wife, p178). Amit could make out the changes in her and felt that it was because of culture shock. And her depression starts growing. She hides everything from Amit whatever is going on in her mind: She does not tell him about these imaginary beginnings. She did not tell him about her immoderate day time sleeping either. They were unspeakable failings. She thought of them as deformities-sinister, ugly, and wicked (Wife, p115). She started planning the murder of her husband. She becomes violent. She wanted to kill her husband just like how she sees on television. Moreover, she has become neurotic as killing of her husband becomes interesting to her. She is not in position differentiate the reality and the imaginary world.

Dimple cultural values are erased during her relation with Milt. On the other she was driven by guilt, passion, and revenge, she finally kills her husband by stabbing him for seven times. She becomes a victim of neurotic disorder by watching the advertisements. Her emotions brought a kind of madness, nightmares extramarital affairs in her. She takes revenge of her unfulfilled desires by murdering her husband. She becomes mentally unstable and indulges in such a violent act. She was very much conscious of being more and more alienated from the surroundings: "she was a pitiful immigrant among demanding appliances."(Wife 186) in her flat that expatriation to America had brought her to downfall in life.

In the same regard, Mukherjee herself states that the kinds of women she writes about are those who are adjusting. Indian daughters have been raised to please, trained to be adaptable wives, and that adaptability is working to the women's advantage when they come over as immigrants. Further, in the novel, *Jasmine* the protagonists assimilates with the culture and she changes for her existence in alien soil with new names and people. She knows how to live in life whereas Dimple in novel *wife*, who is very dim, does not adjust with new culture as more violence and vulgarity were shown on television she begin to imagine it as real and unable to differentiate the both world. She feels alienated and on other loneliness has made neurotic in sense. Further, she murders her husband. These two novels narrate the story of immigrant women and their lives in alien soil. One adjusts and assimilates with new and other becomes neurotic and murder.

REFERENCE

1. Mukherjee, Bharati. *Jasmine.* New York: Groove, 1989. Print.

2. Mukherjee, Bharati. *Wife,* Delhi: Sterling, 1976. Print.